GOD'S BEST

BEST

Secrets

GOD'S BEST
Secrets

ANDREW MURRAY

Whitaker House

GOD'S BEST SECRETS

ISBN: 0-88368-559-0
Printed in the United States of America
© 1998 by Whitaker House

Whitaker House
30 Hunt Valley Circle
New Kensington, PA 15068

Library of Congress Cataloging-in-Publication Data

Murray, Andrew, 1812–1878.
    God's best secrets / by Andrew Murray.
        p.   cm.
    Originally published: Los Angeles : Biola Book, 1923.
    ISBN 0-88368-559-0 (trade paper : alk. paper)
    1. Devotional calendars. I. Title.
    [BV4811.M82   1998]
    242'.2—dc21   98-47552

3 4 5 6 7 8 9 10 11 12 13 14 / 09 08 07 06 05 04 03 02 01

CONTENTS

INTRODUCTION

The more I think of and pray about the state of religion in the world, the deeper my conviction becomes that the low state of the spiritual life of Christians is due to the fact that they do not realize that the purpose of conversion is to bring the soul on earth to a daily fellowship with the Father in heaven. Once this truth has been accepted, the believer will perceive how indispensable it is to the spiritual life of a Christian to take time each day with God's Word and in prayer, to wait upon God for His presence and His love to be revealed.

But how can Christians be taught this lesson and learn how to live in obedience to it? The first thing is that they must be convinced of the great need for daily fellowship with God. They must be brought under the impression that it is not enough at conversion to accept forgiveness of sins, or even to surrender themselves to God. These things are only a beginning.

The young believer must understand that he has no power of his own to maintain his spiritual life. Rather, he needs each day to receive new grace from heaven through communion with the Lord Jesus. This cannot be obtained by a hasty prayer or a superficial reading of a few verses from God's Word. He must take time quietly and deliberately to come into God's presence, to feel his weakness and his need, and to wait upon God through His Holy Spirit to renew the heavenly light and life in his heart. Only then may he expect to be kept by the power of Christ throughout the day—and kept from all its temptations.

It has been my aim in writing this book to help Christians to see the absolute necessity of fellowship with the Lord Jesus. Without this, the joy and power of God's Holy Spirit in daily life cannot be experienced. Many of God's children long for a better life, but they do not realize that they must give God time, each day in their inner chambers through His Spirit, in order to renew and sanctify their lives.

Meditate on this thought: the feeble state of your spiritual life is mainly due to the lack of time spent in daily fellowship with God. New life will dawn in many souls as a result of time spent in prayer alone with God.

I pray that any reader who finds a blessing in reading this book will share the blessing with others. If you have accepted the message that the Lord Jesus will daily grant you His presence and love, pass it on to others. However weak and powerless you feel, your faith will be strengthened as you help others to realize the need for daily fellowship with Jesus.

As you think of the need of our country and the church, as you think of souls around you, as you think of the spreading of God's Gospel, I ask you, Christian, to help find volunteers who, as true soldiers of the cross, will persevere continually in prayer, until God pours out His blessing upon us all.

Your servant in the love of Christ and in prayer,
ANDREW MURRAY

Section One

❧

The Secret of Fellowship

FROM DAY TO DAY

The inward man is being renewed day by day.
—2 Corinthians 4:16

There is one lesson that all young Christians should learn, and that is the absolute necessity of fellowship with Jesus each day. This lesson is not always taught at the beginning of the Christian life, nor is it always understood by the young convert. He should realize that the grace he has received—the forgiveness of his sins, his acceptance as God's child, his joy in the Holy Spirit—can only be preserved by daily renewal in fellowship with Jesus Christ Himself.

Many Christians backslide because this truth is not clearly taught. They are unable to stand against the temptations of the world and of their old nature. They strive to do their best to fight against sin and to serve God, but they have no strength. They have never really grasped the secret that the Lord Jesus in heaven will continue His work in them every day, but only on one condition: every soul must give Him time each day to impart His love and His grace. Time alone with the Lord Jesus each day is the indispensable condition of growth and power.

Read Matthew 11:25–30. Christ says, *"Come to Me...and I will give you rest....Learn from Me...and you will find rest for your souls"* (vv. 28–29). The Lord will teach us just how meek and humble He is. Bow before Him, tell Him that you long for Him and His love, and He will let His love rest on you. This is a thought not only for young Christians, but also for all who love the Lord.

If you desire to live this life of fellowship with Christ, if you wish to enjoy this blessed experience each day, then learn the lesson of spending time each day, without exception, in fellowship with your Lord. In this way, your inner man will be renewed from day to day.

FELLOWSHIP WITH GOD

❧

The three persons in the Godhead are the Father, the Son, and the Holy Spirit. Each one is different from the others, just as each one of us is an individual, distinct from others and standing in certain relations to others. God desires to reveal Himself as a person; He will reveal Himself, and it is our holy calling to enter into fellowship with Him.

God greatly desires this fellowship with man. But sin has come between man and his God. Even in the Christian, who thinks he knows God, there is often great ignorance of and even indifference to this personal relationship of love for God.

People believe that at conversion their sins are forgiven, that God accepts them so that they may go to heaven, and that they should try to do God's will. But the idea is strange to them that they may and must each day have this blessed fellowship with God, just as a father and his child on earth have pleasure in fellowship.

God gave us Christ His Son in order to bring us to Himself. But this is only possible when we live in close fellowship with Jesus Christ. Our relationship to Christ rests on His deep, tender love for us. We are not able in ourselves to reciprocate this love to Him. But the Holy Spirit will do the work in us. For this we need to separate ourselves each day from the world and turn in faith to the Lord Jesus, so that He may pour out His love in our hearts (Rom. 5:5), and so that we may be filled with a great love for Him.

Dear soul, meditate quietly on this thought. Read the words of Christ in John 14:21: *"He who loves Me will be loved by My Father, and I will love him."* Take time to believe in this personal fellowship. Tell God of your love. Say to Him, "Lord, You have loved me dearly; therefore, I earnestly desire to love You above all others."

JESUS

❧

*You shall call His name JESUS, for
He will save His people from their sins.
—Matthew 1:21*

Because the Lord Jesus was a person, He had His own individual name. His mother, His disciples, and all His friends called Him by this name, Jesus. But they probably thought little of what that name meant. And the majority of Christians today hardly know what a treasure is contained in that name, Jesus: *"He will save His people from their sins."*

Many think of His death on the cross or of His work in heaven as our Intercessor, but they do not realize that Jesus is a living person in heaven who thinks of us each day and longs to reveal Himself. He desires us to bring Him our love and adoration each day.

Christians pray to Christ to save them from their sins, but they know very little how the blessed work is done. The living Christ reveals Himself to us, and through the power of His love, the love of sin is expelled. It is through personal fellowship with Him that Jesus saves us from our sins. I must come as an individual, with my heart and all the sin that is in it, to Jesus as an almighty personal Savior in whom God's holiness dwells. And as He and I commune together in the expression of mutual love and desire, by the work of His Holy Spirit in my heart, His love will expel and conquer all the sin.

O Christian, you will find the secret of happiness and holiness in fellowship with Jesus each day. Your heart will long for the hour of prayer as the best hour of the day. As you learn to take time to be alone with Him each day, you will experience His presence, enabling you to love Him, to serve Him, and to walk in His ways throughout the day. Through this unbroken fellowship, you will learn the secret of the power of a truly godly life.

THE INNER CHAMBER

*When thou prayest, enter into thine inner chamber, and
having shut thy door, pray to thy Father which is in secret,
and thy Father which seeth in secret shall recompense thee.*
—*Matthew 6:6 RV*

Have you ever thought what a wonderful privilege it is that
everyone each day, and each hour of the day, has the liberty of
asking God to meet him in the inner chamber and to hear what he
has to say? We imagine that every Christian uses such a privilege
gladly and faithfully. But how many really do take advantage of the
privilege?

"When thou prayest," said Jesus, *"enter into thine inner chamber, and having shut thy door, pray to thy Father which is in secret."* This means two things. First, shut the world out, and
withdraw from all worldly thoughts and activities. Second, shut
yourself in alone with God, to pray to Him in secret. Let this be
your chief aim in prayer: to realize the presence of your heavenly
Father. Let your watchword be, "Alone with God."

This is only the beginning. As you take time to realize His
presence with you and to pray to *"thy Father which seeth in secret,"*
you can do so in the full assurance that He knows how you long for
His help and guidance, and that He will incline His ear to you.

Then follows the great promise: *"Thy Father which seeth in
secret shall recompense thee."* The Father will see to it that your
prayer is not in vain. All through the activities of a busy day, the
answer to your prayer will be granted. Prayer in secret will be followed by the secret working of God in your heart.

The Lord Jesus has given us the promise of His presence, and
He shows us the way to the inner chamber. Therefore, He will
surely be with us to teach us to pray. It is through Him that we
have access to the Father. (See John 14:6.) Be childlike and trustful
in your fellowship with Christ. Confess each sin; bring your every
need. Offer your prayer to the Father in the name of Christ. Prayer
in fellowship with Jesus cannot be in vain.

FAITH

🕸

Only believe.
—Mark 5:36

We have here a lesson of the greatest importance. When we are alone in the inner chamber, we must send up our petitions, trusting implicitly in the love of God and in the power of the Lord Jesus. Take time to ask yourself the question, Is my heart full of a great and steadfast faith in God's love? If this is not the case, do not begin to pray just yet. Faith does not come of itself.

Consider quietly how impossible it is for God to lie. He is ready with infinite love to give you a blessing (Ps. 29:11). Take some passage of Scripture in which God's power, faithfulness, and love are revealed. Take hold of the words and say, "Yes, Lord, I will pray in firm faith in You and in Your great love."

It is a mistake to limit the word *faith* to the forgiveness of sins and to our acceptance as children of God. Faith includes far more than this. We must have faith in all that God is willing to do for us. We must have faith each day according to our special needs. God is infinitely great and powerful, and Christ has so much grace for each new day, that our faith must reach out afresh each day according to the need of the day.

When you enter into the inner chamber, even before you begin to pray, ask yourself, Do I really believe that God is here with me and that the Lord Jesus will help me to pray? Do I believe that I can expect to spend a blessed time in communion with my God?

Jesus often taught His disciples how indispensable faith was to true prayer. He will teach you this lesson, too. Remain in fellowship with Him, and ask Him to strengthen your faith in His almighty power. Christ says to you and to me, as He did to Martha, *"Did I not say to you that if you would believe you would see the glory of God?"* (John 11:40).

THE WORD OF GOD

*Man shall not live by bread alone, but by
every word that proceeds from the mouth of God.*
—Matthew 4:4

In the above verse, our Lord compared the Word of God to our daily bread, thereby teaching us a great lesson. Bread is indispensable to life. We all understand this. However strong a person may be, if he takes no nourishment, he will grow weaker, and he will die. If an illness prevents me from eating, I will die. It is the same with the Word of God. The Word contains a heavenly principle and works powerfully in those who believe.

Bread must be eaten. I may know all about bread. I may have bread and give it to others. I may have bread in my house and on my table in great abundance, but that will not help me unless I eat it. Similarly, a mere knowledge of God's Word and even the preaching of it to others will not benefit me. It is not enough to think about it. Rather, I must feed on God's Word and take it into my heart and life. In love and obedience I must take hold of the words of God and let them take full possession of my heart. Then they will indeed be words of life.

Bread must be eaten daily, and the same is true of God's Word. The psalmist wrote, *"Blessed is the man...*[whose] *delight is in the law of the LORD, and in His law he meditates day and night"* (Ps. 1:1–2); *"Oh, how I love Your law! It is my meditation all the day"* (Ps. 119:97). To secure a strong and powerful spiritual life, an intake of God's Word every day is indispensable.

When He was on earth, the Lord Jesus learned, loved, and obeyed the Word of the Father. If you seek fellowship with Him, you will find Him in His Word. Christ will teach you to commune with the Father through the Word, just as He did on earth. You will learn, like Him, to live solely for the glory of God and the fulfillment of His Word.

HOW TO READ GOD'S WORD

❧

Blessed is the man...[whose] *delight is in the law of*
the LORD, and in His law he meditates day and night.
—*Psalm 1:1–2*

Here are some simple rules for Bible reading. First, read God's Word with great reverence. Meditate a moment in silence on the thought that the words come from God Himself. Bow in deep reverence. Be silent before God. Let Him reveal His Word in your heart.

Second, read with careful attention. If you read the words carelessly, thinking that you can grasp their meaning with your human understanding, you will use the words superficially and will not enter into their depths. When someone tries to explain anything wonderful or beautiful to us, we give our entire attention to try to understand what is said. How much higher and deeper are God's thoughts than our thoughts! *"For as the heavens are higher than the earth, so are...My thoughts than your thoughts"* (Isa. 55:9). We need to give our undivided attention to understand even the superficial meaning of the words. How much harder it is to grasp the spiritual meaning!

Next, read with the expectation of the guidance of God's Spirit. It is God's Spirit alone that can make the Word a living power in our hearts and lives. Read Psalm 119. Notice how earnestly David prayed that God would teach him, open his eyes, give him understanding, and incline his heart to God's ways. As you read, remember that God's Word and God's Spirit are inseparable.

Finally, read with the firm purpose of keeping the Word day and night in your heart and in your life. The whole heart and the whole life must come under the influence of the Word. David said, *"Oh, how I love Your law! It is my meditation all the day"* (Ps. 119:97). In the same manner, in the midst of his daily work, the believer can cherish God's Word in his heart and meditate on it. Read Psalm 119 again, until you accept God's Word with all your heart. Pray that God may teach you to understand it and to carry out its precepts in your life.

THE WORD AND PRAYER

❧

Revive me, O LORD, according to Your word.
—Psalm 119:107

Prayer and the Word of God are inseparable and should always go together in the quiet time of the inner chamber. In His Word, God speaks to me; in prayer, I speak to God. If there is to be true fellowship, God and I must both take part. If I simply pray without using God's Word, I am apt to use my own words and thoughts. To really give prayer its power, I must take God's thoughts from His Word and present them before Him. Then I am enabled to pray according to God's Word. How indispensable God's Word is for all true prayer!

When you pray, you must seek to know God correctly. It is through the Word that the Holy Spirit gives you right thoughts of Him. The Word will also teach you how wretched and sinful you are. It reveals to you all the wonders that God will do for you and the strength He will give you to do His will. The Word teaches you how to pray with strong desire, with firm faith, and with constant perseverance. The Word teaches you not only what you are, but also what you may become through God's grace. Above all, it reminds you each day that Christ is the great Intercessor, and allows you to pray in His name.

O Christian, learn this great lesson, to renew your strength each day in God's Word, and thereby pray according to His will.

Now let us turn to the other side: prayer. We need prayer when we read God's Word: prayer to be taught by God to understand His Word, prayer that through the Holy Spirit we may rightly know and use God's Word, prayer that we may see in the Word that Christ is all in all, and will be all in us.

Blessed inner chamber, where I may approach God in Christ through the Word and prayer! There I may offer myself to God and His service, and be strengthened by the Holy Spirit, so that His love may be poured out in my heart (Rom. 5:5), and I may daily walk in that love.

OBEDIENCE

❧

Obey My voice...and I will be your God.
—Jeremiah 11:4

God gave this command to Israel when He gave them the law. But Israel had no power to keep the law. So God gave them a new covenant, to enable His people to live a life of obedience. We read, *"I will put My law in their minds, and write it on their hearts"* (Jer. 31:33); *"I will put My fear in their hearts so that they will not depart from Me"* (Jer. 32:40); *"I will...cause you to walk in My statutes"* (Ezek. 36:27). These wonderful promises gave Israel the assurance that obedience would be their delight.

See what the Lord Jesus said about obedience: *"He who has My commandments and keeps them, it is he who loves Me"* (John 14:21); *"If anyone loves Me, he will keep My word; and My Father will love him, and We will come to him and make Our home with him"* (v. 23); *"If you keep My commandments, you will abide in My love"* (John 15:10). These words are an inexhaustible treasure. Through faith we can firmly trust Christ to enable us to live such a life of love and obedience.

No father can train his children unless they are obedient. No teacher can teach a child who continues to disobey him. No general can lead his soldiers to victory without prompt obedience. Pray that God will imprint this lesson on your heart: the life of faith is a life of obedience. As Christ lived in obedience to the Father, so we, too, need obedience for a life in the love of God.

But so many people think, "I cannot be obedient; it is impossible." Yes, impossible to you, but not to God. He has promised to *"cause you to walk in* [His] *statutes"* (Ezek. 36:27). Pray and meditate on these words, and the Holy Spirit will enlighten your eyes, so that you will have power to do God's will. Let your fellowship with the Father and with the Lord Jesus Christ have this as its one aim: a life of quiet, determined, unquestioning obedience.

CONFESSION OF SIN

⁋ℇ

*If we confess our sins, He is faithful and just to forgive us
our sins and to cleanse us from all unrighteousness.*
—*1 John 1:9*

Too often the confession of sin is superficial, and often it is quite neglected. Few Christians realize how necessary it is to be sincere about the matter. Some do not feel that an honest confession of sin gives power to live the life of victory over sin. But we, in fellowship with the Lord Jesus, need to confess with a sincere heart every sin that may be a hindrance in our Christian lives.

Read what David said: *"I acknowledged my sin to You....I said, 'I will confess my transgressions to the LORD,' and You forgave the iniquity of my sin....You are my hiding place...You shall surround me with songs of deliverance"* (Ps. 32:5, 7). David spoke of a time when he was unwilling to confess his sin. *"When I kept silent...Your hand was heavy upon me"* (vv. 3–4). But when he had confessed his sin, a wonderful change came.

Confession means not only that you confess your sin with shame, but also that you hand it over to God, trusting Him to take it away. Such a confession implies that you are wholly unable to get rid of your guilt, but by an act of faith you depend on God to deliver you. This deliverance means, in the first place, that you know your sins are forgiven, and secondly, that Christ undertakes to cleanse you from the sin and keep you from its power.

O Christian, if you are seeking to have fellowship with Jesus, do not fear to confess each sin in the confident assurance that there is deliverance. Let there be a mutual understanding between the Lord Jesus and yourself that you will confess each sin and will obtain forgiveness. Then you will know your Lord as Jesus, who saves His people from their sins (Matt. 1:21). Believe that there is great power in the confession of sin, for the burden of sin was borne by our Lord and Savior.

THE FIRST LOVE

🦋

Nevertheless I have this against you,
that you have left your first love.
—Revelation 2:4

In the verses preceding Revelation 2:4, eight signs are mentioned that show the zeal and activity of the church at Ephesus. But there was one bad sign, and the Lord said, *"I will come to you quickly and remove your lampstand from its place; unless you repent"* (v. 5). And what was this sign? *"You have left your first love."*

We find the same lack in the church of the present day. There is zeal for the truth, there is continuous and persevering labor, but what the Lord values most is still missing: the tender, fervent love for Himself.

This is a thought of great significance. A church, or even an individual Christian, may be an example in every good work, and yet the tender love for the Lord Jesus in the inner chamber is missing. There is no personal, daily fellowship with Christ, and all the manifold activities with which people satisfy themselves are nothing in the eyes of the Master Himself.

Dear brother or sister in Christ, this book speaks of the fellowship of love that we can have with Christ in the inner chamber. Everything depends on this. Christ came from heaven to love us with the love with which the Father loved Him (John 17:26). He suffered and died to win our hearts for this love. His love can be satisfied with nothing less than a deep, personal love on our part.

Christ considers this of the highest importance. Let us have the same thought. Many ministers, missionaries, and Christian workers confess with shame that, in spite of all their zeal in the Lord's work, their prayer lives are defective because they have left their first love. I pray that you will write this down on a piece of paper and remember it continually: the love of Jesus must be all— in the inner chamber, in all our work, and in our daily lives.

THE HOLY SPIRIT

⚜

He will glorify Me, for He will take
of what is Mine and declare it to you.
—John 16:14

Our Lord, on the last night that He was with His disciples, promised to send the Holy Spirit as a Comforter. Although His bodily presence was removed, they would realize His presence in them and with them in a wonderful way. The Holy Spirit would so reveal Christ in their hearts, that they would experience His presence with them continually. The Spirit would glorify Christ and would reveal the glorified Christ in heavenly love and power.

How little do Christians understand, believe, and experience this glorious truth! Ministers would fail in their duties if, in a book like this or in their preaching, they encouraged Christians to love the Lord Jesus without at the same time warning them that it is not a duty they can perform in their own strength. No, that is impossible; it is God, the Holy Spirit alone, who will pour out His love in our hearts (Rom. 5:5) and will teach us to love Him fervently. Through the Holy Spirit we may experience the love and abiding presence of the Lord Jesus throughout the day.

But let us remember that the Spirit of God must have entire possession of us. He claims our hearts and our entire lives. He will strengthen us with might in the inner man (Eph. 3:16), so that we may have fellowship with Christ, keep His commandments, and abide in His love.

Once we have grasped this truth, we will begin to feel our deep dependence on the Holy Spirit and will ask the Father to send Him in power into our hearts. The Spirit will teach us to love the Word, to meditate on it, and to keep it. He will reveal the love of Christ to us, so that we may love Him *"fervently with a pure heart"* (1 Pet. 1:22). Then we will begin to see that having the love of Christ in the midst of our daily lives and distractions is a glorious possibility and a blessed reality.

CHRIST'S LOVE FOR US

Even as the Father hath loved me,
I also have loved you: abide ye in my love.
—John 15:9 RV

In fellowship between friends and relations, everything depends on their love for each other. Of what value is great wealth if love is lacking between husband and wife, or between parents and children? And in our religion, of what value is all knowledge and zeal in God's work, without the knowledge and experience of Christ's love? (See 1 Corinthians 13:1–3.) O Christians, the one thing needed in the inner chamber is to know by experience how much Christ loves you, and to learn how you may abide and continue in that love.

Think of what Christ said: *"As the Father hath loved me"*—what a divine, everlasting, wonderful love—*"I also have loved you."* It was the same love with which He had loved the Father and that He always bore in His heart, which He now gave into the hearts of His disciples. He yearns that this everlasting love will rest upon us and work within us, so that we may abide in it day by day. What a blessed life! Christ desires every disciple to live in the power of the very same love of God that He Himself experienced. Reader, do you realize that in your fellowship with Christ in secret or in public, you are surrounded by and kept in this heavenly love? Let your desire reach out for this everlasting love. The Christ with whom you desire fellowship longs unspeakably to fill you with His love.

Read all that God's Word says about the love of Christ. Meditate on the words, and let them sink into your heart. Sooner or later you will begin to realize, "The greatest happiness of my life is that I am loved by the Lord Jesus. I may live in fellowship with Him all day long." Let your heart continually say, "His love for me is unspeakable; He will keep me abiding in His love."

OUR LOVE FOR CHRIST

🙦

Jesus Christ: whom not having seen ye love;
on whom, though now ye see him not, yet believing,
ye rejoice greatly with joy unspeakable and full of glory.
—1 Peter 1:8 RV

What a wonderful description of the Christian life! People had never seen Christ, yet they truly loved Him and believed in Him, so that their hearts were filled with unspeakable joy. Such is the life of a Christian who really loves his Lord.

We have seen that the chief attributes of the Father and the Son are love for each other and love for man. These should be the chief characteristics of the true Christian. The love of God and of Christ is poured out in his heart (Rom. 5:5) and becomes a well of living water, flowing forth as love for the Lord Jesus.

This love is not merely a blessed feeling. It is an active principle. It takes pleasure in doing the will of the beloved Lord. It is joy to keep His commandments. The love of Christ for us was shown by His death on the cross; our love must be exhibited in unselfish, self-sacrificing living. Oh, that we understood this: in the Christian life, love for Christ is everything!

Great love will beget great faith—faith in His love for us, faith in the powerful revelations of His love in our hearts, faith that He through His love will work all His good pleasure in us. The wings of faith and love will lift us up to heaven, and we will be filled with *"joy unspeakable."* The joy of the Christian is an indispensable witness to the world of the power of Christ to change hearts and to fill them with heavenly love and gladness.

Oh, you who love the Lord Jesus, take time daily in the inner chamber with Him to drink in a fresh supply of His heavenly love. It will make you strong in faith, and your joy will be full. Love, joy, faith—these will fill your life each day through the grace of the Lord Jesus.

LOVE FOR FELLOW CHRISTIANS

🐝

A new commandment I give to you, that you love one another;
as I have loved you, that you also love one another.
—John 13:34

The Lord Jesus told His disciples that He loved them just as the Father had loved Him. And now, following His example, we must love one another with the same love.

"By this all will know that you are My disciples, if you have love for one another" (v. 35). Christ later prayed, *"That they all may be one, as You, Father, are in Me, and I in You; that they also may be one in Us, that the world may believe that You sent Me"* (John 17:21). If we exhibit the love that was in God toward Christ, and in Christ toward us, the world will be obliged to confess that our Christianity is genuine and from above.

This is what actually happened in Bible times. The Greeks and Romans, Jews and heathen, hated each other. Among all the nations of the world, there was hardly a thought of love for each other. The very idea of self-sacrifice was a strange one. When the unsaved saw that Christians from different nations, under the powerful workings of the Holy Spirit, became one and loved one another, even to the point of self-sacrifice in time of plague or illness, they were amazed and said, "Behold how these people love one another!" (See John 13:35.)

Among professing Christians, there is a certain oneness of belief and feeling of brotherhood, but Christ's heavenly love is often lacking, and we do not bear one another's burdens or love others as heartily as we should. Pray that you will love your fellow believers with the same love with which Christ loves you. If we abide in Christ's love and let that love fill our hearts, supernatural power will be given to us to love all God's children. As the bond of love between the Father and the Son, and between Christ and His followers, is close, so must the bond of love be between all God's children.

LOVE FOR SOULS

❧

He who turns a sinner from the error of
his way will save a soul from death.
—James 5:20

What a wonderful thought, that I may save a soul from ever-lasting death! How can this be? I must convert him from the error of his ways. This is the calling not only of the minister, but also of every Christian: to work for the salvation of sinners.

When Christ and His love takes possession of our hearts, He gives us this love so that we might bring others to Him. In this way, Christ's kingdom is extended. Everyone who has the love of Christ in his heart is commissioned to tell others. This was the case in the early church. After the Day of Pentecost, people went out and told of the love of Christ, which they had themselves experienced. Heathen writers have told us that the rapid spread of Christianity in the first century was due to the fact that each convert, being filled with the love of Christ, tried to deliver the Good News to others.

What a change has come over the church! Many Christians never try to win others to Christ. Their love is so weak and faint that they have no desire to help others. May the time soon come when Christians will feel constrained to tell of the love of Christ. In a particular revival in Korea, the converts were filled with such a burning love for Christ that they felt bound to tell others of His love. It was even taken as a test of membership that each one should have brought another to the Lord before being admitted to the church.

Reader, examine your heart. Pray that, in fellowship with Christ, you will not only think of your own soul, but having received the gift of God's love, will also pass it on to others. You will then know true happiness, the joy of bringing souls to Christ.

Let us pray earnestly to be so filled with God's love that we may wholeheartedly surrender ourselves to win others for Him.

THE SPIRIT OF LOVE

❧

*The love of God has been poured out in our
hearts by the Holy Spirit who was given to us.*
—*Romans 5:5*

The fruit of the Spirit is love.
—*Galatians 5:22*

When we consider Christ's love for us, our love for Christ, and our love for fellow Christians or for souls around us, the thought sometimes arises: "The demand is too great; it is unattainable; it is impossible for a Christian to live this life of love and to show it to others in the church and to needy souls." And because we deem it impossible, and because of our unbelief and lack of faith in God's promises, we make little progress in this spirit of love.

We need to remind ourselves continually that it is not in our own strength, or even by serious thought, that we can obtain the love of Christ. We must realize the truth, that the love of God is *"poured out in our hearts"* and will be poured out daily by the Spirit of God. Only as we are wholly surrendered to the leading of the Spirit will we be able to live according to God's will. When the inner life of love is renewed from day to day, we will feel compelled to work for souls.

Here is a prayer that you can offer: *"I bow my knees to the Father...that He would grant you...to be strengthened with might through His Spirit in the inner man, that Christ may dwell in your hearts through faith; that you, being rooted and grounded in love, may...know the love of Christ which passes knowledge"* (Eph. 3:14, 16–19). You may be *"rooted and grounded"* in this love and may know the love *"which passes knowledge,"* but only on one condition: you must be strengthened by the Spirit *"in the inner man,"* so that Christ may dwell in your heart. Then you will indeed be *"rooted and grounded in love."*

Christian, take this message from God's Word, and let it influence your life. Unless you wait upon God daily, on your knees, for His Spirit to be revealed in your heart, you cannot live in this love. A life of prayer will cause you to experience the blessed reality of the love of Christ, the love of fellow believers, and love for souls.

Put your confidence each day in secret in the Holy Spirit—the Spirit of love that God will give to those who ask in faith.

PERSEVERING PRAYER

Men always ought to pray and not lose heart.
—Luke 18:1

Continuing steadfastly in prayer.
—Romans 12:12

Pray without ceasing.
—1 Thessalonians 5:17

One of the greatest drawbacks to the life of prayer is that the answer does not come as speedily as we expect. We are discouraged by the thought, "Perhaps I do not pray correctly," and so we do not persevere in prayer. This was a lesson that our Lord taught often and urgently. If we look further into the matter, we can see that there may be a reason for the delay, and the waiting may bring a blessing to our souls. Remember Daniel, who waited twenty-one days for the answer to his prayer. (See Daniel 10:1–15.)

When we pray, our desire must grow deeper and stronger, and we must ask with the whole heart. God puts us into the school of persevering prayer so that our weak faith may be strengthened. Believe that there is a great blessing in the delayed answer to prayer.

Above all, God wants to draw us into closer fellowship with Himself. When our prayers are not answered, we learn to realize that the fellowship, nearness, and love of God are more to us than the answers to our petitions, and we continue in prayer. What a blessing Jacob received through the delay of the answer to his prayer! He saw God face-to-face, and as a prince he had power with God and prevailed (Gen. 32:28).

Christians, listen to this warning. Do not be impatient or discouraged if the answer does not come. Rather, continue in prayer. *"Pray without ceasing."* You will find it an unspeakable blessing to do so. You may ask whether your prayer agrees with God's will and His Word. You may inquire if it is in the right spirit and in the name of Christ. Keep on praying; you will learn that the delay in the answer to prayer is one of the most precious means of grace that God can bestow on you. You will also learn that those who have persevered in pleading God's promises are those who have had the greatest power with God in prayer.

THE PRAYER MEETING

🐜

These all continued with one accord
in prayer and supplication.
—Acts 1:14

And they were all filled with the Holy Spirit.
—Acts 2:4

The value of a genuine prayer meeting is enormous. There God's children meet together, not as in church, to listen to one speaker, but to lift up their hearts unitedly to God. By this means, Christians are drawn closer to each other. Those who are weak are strengthened and encouraged by the testimony of the older and more experienced members, and even young Christians have the opportunity to tell of the joy of the Lord.

The prayer meeting may become a great power for good in a congregation and a spiritual help to both minister and members. By means of intercession, God's blessing is poured out at home and abroad.

But there are also dangers to be considered. Many attend and are edified but never learn to pray themselves. Others go for the sake of social and religious fervor and have a *"form of godliness"* (2 Tim. 3:5) but do not know the hidden life of prayer. Unless there is much and earnest prayer in the inner chamber, attendance at a prayer meeting may be a mere form.

It is well to ask, "What constitutes a living prayer meeting?" There should be hearty love and fellowship between the members.

The leaders should realize how great the influence of such a meeting may be, with its roots nourished by the life of prayer in the inner chamber. Prayer should include God's people and His church all over the world. Above all, as on the Day of Pentecost, there must be waiting on God for the filling of the Holy Spirit.

Dear reader, I aim to help you in your spiritual life. But remember, you do not live for yourself alone; you are part of the body of Christ. You must include all Christians in your intercession. As the roots of the tree hidden deep in the earth are one with the branches that spread out to the sky, so the hidden prayer life is inseparably bound with united prayer.

INTERCESSION

❧

*Praying always...in the Spirit...with all perseverance
and supplication for all the saints.
—Ephesians 6:18*

What an unspeakable blessing there is in intercession! That one should pray down heavenly gifts on himself is a wonder of grace, but that he should bring down blessings on others is indeed an inconceivable honor. But God makes the pouring out of blessing on others dependent on our prayers. Indeed, He makes us His remembrancers and fellow workers. He has taken us into partnership in His work; if we fail in doing our part, others will suffer, and His work will suffer unspeakable loss.

God has appointed intercession as one of the means by which souls are saved, and by which saints and ministers of the Gospel are built up in the faith. Even the ends of the earth will receive life and blessing through our prayers. Should we not expect God's children to strive joyfully and with all their powers, by means of intercession, to bring down blessing on the world?

Christian, begin to use intercession as a means of grace for yourself and for others. Pray for your neighbors. Pray for souls with the definite desire that they may be won for Christ. Pray for your minister, for all ministers and missionaries. Pray for your country and its people. Pray for all men. If you surrender yourself to the guidance of the Holy Spirit and live a life wholly for God, you will realize that the time spent in prayer is an offering well pleasing to God, bringing blessing to yourself and power into the lives of those for whom you pray.

Yes, pray *"always with all prayer and supplication in the Spirit, being watchful to this end with all perseverance and supplication for all the saints"* (v. 18). In so doing, you will learn the lesson that intercession is the chief means of winning souls and of bringing glory to God.

PRAYER AND FASTING

🐾

So Jesus said to them, "Because of your unbelief....However,
this kind does not go out except by prayer and fasting."
—*Matthew 17:20–21*

Our Lord here taught us that a life of faith requires both prayer and fasting. That is, prayer grasps the power of heaven, and fasting loosens the hold on earthly pleasure.

Jesus Himself fasted to get strength to resist the Devil. He taught His disciples that fasting should be in secret and that the heavenly Father would reward openly (Matt. 6:6). Abstinence from food, or moderation in taking it, helps to strengthen the soul for communion with God.

Let us learn this great lesson that abstinence, moderation, and self-denial in temporal things are a help to the spiritual life. After eating a hearty meal, one does not feel much desire to pray. To willingly sacrifice our own pleasure or bodily enjoyment, and to subdue the lust of the flesh and the lust of the eyes, will help to set our minds more fully on heavenly things. The very exertion needed in overcoming the desires of the flesh will give us strength to take hold of God in prayer.

The great lesson is this: our dullness in prayer comes from our fleshly desires for comfort and ease. *"Those who are Christ's have crucified the flesh with its passions and desires"* (Gal. 5:24). Prayer is not easy work. It may easily become a mere form. For the real practice of prayer, to really take hold of God and have communion with Him, it is necessary that all that can please the flesh is sacrificed and given over to death.

Beloved Christian, it is worth any trouble to deny ourselves daily, in order to meet the holy God and receive heavenly blessings from Him.

THE SPIRIT OF PRAYER

❧

The Spirit...makes intercession for the saints.
—Romans 8:27

Prayer is not our work, but God's work, which He works within us by His almighty power. As we consider this statement, our attitude should be one of silent expectation that as we pray, the Holy Spirit will help our weaknesses and will pray within us with *"groanings which cannot be uttered"* (v. 26).

What a thought! When I feel how defective my prayers are, when I have no strength of my own, I may bow in silence before God in the confidence that His Holy Spirit will teach me to pray. The Spirit is the Spirit of prayer. It is not my work, but God's work in me. My desire to pray is a sign that God will hear me.

When God moves to grant our requests, He first works the desire in our hearts, and the Spirit will perfect the work, even in our weakness. We see this in the story of Jacob. The same One who wrestled with him and seemed to withhold the blessing was in reality strengthening him to continue and to prevail in prayer. (See Genesis 32:24–30.) What a wondrous thought! Prayer is the work of the triune God: the Father, who wakens the desire and will give all we need; the Son, who through His intercession teaches us to pray in His name; and the Holy Spirit, who in secret will strengthen our feeble desires.

I have already told you about the Spirit of truth, who will glorify Christ in us, and of the Spirit of love, who will pour out this love in our hearts. Now we have the Spirit of prayer, through whom our lives may be ones of continual prayer. Thank God. The Spirit has been given from heaven to dwell in our hearts and to teach us to pray.

Christian, listen to the leading of the Spirit. Obey His voice in all things. He will make you a man or woman of prayer. You will then realize the glory of your calling as an intercessor, asking great things of God for those around you, for the church, and for the whole unsaved world.

WHOLLY FOR CHRIST

🦚

*One died for all...that they which live
should no longer live unto themselves, but unto
him who for their sakes died and rose again.*
—2 Corinthians 5:14–15 RV

Here we have a threefold life described. First is the life of the Christian who lives according to his old nature: he lives for himself alone. The second is the life of a true Christian: he lives wholly for Christ. Third is the life of Christ in heaven: He lives wholly for us.

Many Christians need to be convinced of the foolishness of living only for themselves. At conversion, they tend to think more of their own salvation and less of the glory of God and the claim that Christ, who has redeemed us with His precious blood, has upon them. Many Christians live for themselves, content with doing a little for the Master. The believer who realizes his high calling and the privilege and blessedness of consecrating His life entirely to God's service will find true happiness.

The great hindrance to such a life is unbelief, which says that complete submission to God is impossible. But when the truth takes hold of us—"Christ in heaven lives wholly for me; He will impart His life to me and will enable me to live wholly for Him"—then we will be able to say joyfully, "Dear Lord Jesus, from this moment let my prayer each day be, 'Wholly for Christ, wholly for Christ.'"

Dear brother or sister, let nothing less than this be your earnest desire, your prayer, and your firm expectation. Say, "Christ has not only died for me, but He also lives in heaven to keep and sanctify me, His purchased possession." Ponder this wonderful thought, that Christ will keep you as a member of His body, to work and live for Him. Pray for grace to live wholly for God in seeking souls and in serving His people. Take time from day to day to be so united to Christ in the inner man that you can say with all your heart, "I live wholly for Him, who gave Himself wholly for me and who now lives in heaven wholly for me."

THE CROSS OF CHRIST

🦋

I have been crucified with Christ.
—Galatians 2:20

The cross of Christ is His greatest glory. Because He humbled Himself to the death of the cross, God has highly exalted Him (Phil. 2:8–9). The cross was the power that conquered Satan and sin.

The Christian shares with Christ in the cross. The crucified Christ lives in him through the Holy Spirit, and the spirit of the cross inspires him. He lives as one who has died with Christ. As he realizes the power of Christ's crucifixion, he lives as one who has died to the world and to sin, and the power becomes a reality in his life. It is as the Crucified One that Christ lives in him.

Our Lord said to His disciples, *"Take up* [your] *cross, and follow Me"* (Matt. 16:24). Did they understand this? They had seen men carrying a cross, and they knew it meant a painful death. All His life, Christ bore His cross—the death sentence that He would die for the world. Similarly, each Christian must bear his cross, acknowledge that he is worthy of death, and believe that he is crucified with Christ and that the Crucified One lives in him. *"Our old man was crucified with Him"* (Rom. 6:6). *"Those who are Christ's have crucified the flesh with its passions and desires"* (Gal. 5:24). When we have accepted this life of the cross, we will be able to say with Paul, *"But God forbid that I should boast except in the cross of our Lord Jesus Christ"* (Gal. 6:14).

This is a deep spiritual truth. Think and pray over it, and the Holy Spirit will teach you. Let the disposition of Christ on the cross, His humility, His sacrifice of all worldly honor, His spirit of self-denial, take possession of you. The power of His death will work in you, you will become like Him in His death, and you will *"know Him and the power of His resurrection"* (Phil. 3:10). Take time, dear reader, so that Christ through His Spirit may reveal Himself as the Crucified One.

THE WORLD

❧

Do not love the world or the things in the world.
If anyone loves the world, the love of the Father is not in him.
—1 John 2:15

John taught us clearly what he meant by *"the world."* He wrote, *"All that is in the world; the lust of the flesh, the lust of the eyes, and the pride of life; is not of the Father but is of the world"* (v. 16).

The world is the disposition or power under which man has fallen through sin. And the god of this world, in order to deceive man, conceals himself under the form of what God has created. The world, with its pleasures, surrounds the Christian each day with temptations.

This was the case with Eve in the Garden of Eden. In Genesis 3:6, we find the three characteristics that John mentioned: first, the lust of the flesh: *"The woman saw that the tree was good for food"*; second, the lust of the eyes: *"It was pleasant to the eyes"*; and third, the pride of life: *"A tree desirable to make one wise."* The world still comes to us offering desirable food and much to please the fleshly appetites. It offers much that the eye desires, including riches, beauty, and luxury. And it offers the pride of life, which is shown when a man imagines he knows and understands everything, and prides himself on it.

Are our lives in the world not full of danger, with the allurements of the flesh, so much to occupy our eyes and our hearts, and so much worldly wisdom and knowledge?

John told us, "Do not love the world, for then the love of the Father is not in you." Our Lord calls us, as He called His disciples, to leave all and follow Him.

Christian, you live in a dangerous world. Cling to the Lord Jesus. As He teaches you to shun the world and its attractions, your love will go out to Him in loyal-hearted service. But remember, there must be daily fellowship with Jesus. His love alone can expel the love of the world. Take time to be alone with your Lord.

PUT ON CHRIST

*For as many of you as were baptized
into Christ have put on Christ.
—Galatians 3:27*

*Put on the Lord Jesus Christ, and make no
provision for the flesh, to fulfill its lusts.
—Romans 13:14*

The word that is translated *"put on"* is the same that is used in regard to putting on clothes. We have *"put on the new man"* (Eph. 4:24), and the new nature is like a garment that is worn so that all can see who we are. Paul said that the Christian, when he has confessed Christ at baptism, has *"put on Christ."* Just as a man may be recognized by the garment he wears, so the Christian is known by the fact that he has put on Christ and exhibits Him in his whole life and character.

"Put on the Lord Jesus," not just at conversion, but also on a daily basis. As I put on my clothes each day and am seen in them, so the Christian must daily put on the Lord Jesus, so that he no longer lives to fulfill the lusts of the flesh, but shows forth the image of his Lord and the new man formed in His likeness.

Put on Christ! This work must be done each day in the inner chamber. I must put on the Lord, the heavenly Jesus. But I need time to put on Christ. Just as my garments cover me and protect me from the wind and the sun, even so Christ Jesus will be my beauty, my defense, and my joy. As I commune with Him in prayer, He imparts Himself to me and strengthens me to walk as one who is in Him and is bound to Him forever.

Reader, take time to meditate on this wonderful truth. Just as your clothing is a necessity as you go out into the world, let it be equally indispensable for you to put on Jesus Christ, to abide in Him, and to walk with Him all day long.

This cannot be done hastily and superficially. It takes time, quiet time in living fellowship with Jesus, to realize that you have put Him on. Take the time and the trouble. Your reward will be great.

THE STRENGTH OF THE CHRISTIAN

🦋

Finally, my brethren, be strong in the Lord
and in the power of His might.
—Ephesians 6:10

As the apostle reached the end of his epistle, he began the last section of it with the words, *"Finally, my brethren, be strong in the Lord."*

The Christian needs strength. This we all know. We also know the truth that the Christian has no strength of his own. Where may strength be obtained? Notice the answer: *"Be strong in the Lord and in the power of His might."*

Paul had spoken of this power in the earlier part of his epistle. He had prayed, "God, give them the Spirit, that they might know *'the exceeding greatness of His power...according to the working of His mighty power which He worked in Christ when He raised Him from the dead'* (Eph. 1:19–20)." This is the literal truth: *"the exceeding greatness of His power,"* which raised Christ from the dead, works in every believer—in me and in you. We hardly believe it, and we experience it even less. This is why Paul prayed, and we must pray with him, that God through His Spirit would teach us to believe in His almighty power. Pray with all your heart: "Father, grant me the Spirit of wisdom, so that I may experience this power in my life."

In Ephesians 3, Paul asked God to grant the Ephesians, *"according to the riches of His glory, to be strengthened with might through His Spirit in the inner man, that Christ may dwell in [their] hearts"* (vv. 16–17). And then he added, *"Now to Him who is able to do exceedingly abundantly above all that we ask or think, according to the power that works in us, to Him be glory"* (vv. 20–21).

Read over these two passages again, and pray for God's Spirit to enlighten your eyes. Believe in the divine power working within you. Pray that the Holy Spirit will reveal it to you, and take hold of the promise that God will manifest His power in your heart, supplying all your needs.

Have you not begun to realize that much time in communion with the Father and the Son is necessary if you want to experience the power of God within you?

THE WHOLE HEART

With my whole heart I have sought You.
—Psalm 119:10

Notice how often the psalmist spoke about the whole heart in Psalm 119: *"Those...who seek Him with the whole heart"* (v. 2); *"I shall observe* [Your law] *with my whole heart"* (v. 34); *"I will keep Your precepts with my whole heart"* (v. 69); *"I cry out with my whole heart"* (v. 145). In seeking God, in observing His law, in crying for His help—each time it is with the whole heart.

When we want to make anything a success in worldly affairs, we put our whole heart into it. Is this not much more necessary in the service of the holy God? Is He not worthy? Does His great holiness, and the natural aversion of our hearts from God, not demand it? The whole heart is needed in the service of God when we worship Him in secret.

And yet how little most Christians think of this! They do not remember how necessary it is in prayer, in reading God's Word, in striving to do His will, to say continually, *"With my whole heart I have sought You."* Yes, when we pray, and when we try to understand God's Word and obey His commands, let us say, "I desire to seek God, to serve Him, and to please Him with my whole heart."

"With my whole heart I have sought You." Dear reader, take these words into your heart. Think over them. Pray over them. Speak them out before God until you feel, "I really mean what I say, and I have the assurance that God will hear my prayer." Say them each morning as you approach God in prayer: "I seek You with my whole heart." You will soon feel the need of waiting in holy stillness upon God, so that He may take possession of your whole heart, and you will learn to love Him with your whole heart and with all your strength.

IN CHRIST

❧

But of [God] *you are in Christ Jesus.*
—1 Corinthians 1:30

The expression *"in Christ"* is often used in the Epistles. The Christian cannot read God's Word correctly, nor experience its full power in his life, until he prayerfully and believingly accepts this truth: I am in Christ Jesus.

The Lord Jesus, on the last night with His disciples, used this expression more than once. He said that when the Spirit had been poured out, *"at that day you will know that I am in My Father, and you in Me"* (John 14:20). And then follows, *"Abide in Me....He who abides in Me, and I in him, bears much fruit"* (John 15:4–5); *"If you abide in Me...you will ask what you desire, and it shall be done for you"* (v. 7). But the Christian cannot take hold of these promises unless he first prayerfully accepts the words, *"in Christ."*

Paul expressed the same thought in Romans: *"We* [are] *buried with Him"* (Rom. 6:4); we are *"dead indeed to sin, but alive to God in Christ Jesus our Lord"* (v. 11); *"There is therefore now no condemnation to those who are in Christ Jesus"* (Rom. 8:1). In Ephesians, Paul wrote that God *"has blessed us with every spiritual blessing...in Christ"* (Eph. 1:3); He *"chose us in Him"* (v. 4); and *"He has made us accepted in the Beloved. In Him we have redemption"* (vv. 6–7). And in Colossians we find: *"In Him dwells all the fullness"* (Col. 2:9); we are *"perfect in Christ Jesus"* (Col. 1:28); *"walk in Him"* (Col. 2:6); and *"you are complete in Him"* (v. 10).

Let your faith take hold of these words: it is God who establishes us in Christ (2 Cor. 1:21). *"Of* [God] *you are in Christ Jesus."* The Holy Spirit will make it your experience. Pray earnestly, and follow the leading of the Spirit. The word will take root in your heart, and you will realize something of its heavenly power. But remember that abiding in Christ is a matter of the heart. It must be cultivated in a spirit of love. Only as you take time from day to day in fellowship with Christ will the abiding in Christ become a blessed reality, and the inner man will be renewed from day to day.

CHRIST IN ME

🦋

Do you not know...that Jesus Christ is in you?
—2 Corinthians 13:5

The apostle Paul wanted each Christian to live in the full assurance of "Christ is in me." What a difference it would make in our lives if we could take time every morning to be filled with the thought, "Christ is in me"! As surely as I am in Christ, Christ is also in me.

On His last night on earth, Christ clearly told His disciples that the Spirit would teach them: *"At that day you will know that I am in My Father, and you in Me, and I in you"* (John 14:20). Through the power of God, all of us who believe were crucified with Christ and raised again with Him. As a result, Christ is in us. But this knowledge does not come easily. Through faith in God's Word, we Christians accept it, and the Holy Spirit will lead us into all truth (John 16:13). Take time this very day to realize and take hold of this blessing in prayer.

Paul clearly expressed this thought in the prayer of Ephesians 3:16–17: *"That* [the Father] *would grant you, according to the riches of His glory"*—notice that it is not the ordinary gift of grace, but a special revelation of the riches of His love and power—*"to be strengthened with might through His Spirit in the inner man, that Christ may dwell in your hearts through faith."* Have you grasped it? Every Christian may really have the experience of being filled with the fullness of God.

Dear Christian, Paul said, *"I bow my knees to the Father"* (v. 14). That is the only way to obtain the blessing. Take time in the inner chamber to realize, "Christ dwells in me. Too little have I experienced this in the past, but I will cry to God and wait upon Him to perfect His work in me. Even in the midst of my daily work, I must look upon my heart as the dwelling place of the Son of God, and say, 'I am crucified with Christ. I live no more; Christ lives in me.' (See Galatians 2:20.) Only in this way will Christ's words, *'Abide in Me, and I in you'* (John 15:4), become my daily experience."

CHRIST IS ALL

🎕

Christ is all and in all.
—Colossians 3:11

In the eternal counsel of God, in the redemption on the cross, and as King on the throne in heaven and on earth, *"Christ is all."* In the salvation of sinners, in their justification and sanctification, in the upbuilding of Christ's body, and in the care for individuals, even the most sinful, *"Christ is all."* Every day and every hour, the child of God is comforted and strengthened when he accepts, in faith, that *"Christ is all."*

Perhaps you have thought, in reading these pages, that the full salvation here described is not meant for you. You feel too weak, too unworthy, too untrustworthy. My dear reader, if you will only accept the Lord Jesus in childlike faith, you will have a Leader and a Guide who will supply all your needs (Phil. 4:19). Believe with your whole heart in the words of our Savior—*"Lo, I am with you alway[s]"* (Matt. 28:20)—and you will experience His presence each day.

However cold and dull your feelings may be, however sinful you are, meet the Lord Jesus in secret, and He will reveal Himself to you. Tell Him how wretched you are, and then trust Him to help and sustain you. Wait before Him until by faith you can rejoice in Him. Read this book over again, and read it with the thought, *"Christ is all."* You may have failed to remember this at times, but each day as you go into secret prayer, let this thought be with you: *"Christ is all."* Take it as your motto, to teach you to pray, to strengthen your faith, to give you the assurance of His love and access to the Father, to make you strong for the work of the day. *"Christ is all."* Yes, Christ, your Christ, is all you need. This will teach you to abide in His love. It will give you the assurance that He dwells in your heart, and you may know *"the love...which passes knowledge"* (Eph. 3:19). God be praised to all eternity! Christ, your Christ, is your all in all!

Section Two

The Secret of Intercession

INTERCESSION

🦋

Pray for one another.
—James 5:16

What a mystery of glory there is in prayer! On the one hand, we see God, in His holiness and love and power, waiting, longing to bless man; on the other, we see sinful man, a worm of the dust, bringing down from God by prayer the very life and love of heaven to dwell in his heart.

But how much greater the glory of intercession! Through it a man comes boldly to God to say what he desires for others, and through it he seeks to bring down on one soul—or even on hundreds and thousands—the power of eternal life with all its blessings.

Intercession! Would you not say that this is the holiest exercise of our boldness as God's children, the highest privilege and enjoyment connected with our communion with God? It is the power of being used by God as instruments for His great work of making men His habitation and showing forth His glory.

Would you not think that the church would consider this one of the chief means of grace, and seek above everything to cultivate in God's children the power of an unceasing prayerfulness on behalf of the perishing world?

Would you not expect that believers, who have to some extent been brought into the secret of intercession, would feel what strength there is in unity, and what assurance there is that God will certainly *"avenge His own elect who cry out day and night to Him"* (Luke 18:7)? When Christians cease from looking for help in external union, and aim at being bound together to the throne of God by an unceasing devotion to Jesus Christ and by an unceasing continuance in supplication for the power of God's Spirit, the church will put on her beautiful garments and her strength (Isa. 52:1), and will overcome the world.

Our gracious Father, hear our prayer, and teach Your church and each of us what is the glory, the blessing, and the all-prevailing power of intercession. Give us, we pray, the vision of what intercession means to You, how it is essential for carrying out Your blessed purpose and in the bringing down of the Spirit in power. Show us what it means to us as the exercise of our royal priesthood, and what it will mean to Your church and to perishing men. Amen.

THE OPENING OF THE EYES

❧

And Elisha prayed, and said, "LORD, I pray, open his
eyes that he may see....LORD, open the eyes
of these men, that they may see."
—2 Kings 6:17, 20

How wonderfully the prayer of Elisha for his servant was answered! The young man saw the mountain full of chariots of fire and horsemen surrounding Elisha. The heavenly host had been sent by God to protect the Lord's servant.

Then Elisha prayed a second time. The Syrian army had been stricken with blindness and were led into Samaria. There Elisha prayed for the opening of their eyes, and they found themselves hopeless prisoners in the hand of the enemy.

We ought to use these prayers in the spiritual sphere. First of all, we ought to ask that our eyes may see the wonderful provision that God has made for His church, in the baptism with the Holy Spirit and with fire. (See Matthew 3:11.) All the powers of the heavenly world are at our disposal in the service of the heavenly kingdom. How little the children of God live in the faith of that heavenly vision—the power of the Holy Spirit on them, with them, and in them, for their own spiritual life and as their strength to joyfully witness for their Lord and His work!

But we will find that we need that second prayer, too, so that God may open the eyes of those of His children who do not yet see the power that the world and sin have upon His people. They are still unaware of the feebleness that marks the church, making it powerless to do the work of winning souls for Christ and building up believers for a life of holiness and fruitfulness. Let us pray especially that God may open all eyes to see what the great and fundamental need of the church is—to bring down His blessing in intercession, so that the power of the Spirit may be known unceasingly in its divine effectiveness and blessing.

Our Father, who is in heaven, You who are so unspeakably willing to give us the Holy Spirit in power, hear our humble prayer. Open our eyes, we pray, so that we may realize fully the low estate of Your church, and that we may know as fully what treasures of grace and power You are willing to bestow in answer to the fervent prayer of a united church. Amen.

MAN'S PLACE IN GOD'S PLAN

🕊

The heaven, even the heavens, are the Lord's;
but the earth He has given to the children of men.
—Psalm 115:16

God created heaven as a dwelling for Himself—perfect, glorious, and most holy. The earth He gave to man as his dwelling—everything very good, but only as a beginning, with the need of being kept and cultivated. Man was to continue and perfect the work God had done. Think of the iron and the coal hidden away in the earth, of the steam hidden away in the water. It was left to man to discover and use all this, as we see in the network of railways that span the world, and the steamers that cover the ocean. God had created everything to be thus used. But He made the discovery and the use of such things dependent on the wisdom and diligence of man. What the earth is today, with its cities and its cornfields, it owes to man. The work God had begun and prepared was to be carried out by man in fulfillment of God's purpose. And so nature teaches us the wonderful partnership to which God calls man for the carrying out of the work of creation to its destined end.

This principle is equally strong in the kingdom of grace. In His great plan of redemption, God has revealed the power of the heavenly life and the spiritual blessings of which heaven is full. But He has entrusted to His people the work of making these blessings known and of making men partakers of them.

What diligence the children of this world show in seeking the treasures that God has hidden in the earth for their use! Will the children of God not be equally faithful in seeking the treasures hidden in heaven, to bring them down in blessings on the world? It is by the unceasing intercession of God's people that His kingdom will come and His will will be done on earth as it is in heaven (Luke 11:2).

Ever blessed Lord, how wonderful is the place You have given man, in trusting him to continue the work You have begun. Open our hearts for the great thought that, through the preaching of the Gospel and the work of intercession, Your people are to work out Your purpose. Lord, open our eyes, for Jesus' sake. Amen.

INTERCESSION IN THE PLAN OF REDEMPTION

O You who hear prayer, to You all flesh will come.
—Psalm 65:2

When God gave the world into the power of man, who was made in His own image and who was to rule over it as a representative under Him, it was His plan that Adam should do nothing without God, and God Himself would do all His work in the world through Adam. Adam was to be the owner, master, and ruler of the earth. When sin entered the world, Adam's power was proved to be a terrible reality, for through him the earth, with the whole race of man, was brought under the curse of sin.

When God established the plan of redemption, His objective was to restore man to the place from which he had fallen. God chose servants who, through the power of intercession, could ask what they desired, and it would be given to them (John 15:7). When Christ became man, it was so that, as man, both on earth and in heaven, He might intercede for man. And before He left the world, He imparted this right of intercession to His disciples, in the sevenfold promise of the Farewell Discourse (John 15–17), that whatever they would ask, He would do for them. God's intense longing to bless seems in some sense to be graciously limited by His dependence on the intercession that rises from the earth. He seeks to rouse the spirit of intercession so that He may be able to bestow His blessings on mankind. God regards intercession as the highest expression of His people's readiness to receive and to yield themselves wholly to the working of His almighty power.

Christians need to realize this as their true nobility and their only power with God—the right to claim and expect that God will hear prayer. Only as God's children begin to see what intercession means in regard to God's kingdom will they realize how solemn their responsibility is.

Each individual believer will be led to see that God waits for him to take his part. He will feel that the highest, the most blessed, the mightiest of all human positions for the fulfillment of the petition, "as in heaven, so on earth," is the intercession that rises day and night, pleading with God for the power of heaven to be sent down into the hearts of men. Oh, that God might burn into our hearts this one thought: intercession in its omnipotent power is according to His will and is most certainly effective!

GOD SEEKS INTERCESSORS

🕬

He saw that there was no man,
and wondered that there was no intercessor.
—Isaiah 59:16

In Old Testament times, God had among His people intercessors to whose voices He had listened and given deliverance. In Isaiah 59, we read of a time of trouble when God sought for an intercessor but found none. And He wondered! Think of what that means—the amazement of God that there was no one who loved the people enough or who had enough faith in His power to deliver, that he would intercede on their behalf. If there had been an intercessor, God would have given deliverance; without an intercessor, His judgments came down. (See Ezekiel 22:30–31.)

Of what infinite importance is the place the intercessor holds in the kingdom of God! Is it not indeed a matter of wonder that God should give men such power, and yet there are so few who know what it is to take hold of His strength and to pray down His blessings on the world?

Let us try to realize this position. When God had in His Son worked out the new creation and Christ had taken His place on the throne, the work of the extension of His kingdom was given into the hands of men. All that Christ was to do in heaven was to be in fellowship with His people on earth. In His divine condescension, God has willed that the working of His Spirit will follow the prayers of His people. He waits for their intercession that shows the preparation of their hearts—where and how much of His Spirit they are ready to receive.

God rules the world and His church through the prayers of His people. God calls for intercessors: in His grace He has made His work dependent on them; He waits for them.

Our Father, open our eyes to see that You invite Your children to have a part in the extension of Your kingdom by their faithfulness in prayer and intercession. Give us such an insight into the glory of this holy calling, so that with our whole hearts we may yield ourselves to its blessed service. Amen.

CHRIST AS INTERCESSOR

He is also able to save to the uttermost those who come to God through Him, since He always lives to make intercession for them.
—*Hebrews 7:25*

When God had said in Isaiah that He wondered that there was no intercessor, there followed these words: *"Therefore His own arm brought salvation for Him....The Redeemer will come to Zion"* (Isa. 59:16, 20). God Himself would provide the true Intercessor, in Christ His Son, of whom it had already been said, *"He bore the sin of many, and made intercession for the transgressors"* (Isa. 53:12).

In His life on earth, Christ began His work as Intercessor. Think of His high-priestly prayer on behalf of His disciples and all who would through them believe in His name. Think of His words to Peter: *"I have prayed for you, that your faith should not fail"* (Luke 22:32)—a proof of how intensely personal His intercession is. And on the cross He spoke as Intercessor: *"Father, forgive them"* (Luke 23:34).

Now that He is seated at God's right hand, He continues, as our great High Priest, the work of intercession without ceasing. But He does so with this difference: He gives His people power to take part in it. Seven times in His farewell discourse He repeated the assurance that what they asked He would do.

The power of heaven was to be at their disposal. The grace and power of God waited for man's asking. Through the leading of the Holy Spirit, they would know what the will of God was. They would learn in faith to pray in His name. He would present their petition to the Father, and through His and their united intercession, the church would be clothed with the power of the Spirit.

Blessed Redeemer, what wonderful grace it is that You call us to share in Your intercession! Arouse in Your redeemed people an awareness of the glory of this calling, and of all the rich blessings that Your church in its powerlessness can, through its intercession in Your name, bring down upon this earth. May Your Holy Spirit work in Your people a deep conviction of the sin of prayerlessness, of the sloth and unbelief and selfishness that are the cause of it, and of Your loving desire to pour out the Spirit of prayer in answer to their petitions, for Your name's sake. Amen.

THE INTERCESSORS GOD SEEKS

I have set watchmen on your walls, O Jerusalem; they shall never
hold their peace day or night. You who make mention of the
LORD, do not keep silent, and give Him no rest.
—Isaiah 62:6–7

Watchmen were ordinarily placed on the walls of a city to give notice to the rulers of coming danger. Similarly, God appoints watchmen not only to warn men—often they will not hear—but also to summon Him to come to their aid, whenever need or enemies may be threatening. The great mark of intercessors is that they are not to hold their peace day or night; they are to take no rest, and to give God no rest, until the deliverance comes. In faith they may be assured that God will answer their prayers.

It is concerning this that our Lord Jesus said, *"Shall God not avenge His own elect who cry out day and night?"* (Luke 18:7). From every land the voice is heard that the church of Christ, under the influence of the power of the world and the earthly-mindedness it brings, is losing its influence over its members. There is little proof of God's presence in the conversion of sinners or in the holiness of His people. With the great majority of Christians, there is an utter neglect of Christ's call to take part in the spreading of His Gospel. The power of the Holy Spirit is experienced very little.

Amid all the discussions as to what can be done to interest young and old in the study of God's Word, or to awaken love for the services of His house, one seldom hears of the indispensable necessity of the power of the Holy Spirit in the ministry and the membership of the church. Few people are truly convinced that it is owing to the lack of prayer that the workings of the Spirit are so feeble, and many people fail to see that only by united fervent prayer can a change be brought about. If ever there was a time when God's elect should cry day and night to Him, it is now. Will you not, dear reader, offer yourself to God for this blessed work of intercession, and learn to consider it the highest privilege of your life to be a channel through whose prayers God's blessings can be brought down to earth?

Ever blessed Father, hear us, we pray, and raise up the intercessors that You require. Give us men and women to act as Your watchmen, taking no rest and giving You no rest, until Your church again is praised in the earth. Blessed Father, let Your Spirit teach us how to pray. Amen.

THE SCHOOL OF INTERCESSION

❧

*Who, in the days of His flesh, when He had offered
up prayers and supplications, with vehement cries and
tears...was heard because of His godly fear.*
—Hebrews 5:7

Christ, as the Head of the church, is Intercessor in heaven; we, as the members of His body, are partners with Him on earth. Let no one imagine that it cost Christ nothing to become an intercessor. He is our example because of the enormous price He paid. What do we read about Him? *"When You make His soul an offering for sin, He shall see His seed....He shall see the labor of His soul....I will divide Him a portion with the great...because He poured out His soul unto death"* (Isa. 53:10–12). Notice the repeated expression in regard to the pouring out of His soul.

The pouring out of the soul is the divine meaning of intercession. Nothing less than this was needed if His sacrifice and prayer were to have power with God. This giving over of Himself to live and die so that He might save the perishing was a revelation of the spirit that has power to prevail with God.

If we as helpers and fellow laborers with the Lord Jesus are to share His power of intercession, we will need to have the travail of soul that He had, the same giving up of our life and its pleasures for the one supreme work of interceding for our fellowmen. Intercession must not be a passing interest; it must become an ever growing object of intense desire, for which we long and live above everything else. It is the life of consecration and self-sacrifice that will indeed give power for intercession.

The longer we study this blessed truth and think of what it means to exercise this power for the glory of God and the salvation of men, the deeper our conviction will become that it is worth giving up everything to take part with Christ in His work of intercession.

Blessed Lord Jesus, teach us how to unite with You in calling upon God for the souls You have bought. Let Your love fill us and all Your saints, so that we may learn to plead for the power of Your Holy Spirit to be made known. Amen.

THE NAME OF JESUS:
THE POWER OF INTERCESSION

Until now you have asked nothing in My name.
Ask, and you will receive, that your joy may be full....
In that day you will ask in My name.
—John 16:24, 26

During Christ's life upon earth, the disciples had known little of the power of prayer. In Gethsemane, Peter and the others utterly failed. They had no conception of what it meant to ask in the name of Jesus and to receive. The Lord promised them that in the day that was coming, they would be able to pray with such a power in His name, that they would ask what they desired and it would be given to them.

"Until now...nothing." *"In that day you will ask in My name"* and *"will receive."* These two conditions are still found in the church. With the great majority of Christians, there is such a lack of knowledge of their oneness with Christ Jesus, and of the Holy Spirit as the Spirit of prayer, that they do not even attempt to claim the wonderful promises Christ gave here. But when God's children know what it means to abide in Christ in vital union with Him and to yield to the Holy Spirit's teaching, they begin to learn that their intercession is effective and that God will give the power of His Spirit in answer to their prayers.

It is faith in the power of Jesus' name and in our right to use it that will give us the courage to follow where God invites us—to the holy office of intercessors. When our Lord Jesus, in His farewell discourse, gave His unlimited prayer promise, He sent the disciples out into the world with this thought: "He who sits upon the throne and lives in my heart has promised that what I ask in His name I will receive. He will do it."

Oh, if Christians only knew what it means to yield themselves wholly and absolutely to Jesus Christ and His service, how their eyes would be opened to see that intense and unceasing prayerfulness is the essential mark of the healthy spiritual life! They would see that the power of all-prevailing intercession will indeed be the portion of those who live only in and for their Lord.

Blessed Savior, give us the grace of the Holy Spirit to live in You, with You, and for You to such a degree that we may boldly look to You for the assurance that our prayers are heard. Amen.

PRAYER: THE WORK OF THE SPIRIT

🦢

God has sent forth the Spirit of His Son into
your hearts, crying out, "Abba, Father!"
—Galatians 4:6

We know what *"Abba, Father"* meant in the mouth of Christ at Gethsemane. It was the entire surrender of Himself to death, so that the holy will of God's love in the redemption of sinners might be accomplished. In His prayer, He was ready for any sacrifice, even the yielding of His life. In that prayer, the heart of Him whose place is at the right hand of God is revealed to us, with the wonderful power of intercession that He exercises there, and the power to pour down the Holy Spirit.

The Holy Spirit has been bestowed by the Father to breathe the very Spirit of His Son into our hearts. Our Lord desires us to yield ourselves as wholly to God as He did—to pray as He did, that God's will of love would be done on earth at any cost. As God's love is revealed in His desire for the salvation of souls, so also the desire of Jesus was made plain when He gave Himself for them. And He now asks that the same love would fill His people, too, so that they give themselves wholly to the work of intercession and, at any cost, pray down God's love upon the perishing world.

Lest anyone should begin to think that this is beyond his reach, the Holy Spirit of Jesus is actually given into our hearts so that we may pray in His likeness, in His name, and in His power. It is the man who yields himself wholly to the leading of the Holy Spirit who will feel urged, by the compulsion of a divine love, to surrender himself completely to a life of continual intercession, because he knows that it is God who is working in Him.

Now we can understand how Christ could give such unlimited promises of answer to prayer to His disciples: they were first going to be filled with the Holy Spirit. Now we understand how God can give such a high place to intercession in the fulfillment of His purpose of redemption. It is the Holy Spirit who breathes God's own desire into us and enables us to intercede for souls.

"Abba, Father!" Grant that by Your Holy Spirit there may be maintained in us the unceasing intercession of love for the souls for whom Christ died. Give to Your children the vision of the blessedness and power that come to those who yield themselves to this high calling. Amen.

CHRIST: OUR EXAMPLE IN INTERCESSION

🦋

He shall divide the spoil with the strong, because...He bore
the sin of many, and made intercession for the transgressors.
—Isaiah 53:12

Christ *"made intercession for the transgressors."* What did that
mean to Him? Think of what it cost Him to pray that prayer effectively. He had to pour out His soul as an offering for sin, and He
had to cry at Gethsemane, "Father, Your holy will of love be done."

Think of what moved Him thus to sacrifice Himself to the very
uttermost! It was His love for the Father, so that His holiness
might be manifested, and His love for souls, so that they might be
partakers of His holiness.

Think of the reward He won! As Conqueror of every enemy, He
is seated at the right hand of God with the power of unlimited and
assured intercession. And He desires to *"see His seed"* (Isa. 53:10),
a generation of those who have the same mind as Himself, whom
He can train to share in His great work of intercession.

And what does this mean for us, when we seek to pray for the
transgressors? That we, too, yield ourselves wholly to the glory of
the holiness and the love of the Father; that we, too, say, "God's
will be done, no matter what it may cost"; that we, too, sacrifice
ourselves, even to pouring out our souls unto death.

The Lord Jesus has taken us up into a partnership with Himself in carrying out the great work of intercession. He in heaven
and we on earth must have one mind, one aim in life: that we, out
of love for the Father and for the lost, consecrate our lives to intercession for God's blessing. The burning desire of Father and Son
for the salvation of souls must be the burning desire of our hearts,
too.

What an honor! What blessedness! And what a power for us to
do the work because He lives and because, by His Spirit, He pours
forth His love into our hearts (Rom. 5:5)!

Everlasting God of love, open our eyes to the vision of the glory
of Your Son, who always lives to pray (Heb. 7:25). Open our eyes to
the glory of the grace that enables us to live in His likeness so that
we may pray for the transgressors. For Jesus' sake. Amen.

GOD'S WILL AND OURS

❧

Your will be done.
—Matthew 26:42

It is the high prerogative of God that everything in heaven and earth is to be done according to His will and as the fulfillment of His desires. When He made man in His image, man's desires were intended to be in perfect accord with the desires of God. This is the high honor of being made in the likeness of God—that we are to feel and wish just as God does. In human flesh, man was to be the embodiment and fulfillment of God's desires.

When God created man with the power of willing and choosing what he should be, He limited Himself in the exercise of His will. And when man had fallen and yielded himself to the will of God's enemy, God in His infinite love set about the great work of winning man back, and of making the desires of God his own. As desire is the great motivating power in God, so it is in man. And just as man had yielded himself to a life of desire after the things of the earth and the flesh, God had to redeem him and educate him into a life of harmony with Himself. His one aim was that man's desires would be in perfect accord with His own.

The great step in this direction was when the Son of the Father came into this world. He reproduced the divine desires in His human nature and in His prayer to yield Himself up to the perfect fulfillment of all that God wished and willed. The Son, as Man, said in agony and blood, *"Your will be done,"* and made the surrender even to being forsaken by God, so that the power that had deceived man might be conquered and deliverance might be procured. It was in the wonderful and complete harmony between the Father and the Son when the Son said, *"Your will* [of love] *be done,"* that the great redemption was accomplished.

In taking hold of that redemption, believers have to say, first of all for themselves and then in lives devoted to intercession for others, "Your will be done in heaven as on earth." (See Matthew 6:10.) As we plead for the church, its ministers, and its missionaries, its strong Christians or its young converts, and for the unsaved, whether nominally Christian or unchurched, we have the privilege of knowing that we are pleading for what God wills, and that through our prayers His will is to be done on earth as in heaven.

THE BLESSEDNESS OF A LIFE OF INTERCESSION

🥀

*You who make mention of the LORD, do not keep
silent, and give Him no rest till He establishes and
till He makes Jerusalem a praise in the earth.*
—Isaiah 62:6–7

What unspeakable grace to be allowed to deal with God in intercession for the supply of the needs of others!

What a blessing, in close union with Christ, to take part in His great work as Intercessor, and to mingle my prayers with His! What an honor to have power with God in heaven over souls, and to obtain for them what they do not know or think!

What a privilege, as a steward of the grace of God, to bring to Him the state of the church or of individual souls, of the ministers of the Word or His messengers working among the unsaved, and plead on their behalf until He entrusts me with the answer!

What blessedness, in union with other children of God, to strive together in prayer until the victory is gained over difficulties here on earth, or over the powers of darkness in high places!

It is indeed worth living for, to know that God will use me as an intercessor, to receive and dispense here on earth His heavenly blessing and, above all, the power of His Holy Spirit.

This is the life of heaven, the life of the Lord Jesus Himself, in His self-denying love, taking possession of me and urging me to yield myself wholly to bear the burden of souls before Him, and to plead that they may live.

For too long we have thought of prayer simply as a means for supplying our needs in life and service. May God help us to see the place intercession takes in His divine counsel and in His work for the kingdom. And may our hearts indeed feel that there is no honor or blessedness on earth at all equal to the unspeakable privilege of waiting upon God, and of bringing down from heaven the blessings He delights to give!

O my Father, let Your life flow down to this earth, and fill the hearts of Your children! As the Lord Jesus pours out His love in His unceasing intercession in heaven, let it be the same with us also upon earth—a life of overflowing love and never ending intercession. Amen.

THE PLACE OF PRAYER

❧

*These all continued with one accord in
prayer and supplication.*
—Acts 1:14

Christ instructed His disciples to *"wait for the Promise of the Father"* (v. 4). He also said, *"You shall receive power when the Holy Spirit has come upon you; and you shall be witnesses to Me in Jerusalem…and to the end of the earth"* (v. 8).

United and unceasing prayer, the power of the Holy Spirit, living witnesses to the living Christ, from Jerusalem to the end of the earth—such are the marks of the true Gospel, the true ministry, the true church of the New Testament.

A church of united and unceasing prayerfulness, a ministry filled with the Holy Spirit, the members living witnesses to a living Christ, with a message to every creature on earth—such was the church that Christ founded, and such was the church that went out to conquer the world.

When Christ had ascended to heaven, the disciples knew at once what their work was to be: continuing *"with one accord in prayer and supplication."* They were to be bound together, by the love and Spirit of Christ, into one body. This gave them their wonderful power in heaven with God, and upon earth with men.

Their own duty was to wait in united and unceasing prayer for the power of the Holy Spirit, the power to be witnesses for Christ to the end of the earth. A praying church, a Spirit-filled church, a witnessing church, with all the world as its sphere and aim—such is the church of Jesus Christ.

As long as it maintained this character, the church had power to conquer. However, as it came under the influence of the world, how much it lost of its heavenly, supernatural beauty and strength! How unfaithful in prayer, how feeble the workings of the Spirit, how formal its witness to Christ, and how unfaithful to its worldwide mission!

Blessed Lord Jesus, have mercy upon Your church, and give us the Spirit of prayer and supplication as the early church had, so that we may prove what is the power from You that rests upon us and our testimony for You, to win the world to You. Amen.

PAUL AS AN INTERCESSOR

🦎

*I bow my knees to the Father...that He would grant
you...to be strengthened with might through His Spirit.
—Ephesians 3:14, 16*

We think of Paul as the great missionary, the great preacher, the great writer, the great apostle *"in labors more abundant"* (2 Cor. 11:23). We do not sufficiently think of him as the intercessor who sought and obtained, by his supplication, the power that rested upon all his other activities, and brought down the blessing that rested on the churches that he served.

Look beyond what he wrote to the Ephesians. Think of what he said to the Thessalonians: *"Night and day praying exceedingly that we may see your face and perfect what is lacking in your faith...so that He may establish your hearts blameless in holiness"* (1 Thess. 3:10, 13). To the Romans he said, *"Without ceasing I make mention of you always in my prayers"* (Rom. 1:9). To the Philippians he wrote, *"Always in every prayer of mine making request for you all with joy"* (Phil. 1:4). And to the Colossians it was, *"[We] do not cease to pray for you....I want you to know what a great conflict I have for you"* (Col. 1:9; 2:1).

Day and night he cried to God in his intercession for them, that the light and the power of the Holy Spirit might be in them. As earnestly as he believed in the power of his intercession for them, so did he also believe in the blessings that their prayers would bring upon him: *"I beg you...that you strive together with me in prayers to God for me"* (Rom. 15:30); *"[God] will still deliver us, you also helping together in prayer for us"* (2 Cor. 1:10–11); *"Praying...[also] for me...that I may open my mouth boldly"* (Eph. 6:18–19); *"This will turn out for my deliverance through your prayer"* (Phil. 1:19).

The whole relationship between pastor and people depends on their united, continual prayerfulness. Their whole relationship to each other is a heavenly one, spiritual and divine, and can only be maintained by unceasing prayer. When ministers and people wake up to see that the power and blessing of the Holy Spirit are waiting for their united and unceasing prayer, the church will begin to know something of what Pentecostal apostolic Christianity is.

Ever blessed Father, we humbly pray that You will restore again graciously to Your church the spirit of supplication and intercession, for Jesus' sake. Amen.

INTERCESSION FOR LABORERS

*The harvest truly is plentiful, but the laborers
are few. Therefore pray the Lord of the harvest
to send out laborers into His harvest.
—Matthew 9:37–38*

The disciples understood very little of what these words meant. Christ gave these words as seeds, to be lodged in their hearts for later use. At Pentecost, as they saw how many of the new converts were ready in the power of the Spirit to testify of Christ, they must have felt that the ten days of continuous united prayer had brought this blessing of laborers in the harvest as the fruit of the Spirit's power.

Christ meant to teach us that, however large the field may be and however few the laborers, prayer is the best, the sure, the only means for supplying the need.

What we need to understand is that prayer must be sent up not only in the time of need, but also in the time of plenty. The whole work is to be carried on in the spirit of prayer, so that the prayer for laborers will be in perfect harmony with the whole of our lives and efforts.

At one time in the China Inland Mission, the number of missionaries had risen to two hundred. But there was still such a deep need for more laborers in some districts that, after much prayer, the attendees at a certain conference felt at liberty to ask God to give them, within a year, one hundred additional laborers and £10,000 to meet the expenses. They agreed to continue in prayer every day throughout the year. At the end of the time, the one hundred suitable men and women had been found, along with £11,000.

To meet the need of the world, its open fields, and its waiting souls, the churches all complain of the lack of laborers and of funds. Does not Christ's voice call us to the united and unceasing prayer that the first disciples had? God is faithful, by the power of His Spirit, to supply every need. Let the church take the posture of united prayer and supplication. God hears prayer.

Blessed Lord Jesus, teach Your church what it means to live and work for You in the spirit of unceasing prayerfulness, so that our faith may rise to the assurance that You will, in a way surpassing all expectations, meet the crying need of a dying world. Amen.

INTERCESSION FOR INDIVIDUAL SOULS

You will be gathered one by one, O you children of Israel.
—*Isaiah 27:12*

In our bodies, every member has its appointed place. The same is true in society and in the church. The work must always aim at the welfare and the highest perfection of the whole, through the cooperation of every individual member.

In the church, the thought is too prevalent that the salvation of men is the work of the minister. But the minister generally only deals with the crowd, seldom reaching the individual. This is the cause of a twofold evil. First, the individual believer does not understand that it is necessary for him to testify to those around him, for the nourishment and strengthening of his own spiritual life and for the ingathering of souls. Second, unconverted souls suffer unspeakable loss because Christ is not personally brought to them by each believer they meet.

Intercession for those around us is far too rare. Its restoration to its right place in the Christian life—how much that would mean to the church and its missions! Oh, when will Christians learn the great truth that what God desires to do needs prayer on earth? As we realize this, we will see that intercession is the chief element in the conversion of souls. All our efforts are futile without the power of the Holy Spirit given in answer to prayer. Only when ministers and people unite in a covenant of prayer and testimony will the church flourish, and every believer will understand the part he has to take.

And what can we do to stir up the spirit of intercession? There is a twofold answer. Every Christian, as he begins to get insight into the need and the power of intercession, must begin to intercede on behalf of single individuals. Pray for your children, for your relatives and friends, for all with whom God brings you into contact. If you find that you do not have the power to intercede, let this discovery humble you and drive you to the mercy seat. God wants every redeemed child of His to intercede for the perishing. Prayer is the vital breath of the normal Christian life, the proof that it is born from above.

Then pray intensely and persistently that God may give the power of His Holy Spirit to you and His children around you, so that the power of intercession may have the place that God will honor.

INTERCESSION FOR MINISTERS

❧

And for me.
—Ephesians 6:19

Praying also for us.
—Colossians 4:3

Finally, brethren, pray for us.
—2 Thessalonians 3:1

These expressions of Paul suggest the strength of his conviction that the Christians had power with God and that their prayers would bring new strength to him in his work. Paul had such a sense of the actual unity of the body of Christ, of the interdependence of each member—even the most honorable—on the life that flowed through the whole body, that he sought to rouse Christians, for their own sakes and for his sake and for the sake of the kingdom of God, with this call: *"Continue earnestly in prayer, being vigilant in it with thanksgiving; meanwhile praying also for us"* (Col. 4:2–3).

The church depends on the ministry to an extent that we very little realize. The place of the minister is so high—he is the steward of the mysteries of God, the ambassador for God to beseech men in Christ's name to be reconciled to Him—that any unfaithfulness or inefficiency in him must bring a terrible blight on the church that he serves. If Paul, after having preached for twenty years in the power of God, still needed the prayers of the church, how much more does the ministry in our day need them?

The minister needs the prayers of his people. He has a right to them. He is dependent on them. It is his task to train Christians for their work of intercession on behalf of the church and the world. He must begin by training them to pray for himself. He may even have to begin still further back and learn to pray more for himself and for them.

Let all intercessors who are seeking to enter more deeply into their blessed work give a larger place to the ministers, both of their own church and of other churches. Let them plead with God for individual men and for special circles. Let them continue in prayer, so that ministers may be men of power, men of prayer, and men full of the Holy Spirit. Fellow Christians, pray for the ministers!

Our Father who is in heaven, we humbly ask You to arouse believers to a sense of their calling to pray for the ministers of the Gospel in the spirit of faith. Amen.

PRAYER FOR ALL BELIEVERS

❧

*With all prayer and supplication praying at all
seasons in the Spirit, and watching thereunto in all
perseverance and supplication for all the saints.*
—*Ephesians 6:18* RV

Notice how Paul repeated the words in the intensity of his desire to reach the hearts of his readers: *"With all prayer and supplication praying at all seasons...watching thereunto in all perseverance and supplication."* It is *"all prayer...all seasons...all perseverance and supplication."*

Paul felt so deeply the unity of the body of Christ, and he was so sure that that unity could only be realized in the exercise of love and prayer, that he pleaded with the believers at Ephesus to pray unceasingly and fervently for all believers, not only all believers in their immediate circle, but also all believers in all the church of Christ of whom they might hear. Paul knew that unity is strength. As we exercise this power of intercession with all perseverance, we will be delivered from self with all its feeble prayers, and our hearts will be enlarged so that the love of Christ can flow freely and fully through us.

The great lack in true believers often is that, in prayer, they are occupied with themselves and with what God must do for them. Here we have a call to every believer to give himself without ceasing to the exercise of love and prayer. As we forget ourselves, in the faith that God will take charge of us, and as we yield ourselves to the great and blessed work of calling down the blessings of God on our fellowmen, the whole church will be equipped to do its work in making Christ known to every creature. This alone is the healthy and blessed life of a child of God who has yielded himself wholly to Christ Jesus.

Pray for God's children and the church around you. Pray for all the work in which they are engaged, or ought to be. Pray *"at all seasons in the Spirit"* for all believers. There is no blessedness greater than that of abiding communion with God. And there is no way that leads to the enjoyment of this more surely than the life of intercession for which these words of Paul appeal so pleadingly.

MISSIONARY INTERCESSION

❧

*Then, having fasted and prayed, and laid
hands on them, they sent them away.*
—Acts 13:3

The supreme question of foreign missions is, How do we multiply the number of Christians who will individually and collectively wield this force of intercession for the conversion and transformation of men? Every other consideration and plan is secondary to that of wielding the forces of prayer.

We take for granted that those who love this work and who bear it in their hearts will follow the scriptural command to pray unceasingly for its triumph. With unceasing devotion and intercession, God's people need to approach Him with an attitude that refuses to let God go until He crowns His workers with victory.

Missions has its root in the love of Christ, which was proved on the cross and now lives in our hearts. As men are so earnest in seeking to carry out God's plans for the natural world, so God's children should be at least as wholehearted in seeking to bring Christ's love to all mankind. Intercession is the chief means appointed by God to bring the great redemption within the reach of all.

Pray for missionaries, that the life of Christ may be clear and strong, and that they may be people of prayer, filled with love, people in whom the power of the spiritual life is obvious.

Pray for Christians, that they may know *"the glory of this mystery among the Gentiles* [the unsaved]: *which is Christ in you, the hope of glory"* (Col. 1:27).

Pray for the teaching of God's Word, that it may be in power. Pray especially for pastors and evangelists, that the Holy Spirit may fill them to be witnesses for Christ among their fellowmen.

Pray, above all, for the church of Christ, that it may be lifted out of its indifference, and that every believer may be brought to understand that the one purpose of his life is to help to make Christ King on the earth.

Our gracious God, our eyes are focused on You. Will You not in mercy hear our prayers, and by the Holy Spirit reveal the presence and the power of Christ in the work of Your servants? Amen.

THE GRACE OF INTERCESSION

🙰

Continue earnestly in prayer, being vigilant in
it with thanksgiving; meanwhile praying also for us.
—*Colossians 4:2–3*

Nothing can bring us nearer to God and lead us deeper into His love than the work of intercession. Nothing can give us a higher experience of the likeness of God than the power of pouring out our hearts to God in prayer for those around us. Nothing can so closely link us to Jesus Christ, the great Intercessor, and give us the experience of His power and Spirit resting on us, as the yielding of our lives to the work of bringing the great redemption into the hearts and lives of our fellowmen. There is nothing in which we will know more of the powerful working of the Holy Spirit than the prayer breathed by Him into our hearts, *"Abba, Father"* (Mark 14:36), in all the fullness of meaning that it had for Christ at Gethsemane. Nothing can so help us to prove the power and faithfulness of God to His Word, as when we reach out in intercession to the multitudes, either in the church of Christ or in the darkness of heathenism. As we pour out our souls as living sacrifices before God, with the one persistent plea that He will open the windows of heaven and send down His abundant blessings in answer to our pleas, God will be glorified, our souls will reach their highest destiny, and God's kingdom will come.

Nothing will help us to understand and experience the living unity of the body of Christ, and the irresistible power that it can exert, so much as uniting with God's children in the persistent plea that God will arise and have mercy upon Zion (Ps. 102:13), and will make her a light to those who are sitting in darkness (Luke 1:79). My brothers and sisters in Christ, how little we realize what we are losing by not living in fervent intercession! Think of what we will gain for ourselves and for the world if we allow God's Spirit, as a Spirit of grace and of supplication, to master our whole beings!

In heaven, Christ lives to pray (Heb. 7:25). His whole fellowship with His Father is prayer—an asking and receiving of the fullness of the Spirit for His people. God delights in nothing so much as prayer. Will we not learn to believe that the highest blessings of heaven will be unfolded to us as we pray more?

Blessed Father, pour down the Spirit of supplication and intercession on Your people, for Jesus Christ's sake. Amen.

UNITED INTERCESSION

There is one body and one Spirit.
—Ephesians 4:4

Our own bodies teach us how essential it is for every member to seek the welfare of the whole. It is the same in the body of Christ. There are, unfortunately, too many who look upon salvation only in connection with their own happiness. There are also those who know that they do not live for themselves, and they truly seek to bring others to share in their happiness; but they do not yet understand that, in addition to their personal circle or church, they have a calling to include the whole body of Christ Jesus in their love and their intercession.

Yet this is what the Spirit and the love of Christ will enable them to do. Only when intercession for the whole church, by the whole church, ascends to God's throne, can the Spirit of unity and of power have His full influence. The desire that has been awakened for closer union among the different branches of the church of Christ is cause for thanksgiving. And yet the difficulties are so great and, in the case of different nationalities of the world, so apparently insurmountable, that the thought of a united church on earth appears beyond reach.

Let us bless God that there is unity in Christ Jesus, deeper and stronger than any visible manifestation could make it. Let us thank Him that there is a way in which, even now, amid the diversity of denominations, the unity can be practically exemplified and utilized in order to access previously unknown divine strength and blessings in the work of the kingdom. Only in the cultivation and increase of intercession can true unity be realized. As believers are taught what is the meaning of their calling as *"a royal priesthood"* (1 Pet. 2:9), they are led to see that God's love and promises are not confined to their limited spheres of labor. Rather, He invites them to enlarge their hearts, and like Christ—and also like Paul, I might say—to pray for all who believe, or who may still be brought to believe, that this earth and the church of Christ in it will by intercession be bound to the throne of heaven as it has never been before.

Christians and ministers must bind themselves together for this worldwide intercession. This unity will strengthen the confidence that prayer will be heard and that their prayers will become indispensable for the coming of the kingdom.

UNCEASING INTERCESSION

Pray without ceasing.
—1 Thessalonians 5:17

How different is the standard of the average Christian, with regard to a life in the service of God, from that which Scripture gives us! In the former the chief thought is personal safety—grace to pardon his sin and to live the kind of life that will secure his entrance into heaven. How high above this is the Bible standard—a Christian surrendering himself with all his powers, with his time, thoughts, and love wholly yielded to the glorious God who has redeemed him! He now delights in serving this God, in whose fellowship heaven is begun.

To the average Christian, the command, *"Pray without ceasing,"* is simply a needless and impossible life of perfection. Who can do it? We can get to heaven without it. To the true believer, on the contrary, it holds out the promise of the highest happiness, of a life crowned by all the blessings that can be brought down on other souls through his intercession. And as he perseveres, unceasing intercession becomes increasingly his highest aim upon earth, his highest joy, his highest experience of the wonderful fellowship with the holy God.

"Pray without ceasing." Let us take hold of these words with a large faith, as a promise of what God's Spirit will work in us, of how close and intimate our union to the Lord Jesus can be, and of our likeness to Him, in His ever blessed intercession at the right hand of God. Let these words become to us one of the chief elements of our heavenly calling, to be consciously the stewards and administrators of God's grace to the world around us. As we think of how Christ said, *"I in them, and You in Me"* (John 17:23), let us believe that just as the Father worked in Him, so Christ the interceding High Priest will work and pray in us. As the faith of our high calling fills our hearts, we will begin literally to feel that there is nothing on earth for one moment to be compared to the privilege of being God's priests, walking without intermission in His holy presence, bringing the burdens of the souls around us to the footstool of His throne, and receiving at His hands the power and blessing to dispense to our fellowmen.

This is indeed the fulfillment of the Scriptures that say, "Man was created in the likeness and the image of God." (See Genesis 1:26–27.)

INTERCESSION: THE LINK BETWEEN HEAVEN AND EARTH

Your will be done on earth as it is in heaven.
—*Luke 11:2*

When God created heaven and earth, He meant heaven to be the divine pattern to which earth was to be conformed; *"on earth as it is in heaven"* was to be the law of its existence.

This Scripture calls us to think of what constitutes the glory of heaven. God is all in all there. Everything lives in Him and for His glory. As we think of what this earth has now become—with all its sin and misery, with the great majority of people lacking any knowledge of the true God, and with the remainder living only as nominal Christians who are for the greater part utterly indifferent to His claims and are estranged from His holiness and love—we feel what a miracle is needed if these words are to be fulfilled: *"On earth as it is in heaven."*

How is this ever to come true? Only through the prayers of God's children. Our Lord taught us to pray for it. Intercession is to be the great link between heaven and earth. The intercession of the Son, begun on earth, continued in heaven, and carried on by His redeemed people on earth, will bring about the mighty change—*"on earth as it is in heaven."* Christ's redeemed ones, who yield themselves fully to His mind and Spirit, make His prayer their own and unceasingly send up the cry, *"Your will be done on earth as it is in heaven."*

Every prayer of a parent for a child, every prayer of a believer for the saving of the lost or for more grace for those who have been saved, is part of the great unceasing cry going up day and night from this earth: *"On earth as it is in heaven."*

But when God's children not only learn to pray for their immediate circles and interests, but also enlarge their hearts to take in the whole church and the whole world, then their united supplication will have power with God and will hurry the day when it will indeed be *"on earth as it is in heaven"*—the whole earth filled with the glory of God. Child of God, will you not yield yourself, like Christ, to live with this one prayer: "Father, *'Your will be done on earth as it is in heaven'"*?

"Our Father in heaven, Hallowed be Your name. Your kingdom come. Your will be done on earth as it is in heaven" (Luke 11:2). Amen.

THE FULFILLMENT OF GOD'S DESIRE

*The LORD has chosen Zion; He has desired it for His
dwelling place....Here I will dwell, for I have desired it.*
—*Psalm 132:13–14*

Here you have the one great desire of God that moved Him in
the work of redemption. His heart longed for man; He desired to
dwell with him and in him.

To Moses He said, *"Let them make Me a sanctuary, that I may
dwell among them"* (Exod. 25:8). And just as Israel had to prepare
the dwelling for God, His children are now called to yield themselves to God so that He might dwell in them and they might win
others to become His habitation. As the desire of God toward us
fills our hearts, it will waken within us the desire to gather others
around us to become His dwelling, too.

What an honor! What a high calling, to count my worldly business as entirely secondary, and to find my life and my delight in
winning souls in whom God may find His heart's delight! *"Here I
will dwell, for I have desired it."*

And this is what I can do through intercession. I can pray for
those around me, that God would give them His Holy Spirit. God's
great plan is that man himself will build Him a habitation. In answer to the unceasing intercession of His children, God will give
His power and blessing. As this great desire of God fills us, we will
give ourselves wholly to work for its fulfillment.

When David thought of God's desire to dwell in Israel, he said,
*"I will not give sleep to my eyes or slumber to my eyelids, until I find
a place for the LORD, a dwelling place for the Mighty One of Jacob"*
(Ps. 132:4). And since it has been revealed to us what that indwelling of God may be, should we not give our lives for the fulfillment of His heart's desire?

Oh, let us begin, as never before, to pray for our children, for
the souls around us, and for all the world—not only because we
love them, but especially because God longs for them and gives us
the honor of being the channels through whom His blessings are
brought down upon them. Children of God, awaken to the realiza-
tion that God is seeking to train you as intercessors, through whom
the great desire of His loving heart can be satisfied!

O God, who has said of human hearts, *"Here I will dwell, for I
have desired it,"* teach us to pray, day and night, that the desire of
Your heart may be fulfilled. Amen.

THE FULFILLMENT OF MAN'S DESIRES

🦚

Delight yourself also in the LORD, and
He shall give you the desires of your heart.
—Psalms 37:4

God is love, an ever flowing fountain out of which streams the unceasing desire to make His creatures the partakers of all the holiness (Heb. 12:10) and blessedness in Himself. This desire for the salvation of souls is God's perfect will, His highest glory.

To all His children who are willing to yield themselves wholly to Him, God imparts His loving desire to take His place in the hearts of all men. It is in this that the likeness and image of God consist: to have a heart in which His love takes complete possession and leads us to find our highest joy in loving as He does.

It is thus that our text finds its fulfillment: *"Delight yourself also in the LORD"* and in His life of love, *"and He shall give you the desires of your heart."* You can be sure that the intercession of love, rising up to heaven, will be met with the fulfillment of the desires of our hearts. As we delight in what God delights in, such prayer is inspired by God and will have its answer. And our prayer becomes unceasingly, "Your desires, my Father, are mine. Your holy will of love is my will, too."

In fellowship with Him, we acquire the courage to bring our concerns before the Lord in an ever growing confidence that our prayers will be heard. As we reach out in yearning love, we will obtain power to take hold of the will of God to bless. We will also begin to believe that God will work out His own blessed will in giving us the desires of our hearts, because the fulfillment of His desire has been the delight of our souls.

We then become, in the highest sense of the word, God's fellow laborers. Our prayers become part of God's divine work of reaching and saving the lost. And we learn to find our happiness in losing ourselves in the salvation of those around us.

Dear Father, teach us that nothing less than delighting ourselves in You, and in Your desires toward men, can inspire us to pray correctly or can give us the assurance of an answer. Amen.

MY GREAT DESIRE

*One thing I have desired of the LORD, that will I seek: that
I may dwell in the house of the LORD all the days of my life,
to behold the beauty of the LORD, and to inquire in His temple.*
—Psalm 27:4

Here we have man's response to God's desire to dwell in us.
When the desire of God toward us begins to rule our lives and
hearts, our desire is fixed on one thing, and that is to dwell in the
house of the Lord all the days of our lives, to behold the beauty of
the Lord, to worship Him in the beauty of holiness, and then to inquire in His temple and to learn what He meant when He said, *"I,
the LORD, have spoken it, and I will do it....I will also let the house
of Israel inquire of Me to do this for them"* (Ezek. 36:36–37).

The more we realize the desire of God's love to put His rest in
our hearts, and the more we desire to dwell every day in His temple
and to behold His beauty, the more the Spirit of intercession will
grow upon us, to claim all that God has promised in His new covenant. Whether we think of our church or country, of our home or
school, of people close to us or far away; whether we think of the
saved and all their needs or the unsaved and their danger, the
thought that God is longing to find His home and His rest in the
hearts of men, if we only *"inquire"* of Him, will rouse us entirely.
All the thoughts of our feebleness and unworthiness will be swal-
lowed up in the wonderful assurance that He has said of human
hearts, *"This is My resting place forever; here I will dwell, for I
have desired it"* (Ps. 132:14).

As we see by faith how high our calling is, how indispensable
God has made fervent, intense, persistent prayer as the condition of
His purpose being fulfilled, we will be drawn to give up our lives to
a closer walk with God, to an unceasing waiting upon Him, and to a
testimony to our fellowmen of what God will do in them and in us.

Is it not wonderful beyond all thought, this divine partnership
in which God commits the fulfillment of His desires to our keeping?
We should be utterly ashamed that we have so little realized it!

Our Father in heaven, we ask that You would give, give in
power, the Spirit of grace and supplication to Your people, for Jesus' sake. Amen.

INTERCESSION DAY AND NIGHT

Shall God not avenge His own elect who cry out day
and night to Him, though He bears long with them?
—Luke 18:7

When Nehemiah heard of the destruction of Jerusalem, he cried to God, *"Hear the prayer of Your servant which I pray before You now, day and night"* (Neh. 1:6). Concerning the watchman set on the walls of Jerusalem, God said, *"They shall never hold their peace day or night"* (Isa. 62:6). And Paul wrote, *"Night and day praying exceedingly...that He may establish your hearts blameless in holiness before our God and Father"* (1 Thess. 3:10, 13).

Is such prayer really needed and really possible? Yes. It is needed when the heart is so entirely possessed by some desire that it cannot rest until the desire is fulfilled. And it is possible when one's life has so come under the power of the heavenly blessing to such a degree that nothing can keep it from sacrificing all to obtain it.

When a child of God begins to get a real vision into the need of the church and of the world—a vision of the divine redemption that God has promised in the outpouring of His love into our hearts, a vision of the power of true intercession to bring down the heavenly blessing, and a vision of the honor of being allowed as intercessors to take part in that work—it naturally follows that he regards as the most heavenly thing upon earth his work of crying day and night to God for the revelation of His mighty power.

Let us learn from David, who said, *"Zeal for Your house has eaten me up"* (Ps. 69:9). Let us learn from Christ our Lord, of whom these words were so intensely true. There is nothing so much worth living for as satisfying the heart of God in His longing for human fellowship and affection, and winning hearts to be His dwelling places. How can we rest until we have found a place for the Mighty One in our hearts and have yielded ourselves to the great work of intercession for so many after whom the desires of God are going out?

God grant that our hearts may be so brought under the influence of these divine truths, that we will yield ourselves in pure devotion to Christ. May our longing to satisfy the heart of God be the chief aim of our lives.

Lord Jesus, the great Intercessor, breathe Your own Spirit into our hearts, for Your name's sake. Amen.

THE HIGH PRIEST AND HIS INTERCESSION

&c⃝

We have such a High Priest...[who is] *able to save*
to the uttermost those who come to God through Him,
since He always lives to make intercession for them.
—Hebrews 8:1; 7:25

In Israel, what a difference there was between the high priest and the priests and Levites! The high priest alone had access to the Holiest of All. He bore on his forehead the golden crown, *"HO-LINESS TO THE LORD"* (Exod. 28:36), and by his intercession on the great Day of Atonement he bore the sins of the people. The priests, in contrast, brought the daily sacrifices, stood before the Lord, and came out to bless the people. Though the difference between high priest and priest was great, their unity was even greater. The priests formed one body with the high priest, sharing with him the power to appear before God to receive and dispense His blessings to His people.

It is the same with our great High Priest. Jesus alone has power with God, in a never ceasing intercession, to obtain from the Father what His people need. Though there is infinite distance between Him and the *"royal priesthood"* (1 Pet. 2:9) that surrounds Him for His service, the unity and the fellowship into which His people have been taken up with Him is no less infinite. When He obtains blessings from His Father for us, He holds them so that His people may receive from Him through their fervent supplication.

As long as Christians simply think of being saved, and of a life that will make that salvation secure, they will never understand the mystery of the power of intercession to which they are called.

But once they see that salvation means a vital union with Jesus Christ—an actual sharing of His life dwelling and working in us, and the consecration of our whole beings to live and labor, to think and will, and to find our highest joy in living as a royal priesthood—the church will "put on her strength" (see Isaiah 52:1) and will prove, in fellowship with God and man, how truly the likeness and the power of Christ dwell in her.

Oh, that God would open our hearts to know what our royal priesthood is and what the real meaning is of our living and praying in the name of Jesus, so that what we ask will indeed be given to us! Lord Jesus, our holy High Priest, breathe the spirit of Your own holy priesthood into our hearts. Amen.

A ROYAL PRIESTHOOD

*Call to Me, and I will answer you, and show
you great and mighty things, which you do not know.*
—Jeremiah 33:3

As you ask God for the great mercies of the new covenant to be bestowed, keep the following thoughts in mind.

1. THE INFINITE WILLINGNESS OF GOD TO BLESS. His very nature is a pledge of it. *"He delights in mercy"* (Mic. 7:18). He waits to be gracious. His promises and the experience of His saints assure us of it.

2. WHY THE BLESSING SO OFTEN TARRIES. In creating man with a free will, and in making him a partner in the rule of the earth, God limited Himself. He made Himself dependent on what man would do. Man's prayer would hold the measure of what God could do in blessing.

3. GOD IS HINDERED AND DISAPPOINTED WHEN HIS CHILDREN DO NOT PRAY, OR PRAY VERY LITTLE. The low, feeble life of the church, the lack of the power of the Holy Spirit for conversion and holiness, is all owing to the lack of prayer. How different the state of the church and of the world would be if God's people were to take no rest in calling upon Him!

4. YET GOD HAS BLESSED, JUST UP TO THE MEASURE OF THE FAITH AND THE ZEAL OF HIS PEOPLE. They should never be content with this as a sign of His approval. Rather, they should say, "If God has thus blessed our feeble efforts and prayers, what will He not do if we yield ourselves wholly to a life of intercession?"

5. WHAT A CALL TO PENITENCE AND CONFESSION THAT OUR LACK OF CONSECRATION HAS KEPT BACK GOD'S BLESSING FROM THE WORLD! He was ready to save men, but we were not willing for the sacrifice of a wholehearted devotion to Christ and His service.

Dear readers, God depends on you to take your place before His throne as intercessors. Awake to your holy calling as *"a royal priesthood"* (1 Pet. 2:9). Begin to live a new life in the assurance that intercession, in fellowship with the interceding Lord Jesus in heaven, is the highest privilege a man can desire. In this spirit, hold this near to your heart: *"Call to Me, and I will answer you, and show you great and mighty things, which you do not know."*

Are you not willing—do you not desire supremely—to give yourself wholly to this blessed calling, and in the power of Jesus Christ to make intercession for God's church and people, and for a dying world, the one chief aim of your life? Is this asking too much? Is it too much to yield your life for this holy service of the royal priesthood, to that blessed Lord who gave Himself for us?

INTERCESSION: A DIVINE REALITY

Then another angel...came...[and] *he was given much incense,*
that he should offer it with the prayers of all the saints
upon the golden altar which was before the throne.
—Revelation 8:3

Intercession is, by amazing grace, an essential element in God's redeeming purpose—to such a degree that, without it, the failure of its accomplishment may lie at our door. Christ's intercession in heaven is essential to His carrying out the work He began on earth, but He calls for the intercession of the saints in the attainment of His purpose. Just think of what we read: *"All things are of God, who has reconciled us to Himself through Jesus Christ, and has given us the ministry of reconciliation"* (2 Cor. 5:18). As the reconciliation was dependent on Christ's doing His part, so in the accomplishment of the work He calls on the church to do her part. Paul regarded unceasing intercession as indispensable to the fulfillment of the work that had been entrusted to him. It is just one aspect of the mighty power of God that works in the hearts of His believing people.

Intercession is indeed a divine reality. Without it, the church loses one of its chief beauties, loses the joy and the power of the Spirit life for achieving great things for God. Without it, the command to preach the Gospel to every creature can never be carried out. Without it, there is no power for the church to recover from her sickly, feeble life and to conquer the world. And in the life of the believer, there can be no entrance into the abundant life and joy of daily fellowship with God unless he takes his place among God's elect—the watchmen and remembrancers of God who cry to Him *"day and night"* (Luke 18:7).

Church of Christ, awaken! Listen to the call: *"Pray without ceasing"* (1 Thess. 5:17). Take no rest, and give God no rest. Even though it may be with a sigh from the depths of the heart, let the answer be, *"For Zion's sake I will not hold My peace"* (Isa. 62:1). God's Spirit will reveal to us the power of a life of intercession as a divine reality, an essential and indispensable element of the great redemption and therefore also of the true Christian life.

May God help us to know and fulfill our calling!

Section Three

❧

The Secret of Adoration

THE SECRET OF ADORATION

In prayer, there are two parties: God and man—God in His inconceivable holiness, glory, and love; man in his littleness, his sinfulness, his powerlessness. Our definition of prayer depends on our point of view. If, as is usually done, we just think of our own needs and desires, of our own efforts to pray, and of our own faith regarding the certainty of an answer, we will soon find that there is no real power in our prayer. Only when we regard prayer in the light of God—the deep interest He takes in us, the wonderful love with which He waits to answer prayer, the almighty power that is the pledge of what He can and will do, and above all, the grace of our Lord Jesus Christ and the Holy Spirit by which He Himself will strengthen us for the faith and perseverance that are needed—will we be able to know the joy and power in prayer. And we will begin to see what an infinite difference it makes whether we look at prayer in the light of earth or heaven, in the light of man's littleness or the infinite glory of the living God.

Once a Christian sees the difference, he may be in danger of attempting to pray a little more or a little better than he has before, but find that his efforts end in failure. He needs to realize that two paths are set before him. The one is of prayer as a means by which man can get what he needs from heaven. The other is of prayer as an infinite grace of God lifting us up into His fellowship and love, and then when He has brought us to Himself, bestowing upon us the blessings we need. In the former case, the gifts that I can receive through prayer are the chief things. In the latter, God and His love, communion with Him, and the surrender of the one who prays to His glory and His will, will be supreme.

Once the child of God understands this, he sees that there is a great decision to be made: Will it be the human or the divine aspect of prayer that will rule my life? Will it be man or God who is first in every prayer? The believer will feel the need of coming to a definite decision as to which of these two paths he will choose. He will feel that it is no trivial matter to change from the one to the other. Only by the intervention of God's mighty power, and by a surrender on the believer's part in the faith of what God will do, is it possible for him to walk with God as he has never yet done. Nothing but the firm decision to part with the self-life in prayer and to yield himself wholly to the life and leading of the Spirit, will enable him truly to become the man of prayer that God and Christ want him to be.

This section was written with the intention of providing very simple help for all believers who are longing to enter into the wonderful privilege that is open to them through prayer. It aims at reminding the reader that, in prayer, God must be first. To this end, there must be secret prayer, where God and you can meet in private. The first thing must be to bow in lowly reverence before God in His glory, the Father whose name is to be hallowed, and so offer Him your adoration and worship. When you have secured some sense of His presence, you may utter your petitions in the hope, in the assurance, that He hears and accepts them and in due time will send you His answer.

Above all, we have felt the need for the unceasing repetition of the loving message: take time. Give God time to reveal Himself to you. Give yourself time to be silent and quiet before Him, waiting to receive through the Spirit the assurance of His presence with you, of His power working in you. Take time to read His Word, so that from it you may know what He asks of you and what He promises you.

Let the Word create around you and within you a holy atmosphere, a holy heavenly light in which your soul will be refreshed and strengthened for daily life. Yes, take time, so that God may let His holy presence enter into your heart and that your whole being may be permeated with the life and love of heaven.

I feel deeply the need for Christians to be trained to pray if their intercession is to be effective (James 5:16). They need only to learn how to live with God in the daily exercise of fellowship with Him through the prayer of faith. Then they will find that the path of prayer in which God is always first is the path not only of great peace and joy, but also of true power for intercession on behalf of those who have yet to be won for Him.

TRUE WORSHIP

🦋

Worship God.
—Revelation 22:9

Those who have read the previous section on the secret of intercession have undoubtedly asked more than once, "What is the reason that prayer and intercession are not a greater joy and delight to Christians? Is there any way in which we may be more inclined to make fellowship with God our chief joy, and as intercessors to bring down His power and blessing on those for whom we pray?"

There may be more than one answer to these questions. But the chief answer is undoubtedly, We know God too little. In our prayers, our hearts are not set chiefly on waiting for His presence. And yet it should be so. We think mostly of ourselves, our needs and weaknesses, our desires and prayers. But we forget that in every prayer God must be first, must be all. To seek Him, to find Him, to wait in His presence, to be assured that His holy presence rests upon us, that He actually listens to what we say and is working in us—this alone gives the inspiration that makes prayer as natural and easy to us as the fellowship of a child with his father.

How is one to reach this nearness to God and fellowship with Him? The answer is simple: we must give God time to make Himself known to us. Believe with all your heart that, just as you present yourself to God in prayer, so God presents Himself to you as the Hearer of prayer. But you cannot realize this unless you give Him time and quiet. It is not the volume or the earnestness of your words in which prayer has its power, but in the living faith that God Himself is taking you and your prayer into His loving heart. He Himself will give the assurance that, in His time, your prayer will be heard.

The purpose of this section is to help you to know the way to meet God in every prayer. In it I give you Scriptures with which your heart can bow before God, waiting on Him to make them living and true in your experience.

Begin today with this verse: *"To You, O LORD, I lift up my soul"* (Ps. 25:1). Bow before Him in stillness, believing that He looks on you and will reveal His presence.

"My soul thirsts for God, for the living God" (Ps. 42:2).

GOD IS A SPIRIT

✎

God is Spirit, and those who worship Him
must worship in spirit and truth.
—John 4:24

When God created man and breathed into him His own spirit, man became a living soul. The soul stood midway between the spirit and the body, to yield either to the spirit to be lifted up to God, or to the flesh and its lusts. In the Fall, man refused to listen to his own spirit, and so it became the slave of the body. The spirit in man became utterly darkened.

In regeneration, it is this spirit that is quickened and born again from above. In the regenerated life and in fellowship with God, it is the spirit of man that must continually yield itself to the Spirit of God. Man's spirit is the deepest inward part of the human being. The Scriptures read, *"You desire truth in the inward parts, and in the hidden part You will make me to know wisdom"* (Ps. 51:6), and *"I will put my law in their inward parts"* (Jer. 31:33 KJV). Also concerning this, Isaiah said, *"With my soul I have desired You in the night, yes, by my spirit within me I will seek You early"* (Isa. 26:9). The soul must sink down into the depths of the hidden spirit and must stir itself to seek God.

God is a Spirit, most holy and most glorious. He gave us a spirit with the one purpose of holding fellowship with Himself. Through sin, that purpose has been darkened and nearly quenched. There is no way for it to be restored except by presenting the soul in stillness before God for the working of His Holy Spirit in our spirits. Deeper than our thoughts and feelings, God will in our inward parts, in our spirits within us, teach us to worship Him *"in spirit and truth."*

"The Father is seeking such to worship Him" (John 4:23). He Himself by the Holy Spirit will teach us this if we wait upon Him. In this quiet hour, be still before God, and yield yourself with your whole heart to believe in and to receive the gentle working of His Spirit. And breathe out such words as these: *"With my soul I have desired You in the night, yes, by my spirit within me I will seek You early"* (Isa. 26:9); *"On You I wait all the day"* (Ps. 25:5).

INTERCESSION AND ADORATION

Worship the LORD in the beauty of holiness!
—Psalm 96:9

The better we know God, the more wonderful our insight into the power of intercession becomes. We begin to understand that it is the great means by which man can take part in the carrying out of God's purpose. God has commissioned His people to make known and communicate to men the whole plan of redemption through Christ. In all this, intercession is the chief and essential element, because in it His servants enter into the full fellowship with Christ, and they receive the power of the Spirit and of heaven as their power for service.

It is easy to see why God has so ordered it. He desires to renew us after His image and likeness. And there is no other way to do this but by our making His desires our own, so that we breathe His character; and by sacrificing ourselves in love, so that we may become to some degree like Christ, ever living to make intercession (Heb. 7:25). Such can be the life of the consecrated believer.

The clearer one's insight into this great purpose of God, the more the need will be felt to enter very truly into God's presence in the spirit of humble worship and holy adoration. The more we take time to abide in God's presence, to enter fully into His mind and will, to get our whole souls possessed by the thought of His glorious purpose, the stronger our faith will become that God will Himself work out all the good pleasure of His will (Phil. 2:13) through our prayers. As the glory of God shines upon us, we will become conscious of the depths of our helplessness, and so we will rise up into the faith that believes that God will do *"above all that we ask or think"* (Eph. 3:20).

Intercession will lead us to feel the need for a deeper adoration. Adoration will give new power for intercession. A true intercession and a deeper adoration will always be inseparable.

The secret of true adoration can only be known by the individual who spends time waiting in God's presence, yielding to God so that He may reveal Himself. Adoration will indeed equip us for the great work of making God's glory known.

"Oh come, let us worship and bow down; let us kneel before the LORD our Maker. For He is our God" (Ps. 95:6–7).

"Give to the LORD the glory due His name" (1 Chron. 16:29).

THE DESIRE FOR GOD

With my soul I have desired You in the night.
—Isaiah 26:9

What is the chief thing, the greatest and most glorious, that man can see or find upon earth? Nothing less than God Himself.

And what is the chief, the best, the most glorious thing that a man can and needs to do every day? Nothing less than to seek, to know, to love, and to praise this glorious God. As glorious as God is, so is the glory that begins to work in the heart and life of the man who gives himself to live for God.

My brother or sister in Christ, have you learned the first and greatest thing you have to do every day? Nothing less and nothing greater than to seek this God, to meet Him, to worship Him, to live for Him and for His glory. It is a great step in the life of a Christian when he truly sees this truth and yields himself to consider fellowship with God every day as the chief purpose of his life.

Take time and ask whether this is not the highest wisdom, and the one thing for which a Christian is to live above all—to know his God rightly, and to love Him with his whole heart. Believe not only that it is true, but also that God's greatest desire is for you to live thus with Him. In answer to prayer, He will indeed enable you to do so.

Begin today, and take a word from God's Book to speak to Him in the stillness of your soul: *"O God, You are my God; early will I seek You; my soul thirsts for You; my flesh longs for You....My soul follows close behind You"* (Ps. 63:1, 8); *"With my whole heart I have sought You"* (Ps. 119:10).

Repeat these words in deep reverence and childlike longing until their spirit and power enter your heart. Then wait upon God until you begin to realize the blessedness of meeting with Him in this way. As you persevere, you will learn to expect that the fear and the presence of God can abide with you throughout the day.

"I waited patiently for the LORD; and He inclined to me, and heard my cry" (Ps. 40:1).

SILENT ADORATION

❧

My soul silently waits for God....My soul, wait
silently for God alone, for my expectation is from Him.
—Psalm 62:1, 5

When man in his littleness and God in His glory meet, we all understand that what God says has infinitely more worth than what man says. Yet our prayers so often consist of telling God what we need that we give Him no time to speak to us. Our prayers are often so indefinite and vague. It is a great lesson to learn, that to be silent before God is the secret of true adoration. Let us remember the promise: *"In quietness and confidence shall be your strength"* (Isa. 30:15).

"My soul, wait silently for God alone, for my expectation is from Him."

"I wait for the LORD, my soul waits, and in His word I do hope" (Ps. 130:5).

As the soul bows itself before Him to remember His greatness, His holiness, His power, and His love, and as it seeks to give Him the honor, reverence, and worship that are His due, the heart will be opened to receive the divine impression of the nearness of God and of the working of His power.

O Christian, believe that such worship of God—in which you bow lower and lower in your nothingness, and in which you lift up your thoughts to realize God's presence as He gives Himself to you in Christ Jesus—is the sure way to give Him the glory that is His due and to lead to the highest blessedness that can be found in prayer.

Do not imagine that such worship is time lost. Do not turn from it if at first it appears difficult or fruitless. Be assured that it brings you into the right relation to God. It opens the way to fellowship with Him. It leads to the blessed assurance that He is looking on you in tender love and is working in you with a secret but divine power. As you become more accustomed to it, it will give you the sense of His presence abiding with you all day long. It will make you strong to testify for God. Men will begin to feel that you have been with God. Someone has said, "No one is able to influence others for goodness and holiness beyond the amount of God that is in him."

"But the LORD is in His holy temple. Let all the earth keep silence before Him" (Hab. 2:20).

"Be silent, all flesh, before the LORD, for He is aroused from His holy habitation!" (Zech. 2:13).

THE LIGHT OF GOD'S COUNTENANCE

God is light.
—1 John 1:5

The LORD is my light.
—Psalm 27:1

Every morning the sun rises, and we walk in its light and perform our daily duties with gladness. Whether we think of it or not, the light of the sun shines on us all day.

Every morning the light of God shines upon His children. But in order to enjoy the light of God's countenance, the soul must turn to God and trust Him to let His light shine upon it.

When there is a shipwreck at midnight, with what longing the sailors look for the morning! How often the sigh goes up, "When will the day break?" Similarly, the Christian must wait on God and rest patiently until His light shines upon him.

"My soul waits for the Lord more than those who watch for the morning" (Ps. 130:6).

Dear reader, begin each day with one of these prayers:

"Make Your face shine upon Your servant" (Ps. 31:16).

"LORD, lift up the light of Your countenance upon us" (Ps. 4:6).

"Cause Your face to shine, and we shall be saved!" (Ps. 80:3).

Do not rest until you know that the light of His countenance and His blessing is resting on you. Then you will experience the truth of these words: *"They walk...in the light of Your countenance. In Your name they rejoice all day long"* (Ps. 89:15–16).

Children of God, believe that it is the ardent longing of your Father that you should dwell and rejoice in His light all day long. Just as you need the light of the sun each hour, so the heavenly light, the light of the Father, is indispensable. As surely as we receive and enjoy the light of the sun, so we may confidently know that God is longing to let His light shine on us.

Even when there are clouds, we still have the sun. In the midst of difficulties, the light of God will rest upon you without ceasing. If you are sure that the sun has risen, you count on its light all day. Make sure that the light of God shines upon you in the morning, and you can count on that light being with you all day long.

Do not rest until you have said, *"There are many who say, 'Who will show us any good?' LORD, lift up the light of Your countenance upon us"* (Ps. 4:6). Take time, until that light shines in your heart, and you can truly say, *"The LORD is my light."*

FAITH IN GOD

🙦

So Jesus answered and said to them, "Have faith in God."
—Mark 11:22

As the eye is the organ by which we see the light and rejoice in it, so faith is the power by which we see the light of God and walk in it.

Man was made for God, in His likeness; his whole being was formed according to the divine pattern. Just think of man's wonderful power of discovering all the thoughts of God hidden in nature. Think of the heart, with its unlimited powers of self-sacrifice and love. Man was made for God, to seek Him, to find Him, to grow up into His likeness, and to show forth His glory—in the fullest sense, to be His dwelling. And faith is the eye that, turning away from the world and self, looks up to God and sees light in His light. To the man of faith, God reveals Himself.

How often we toil and try to waken thoughts and feelings concerning God, which are but a faint shadow, and we forget to gaze on the God who is the Incomparable Original! If only we could realize that God reveals Himself in the depths of our souls!

"Without faith it is impossible to please [God]*"* (Heb. 11:6) or to know Him. In our quiet time, we have to pray to our *"Father who is in the secret place"* (Matt. 6:6). There He hides us *"in the secret place of His tabernacle"* (Ps. 27:5). And there, as we wait and worship before Him, He will let His light shine into our hearts.

Let your one desire be to take time and be still before God, believing with an unbounded faith in His longing to make Himself known to you. Feed on God's Word, to make you strong in faith. Let that faith extend itself to think of what God's glory is, of what His power is to reveal Himself to you, and of what His longing love is to get complete possession of you.

Such faith, exercised and strengthened day by day in secret fellowship with God, will become the habit of our lives, keeping us ever in the enjoyment of His presence and the experience of His saving power.

Abraham *"was strengthened in faith, giving glory to God, and being fully convinced that what He had promised He was also able to perform"* (Rom. 4:20–21).

"I believe God that it will be just as it was told me" (Acts 27:25).

"Wait on the LORD; be of good courage, and He shall strengthen your heart; wait, I say, on the LORD!" (Ps. 27:14).

ALONE WITH GOD

And it happened, as He was alone praying.
—Luke 9:18

He departed again to the mountain by Himself alone.
—John 6:15

Man needs to be alone with God. Man fell when, through the lust of the flesh and the world, he was brought under the power of things visible and earthly. His restoration is meant to bring him back to the Father's house, the Father's presence, the Father's love and fellowship. Salvation means being brought to love and to delight in the presence of God.

Man needs to be alone with God. Without this, God cannot have the opportunity to shine into his heart, to transform his nature by His divine working, to take possession of him, and to fill him with His fullness.

Man needs to be alone with God, to yield to the presence and power of His holiness, of His life, and of His love. Christ on earth needed it; He could not live the life of a Son here in the flesh without at times separating Himself entirely from His surroundings and being alone with God. How much more must this be indispensable to us!

When our Lord Jesus gave us the blessed command to enter our inner chamber and shut the door in order to pray to our Father in secret, He gave us the promise that the Father would hear such prayers and would mightily answer them in our lives before men. (See Matthew 6:4.)

Alone with God—that is the secret of true prayer, of true power in prayer, of real living, of face-to-face fellowship with God, and of power for service. There is no true, deep conversion; no true, deep holiness; no clothing with the Holy Spirit and with power; no abiding peace or joy, without being daily alone with God. As someone has said, "There is no path to holiness, but in being much and long alone with God."

The institution of daily, secret prayer is an inestimable privilege. Let it be the one thing our hearts are set on: seeking, finding, and meeting God. Take time to be alone with God. The time will come when you will be amazed at the thought that one could suggest that five minutes was enough.

"Give heed to the voice of my cry, my King and my God, for to You I will pray. My voice You shall hear in the morning, O LORD; in the morning I will direct it to You, and I will look up" (Ps. 5:2–3).

WHOLLY FOR GOD

Whom have I in heaven but You? And there
is none upon earth that I desire besides You.
—Psalm 73:25

Alone with God—this is a lesson of the deepest importance. May we seek grace from God to reach its depths. Then we will learn that there is another lesson of equally deep significance: wholly for God.

As we find that it is not easy to persevere in being alone with God, we begin to see that it is because the other is lacking; we are not "wholly for God." Because He is the only God and is alone the Adorable One, God has a right to demand to have us wholly for Himself. Without this surrender, He cannot make His power known. We read in the Old Testament that His servants, Abraham, Moses, Elijah, and David, gave themselves wholly and unreservedly to God, so that He could work out His plans through them. It is only the fully surrendered heart that can fully trust God for all He has promised.

This world teaches us that if anyone desires to do a great work, he must give himself wholly to it. This law is especially true of the love of a mother for her child. She gives herself wholly to the little one whom she loves. Is it not reasonable that the great God of love should have us wholly for Himself? And will we not take the words *wholly for God* as the keynote for our devotions every morning when we awaken? Just as God gives Himself wholly to us, so does He desire that we give ourselves wholly to Him.

In the inner chamber, let us meditate on these things alone with God, and with earnest desire ask Him by His almighty power to work in us all that is pleasing in His sight.

Wholly for God—what a privilege! What wonderful grace prepares us for it! Wholly for God—separated from men, from work, and from all that might draw us away—what great blessedness as the soul learns what it means, and what God gives with it!

"You shall love the LORD your God with all your heart, with all your soul, and with all your mind" (Matt. 22:37).

They *"sought Him with all their soul; and He was found by them"* (2 Chron. 15:15).

"With my whole heart I have sought You" (Ps. 119:10).

THE KNOWLEDGE OF GOD

❧

This is eternal life, that they may know You.
—John 17:3

The knowledge of God is absolutely necessary for the spiritual life. It is eternal life. It is not the intellectual knowledge we receive from others, or through our own powers of thought, but the living, experiential knowledge in which God makes Himself known to the soul. Just as the rays of the sun on a cold winter's day warm the body, imparting its heat to us, so the living God sheds the life-giving rays of His holiness and love into the heart of one who waits on Him.

Why do we so seldom experience this life-giving power of the true knowledge of God? Because we do not give God enough time to reveal Himself to us. When we pray, we think we know well enough how to speak to God. And we forget that one of the very first things in prayer is to be silent before God, so that He may reveal Himself. By His hidden but mighty power, God will manifest His presence, resting on us and working in us. To know God in the personal experience of His presence and love is life indeed.

Brother Lawrence, author of *The Practice of the Presence of God,* had a great longing to know God, and for this purpose went into a monastery. His spiritual advisers gave him prayer books to use, but he put them aside. "It helps little to pray," he said, "if I do not know the God to whom I pray." And he believed that God would reveal Himself. Brother Lawrence remained in silent adoration for a long time, in order to come under the full impression of the presence of this great and holy Being. He continued in this practice until, later, he lived consciously and constantly in God's presence and experienced His blessed nearness and keeping power. Just as the sun rising each morning is the pledge of light throughout the day, so the quiet time of waiting upon God, yielding ourselves for Him to shine on us, will be the pledge of His presence and His power abiding with us all day long. Be sure that the Sun has risen upon your soul.

Learn this great lesson: as the sun on a cold day shines on us and imparts its warmth, believe that the living God will work in you with His love and His almighty power. God will reveal Himself as life and light and joy and strength to the soul who waits upon Him.

"LORD, *lift up the light of Your countenance upon us*" (Ps. 4:6).
"*Be still, and know that I am God*" (Ps. 46:10).

GOD THE FATHER

*Baptizing them in the name of the Father and of
the Son and of the Holy Spirit.
—Matthew 28:19*

We will do well to remember that the doctrine of the Holy Trinity has a deep devotional aspect. As we think of God, we remember the inconceivable distance that separates Him in His holiness from sinful men, and we bow in deep contrition and holy fear. As we think of Christ the Son, we remember the inconceivable nearness in which He came to be born of a woman, a daughter of Adam, and to die the accursed death, and so to be inseparably joined to us for all eternity. And as we think of the Holy Spirit, we remember the inconceivable blessedness of God having His abode in us, and making us His home and His temple throughout eternity.

When Christ taught us to say, *"Our Father in heaven"* (Matt. 6:9), He immediately added, *"Hallowed be Your name"* (v. 9). As God is holy, so we are to be holy, too. And there is no way of becoming holy but by considering His name most holy and drawing near to Him in prayer.

How often we speak His name without any sense of the unspeakable privilege of our relationship with God! If we would just take time to come into contact with God and to worship Him in His love, how the inner chamber would become to us the gate of heaven!

Child of God, if you pray to your Father in secret, bow very low before Him, and seek to adore His name as most holy. Remember that this is the highest blessedness of prayer.

"Pray to your Father who is in the secret place; and your Father who sees in secret will reward you openly" (Matt. 6:6).

What an unspeakable privilege, to be alone with God in secret and to say, "My Father!" How incredible to have the assurance that He has indeed seen me in secret and will reward me openly. Take time until you can say, *"I have seen God face to face, and my life is preserved"* (Gen. 32:30).

GOD THE SON

🦚

*Grace to you and peace from God our Father
and the Lord Jesus Christ.*
—*Romans 1:7*

It is remarkable that the apostle Paul in each of his thirteen epistles wrote: *"Grace to you and peace from God our Father and the Lord Jesus Christ."* He had such a deep sense of the inseparable oneness of the Father and the Son in the work of grace, that in each opening benediction he referred to both.

This is a lesson of the utmost importance for us. There may be times in the Christian life when we think chiefly of God the Father, and so pray only to Him. But later on, we realize that it may cause spiritual loss if we do not grasp the truth that each day and each hour it is only through faith in Christ and in being united with Him that we can enjoy a full and abiding fellowship with God.

Remember what we read of the Lamb in the midst of the throne. John had seen One sitting on a throne. *"The four living creatures...do not rest day or night, saying: 'Holy, holy, holy, Lord God Almighty, who was and is and is to come!'"* (Rev. 4:8).

Later, John saw *"in the midst of the throne...a Lamb as though it had been slain"* (Rev. 5:6). Of all the worshipping multitude, none could see God without first seeing Christ the Lamb of God. And none could see Christ without seeing the glory of God, the Father and Son inseparably One.

O Christian, if you wish to know and worship God fully, seek Him and worship Him in Christ. And if you seek Christ, seek Him and worship Him in God. Then you will understand what it means to have *"your life...hidden with Christ in God"* (Col. 3:3), and your experience will be that the fellowship and adoration of Christ is indispensable to the full knowledge of the love and holiness of God.

Be still, and speak these words in deepest reverence: *"Grace...and peace"*—all I can desire—*"from God our Father and the Lord Jesus Christ."*

Take time to meditate on this, to believe and to expect all from God the Father who sits upon the throne, and from the Lord Jesus Christ, the Lamb in the midst of the throne. Then you will learn to truly worship God. Return frequently to this sacred scene, to give *"glory...to Him who sits on the throne, and to the Lamb"* (Rev. 5:13).

GOD THE HOLY SPIRIT

🎕

For through Him we both have access
by one Spirit to the Father.
—Ephesians 2:18

In our communion with God in the inner chamber, we must guard against the danger of seeking to know God and Christ in the power of the intellect or the emotions. The Holy Spirit has been given for the sole purpose that *"through Him we...have access by one Spirit to the Father."* Let us beware, lest all our labor be in vain because we do not wait for the teaching of the Spirit.

Christ taught His disciples this truth on His last night. Speaking of the coming of the Comforter, He said, *"In that day you will ask...the Father in My name....Ask, and you will receive, that your joy may be full"* (John 16:23–24). Take hold of the truth that the Holy Spirit was given with the one great purpose of teaching us to pray. He makes the fellowship with the Father and the Son a blessed reality. Be strong in the faith that He is working secretly in you. As you enter the inner chamber, give yourself wholly to His guidance as your Teacher in all your intercession and adoration.

When Christ said to the disciples on the evening of the Resurrection, *"Receive the Holy Spirit"* (John 20:22), it was, for one thing, to strengthen and equip them for the ten days of prayer and for their receiving the fullness of the Spirit. This suggests to us three things we ought to remember when we draw near to God in prayer:

1. WE MUST PRAY IN THE CONFIDENCE THAT THE HOLY SPIRIT DWELLS IN US. And we must yield ourselves definitely, in stillness of soul, to His leading. Take time for this.

2. WE MUST BELIEVE THAT THE *"GREATER WORKS"* (JOHN 5:20) OF THE SPIRIT WILL BE GIVEN IN ANSWER TO PRAYER. Such *"works"* bring us toward the enlightening and strengthening of the spiritual life, toward the fullness of the Spirit.

3. WE MUST BELIEVE THAT THROUGH THE SPIRIT, IN UNITY WITH ALL GOD'S CHILDREN, WE MAY ASK AND EXPECT THE MIGHTY WORKINGS OF THAT SPIRIT ON HIS CHURCH AND PEOPLE.

"He who believes in Me, as the Scripture has said, out of his heart will flow rivers of living water" (John 7:38).

"Do you believe this?" (John 11:26).

THE SECRET OF THE LORD

🦉

*Go into your room, and when you have shut
your door, pray to your Father who is in the secret place;
and your Father who sees in secret will reward you openly.*
—*Matthew 6:6*

Christ greatly desired that His disciples would know God as their Father, and that they would have secret fellowship with Him. In His own life, He found it not only indispensable, but also the highest happiness to meet the Father in secret. And He wants us to realize that it is impossible to be true, wholehearted disciples without daily fellowship with the Father in heaven, who waits for us *"in secret."*

God is a God who hides Himself from the world and all that is of the world. He wants to draw us away from the world and from ourselves. Instead, He offers us the blessedness of close, intimate communion with Himself. Oh, that God's children would understand this!

Believers enjoyed this experience in Old Testament times: *"You are my hiding place"* (Ps. 32:7); *"He who dwells in the secret place of the Most High shall abide under the shadow of the Almighty"* (Ps. 91:1); *"The secret of the LORD is with those who fear Him"* (Ps. 25:14). How much more Christians in the new covenant ought to value this secret fellowship with God! We read: *"Ye are dead, and your life is hid with Christ in God"* (Col. 3:3 KJV). If we really believe this, we will have the joyful assurance that our lives, hidden *"with Christ in God"* in such divine keeping, are safe and beyond the reach of every foe. We should confidently and daily seek the renewal of our spiritual lives in prayer to our Father who is *"in secret."*

Because we are dead with Christ, because we are one with Him in the likeness of His death and of His resurrection, we know that, as the roots of a tree are hidden under the earth, so the roots of our daily lives are hidden deep in God.

O soul, take time to realize: *"You shall hide* [me] *in the secret place of Your presence"* (Ps. 31:20).

Our first thought in prayer should be, "I must know that I am alone with God, and that God is with me."

"In the secret place of His tabernacle He shall hide me" (Ps. 27:5).

HALF AN HOUR OF SILENCE IN HEAVEN

🎵

There was silence in heaven for about half an hour....
Then another angel...came and stood at the altar. He was
given much incense, that he should offer it with the prayers
of all the saints upon the golden altar which was before
the throne. And the smoke of the incense, with the
prayers of the saints, ascended before God.
—Revelation 8:1, 3–4

"There was silence in heaven for about half an hour," to bring the prayers of the saints before God, before the first angel sounded his trumpet. Tens of thousands of God's children have felt the absolute need for silence and detachment from the things of earth for half an hour, in order to present their prayers before God, and in fellowship with Him to be strengthened for their daily work.

How often the complaint is heard that there is no time for prayer! Very often the confession is made that, even if time could be found, one feels unable to spend the time in real fellowship with God. No one needs to ask what it is that hinders growth in the spiritual life. The secret of strength can only be found in living communion with God.

O dear Christian, if you would only obey Christ when He says, *"When you have shut your door, pray to your Father who is in the secret place"* (Matt. 6:6)! If you would only have the courage to be alone with God for half an hour! Do not think to yourself, "I will not know how to spend the time." Just believe that if you begin and are faithful, bowing in silence before God, He will reveal Himself to you.

If you need help, read some passage of Scripture and let God's Word speak to you. Then bow in deepest humility before God, and wait on Him. He will work within you. Read Psalm 61, 62, or 63, and speak the words out before God. Then begin to pray. Intercede for your own household and children, for the congregation, for the church and minister, for schools and missions. Continue praying, though the time may seem long. God will reward you. But above all, be sure you meet God.

God desires to bless you. Is it not worth the trouble to spend half an hour alone with God? In heaven itself, there was need for half an hour's silence to present the prayers of the saints before God. If you persevere, you may find that the half hour that seems the most difficult in the whole day may eventually become the most blessed in your whole life.

"My soul, wait silently for God alone, for my expectation is from Him" (Ps. 62:5).

GOD'S GREATNESS

🦋

You are great, and do wondrous things;
You alone are God.
—Psalm 86:10

When anyone begins an important work, he takes time and gives his attention to consider the greatness of his undertaking. Scientists, in studying nature, require years of labor to grasp the magnitude of, for instance, the sun, the stars, and the planets. Is not our glorious God worthy that we should take time to know and adore His greatness?

Yet how superficial is our knowledge of God's greatness! We do not allow ourselves time to bow before Him and to come under the deep impression of His incomprehensible majesty and glory.

Meditate on the following Scriptures until you are filled with some sense of what a glorious being God is: *"Great is the LORD, and greatly to be praised; and His greatness is unsearchable"* (Ps. 145:3); *"I will declare Your greatness. They shall utter the memory of Your great goodness"* (vv. 6–7).

Do not imagine that it is easy to grasp the meaning of these words. Take time for them to master your heart, until you bow in what may be speechless adoration before God.

"Ah, Lord GOD!...There is nothing too hard for You...the Great, the Mighty God....You are great in counsel and mighty in work" (Jer. 32:17–19). To this God answers, *"Behold, I am the LORD, the God of all flesh. Is there anything too hard for Me?"* (v. 27).

The right understanding of God's greatness will take time. But if we give God the honor that is His due, and if our faith grows strong in the knowledge of what a great and powerful God we have, we will be led to wait in the inner chamber, to bow in humble worship before this great and mighty God. In His abundant mercy, He will teach us through the Holy Spirit to say, *"The LORD is the great God, and the great King above all gods....Oh come, let us worship and bow down; let us kneel before the LORD our Maker"* (Ps. 95:3, 6).

A PERFECT HEART

For the eyes of the LORD run to and fro
throughout the whole earth, to show himself strong
in the behalf of them whose heart is perfect toward him.
—2 Chronicles 16:9 KJV

In worldly matters, we know how important it is that work be done with the whole heart. In the spiritual realm, this rule still holds true. God has given the commandment, *"You shall love the LORD your God with all your heart...and with all your strength"* (Deut. 6:5). In Jeremiah we read, *"You will seek Me and find Me, when you search for Me with all your heart"* (Jer. 29:13).

It is amazing that earnest Christians, who attend to their daily work with all their hearts, are so content to take things easy in the service of God. They do not realize that, if in anything, they should give themselves to God's service with all the power of their wills.

In the words of 2 Chronicles 16:9, we are given insight into the absolute necessity of seeking God with a perfect heart: *"The eyes of the LORD run to and fro throughout the whole earth, to show himself strong in the behalf of them whose heart is perfect toward him."*

What an encouragement this should be to us to humbly wait on God with an upright heart! We may be assured that His eye will be upon us and that He will show forth His mighty power in us and in our work.

O Christian, have you learned this lesson in your worship of God, yielding yourself each morning, yielding your whole heart to do God's will? Pray each prayer with a perfect heart in true wholehearted devotion to Him. Then expect, by faith, the power of God to work in you and through you.

Remember that in order to come to this, you must begin by being silent before God, until you realize that He is indeed working in secret in your heart.

"I wait for my God" (Ps. 69:3).

"In the secret place of His tabernacle He shall hide me" (Ps. 27:5).

THE OMNIPOTENCE OF GOD

I am Almighty God.
—Genesis 17:1

When Abraham heard these words, he fell on his face. God spoke to him and filled his heart with faith in what God would do for him.

O Christian, have you bowed in deep humility before God, until you felt that you were in living contact with the Almighty; until your heart has been filled with the faith that the almighty God is working in you and will perfect His work in you?

Read in the Psalms how believers gloried in God and in His strength: *"I will love You, O LORD, my strength"* (Ps. 18:1); *"God is the strength of my heart"* (Ps. 73:26); *"The LORD is the strength of my life"* (Ps. 27:1); *"It is God who arms me with strength"* (Ps. 18:32); *"God is our refuge and strength"* (Ps. 46:1). Take hold of these words, and take time to adore God as the Almighty One, your strength.

Christ taught us that salvation is the work of God, and quite impossible to man. When the disciples asked, *"Who then can be saved?"* (Matt. 19:25), His answer was, *"With men this is impossible, but with God all things are possible"* (v. 26). If we firmly believe this, we will have courage to believe that God is working in us all that is well pleasing in His sight.

Remember how Paul prayed for the Ephesians, that through the enlightening of the Spirit they might know *"the exceeding greatness of His power toward us who believe, according to the working of His mighty power"* (Eph. 1:19). For the Colossians he prayed that they might be *"strengthened with all might, according to His glorious power"* (Col. 1:11). When a person fully believes that the mighty power of God is working unceasingly within him, he can joyfully say, *"The LORD is the strength of my life"* (Ps. 27:1).

Do you wonder why many Christians complain of weakness and shortcomings? They do not understand that the almighty God must work in them every hour of the day. That is the secret of the true life of faith.

Do not rest until you can say to God, *"I will love You, O LORD, my strength"* (Ps. 18:1). Let God have complete possession of you, and you will be able to say with all God's people, *"You are the glory of their strength"* (Ps. 89:17).

THE FEAR OF GOD

❧

Blessed is the man who fears the LORD,
who delights greatly in His commandments.
—Psalm 112:1

The fear of God—these words characterize the religion of the Old Testament and the foundation that it laid for the more abundant life of the New. The gift of holy fear is still the great desire of each child of God, and it is an essential part of a life that is to make a real impression on the world around. It is one of the great promises of the new covenant in Jeremiah: *"I will make an everlasting covenant with them...[and] I will put My fear in their hearts so that they will not depart from Me"* (Jer. 32:40).

We find the perfect combination of the two in Acts 9:31: *"Then the churches throughout all Judea, Galilee, and Samaria had peace and were edified. And walking in the fear of the Lord and in the comfort of the Holy Spirit, they were multiplied."* More than once, Paul gave the fear of God a high place in the Christian life: *"Work out your own salvation with fear and trembling; for it is God who works in you"* (Phil. 2:12–13); *"Perfecting holiness in the fear of God"* (2 Cor. 7:1).

It has often been said that the lack of the fear of God is one of the things in which our modern times cannot compare favorably with the times of the Puritans. It is no wonder that there is so much cause of complaint in regard to the reading of God's Word, the worship of His house, and the absence of the spirit of continuous prayer that marked the early church. We need texts like the one at the beginning of this devotion to be expounded, and young converts must be fully instructed in the need for and the blessedness of a deep fear of God, leading to an unceasing prayerfulness as one of the essential elements of the life of faith.

Let us earnestly cultivate this grace in the inner chamber. Let us hear these words coming out of the very heavens: *"Who shall not fear You, O Lord, and glorify Your name? For You alone are holy"* (Rev. 15:4).

"Let us have grace, by which we may serve God acceptably with reverence and godly fear" (Heb. 12:28).

"Blessed is the man who fears the LORD." As we take these words into our hearts and believe that this is one of the deepest secrets of blessedness, we will seek to worship Him in holy fear.

"Serve the LORD with fear, and rejoice with trembling" (Ps. 2:11).

GOD INCOMPREHENSIBLE

Behold, God is great, and we do not know Him.
—Job 36:26

As for the Almighty, we cannot find Him;
He is excellent in power.
—Job 37:23

This attribute of God, as a Spirit whose being and glory are entirely beyond our power of comprehension, is one that we ponder all too little. And yet in the spiritual life, it is of the utmost importance to feel deeply that, as the heavens are high above the earth, so God's thoughts and ways are infinitely exalted beyond all our thoughts (Isa. 55:9).

It is only right that we look up to God with deep humility and holy reverence, and then with childlike simplicity yield ourselves to the teaching of His Holy Spirit. *"Oh, the depth of the riches both of the wisdom and knowledge of God! How unsearchable are His judgments and His ways past finding out!"* (Rom. 11:33).

Let our hearts respond, "O Lord, O God of gods, how wonderful You are in all Your thoughts, and how deep in Your purposes!" The study of what God is should always fill us with holy awe, and the sacred longing to know and honor Him rightly.

Just think—

His greatness...	Incomprehensible
His might...	Incomprehensible
His omnipresence...	Incomprehensible
His wisdom...	Incomprehensible
His holiness...	Incomprehensible
His mercy...	Incomprehensible
His love...	Incomprehensible

As we worship, let us cry out, "What an inconceivable glory is in this great Being who is my God and Father!" Confess with shame how little you have sought to know Him fully or to wait upon Him to reveal Himself. Begin in faith to trust that, in a way passing all understanding, this incomprehensible and all-glorious God will work in your heart and life and allow you, in ever growing measure, to know Him fully.

"My eyes are upon You, O GOD the Lord; in You I take refuge" (Ps. 141:8).

"Be still, and know that I am God" (Ps. 46:10).

THE HOLINESS OF GOD IN THE OLD TESTAMENT

Be holy, for I am holy.
—Leviticus 11:45

I am the LORD who sanctifies you.
—Leviticus 20:8

These two ideas are recorded nine times in Leviticus. (See Leviticus 19:2; 20:7; 21:8, 15, 23; 22:9, 16.) Israel had to learn that, just as holiness is the highest and most glorious attribute of God, so it must be the obvious characteristic of His people. He who desires to know God fully and to meet Him in secret must above all desire to be holy as He is holy.

The priests who were to have access to God had to be set apart for a life of holiness. It was the same for the prophet Isaiah who was to speak for Him: *"I saw the Lord sitting on a throne, high and lifted up....[And the seraphim] said: 'Holy holy, holy is the LORD of hosts'"* (Isa. 6:1, 3). This is the voice of adoration.

"So I said: 'Woe is me, for I am undone!...For my eyes have seen the King, the LORD of hosts'" (v. 5). This is the voice of a broken, contrite heart.

Then one of the seraphim touched Isaiah's mouth with a live coal from the altar and said, *"Behold, this has touched your lips; your iniquity is taken away, and your sin purged"* (v. 7). This is the voice of grace and full redemption.

Then follows the voice of God: *"Whom shall I send?"* (v. 8). And the willing answer is, *"Here am I! Send me"* (v. 8). Pause with holy fear, and ask God to reveal Himself as the Holy One. *"For thus says the High and Lofty One who inhabits eternity, whose name is Holy: 'I dwell in the high and holy place, with him who has a contrite and humble spirit'"* (Isa. 57:15).

Be still, and take time to worship God in His great glory and in that deep condescension in which He longs and offers to dwell with us and in us.

Child of God, if you wish to meet your Father in secret, bow low and worship Him in the glory of His holiness. Give Him time to make Himself known to you. It is indeed an unspeakable grace to know God as the Holy One.

"You shall be holy, for I the LORD your God am holy" (Lev. 19:2).

"Holy, holy, holy is the LORD of hosts" (Isa. 6:3).

"Worship the LORD in the beauty of holiness!" (1 Chron. 16:29).

"Let the beauty of the LORD our God be upon us" (Ps. 90:17).

THE HOLINESS OF GOD IN THE NEW TESTAMENT

🦚

*Holy Father, keep through Your name those whom You have
given Me....Sanctify them....And for their sakes I sanctify
Myself, that they also may be sanctified by the truth.*
—John 17:11, 17, 19

Christ always lives to pray this great prayer. Expect and take
hold of God's answer.

Read the words of the apostle Paul in 1 Thessalonians: *"Night
and day praying exceedingly...that He* [the Lord] *may establish
your hearts blameless in holiness before our God"* (1 Thess. 3:10,
13); *"The God of peace Himself sanctify you completely...who also
will do it"* (1 Thess. 5:23–24).

Ponder deeply these words as you read them, and use them as
a prayer to God: "Blessed Lord, strengthen my heart to be *'blameless in holiness.'* Sanctify me wholly. I know that You are faithful,
and You will do it."

What a privilege to commune with God in secret, to speak
these words in prayer, and then to wait upon Him until, through
the working of the Spirit, they live in our hearts and we begin to
know something of the holiness of God!

God's holiness has been revealed in the Old Testament. In the
New, we find the holiness of God's people in Christ, through the
sanctification of the Spirit. Oh, that we understood the blessedness
of God's saying, *"Be holy, for I am holy"* (Lev. 11:45)!

God is saying to us, "With you, My children, as it is with Me,
holiness should be the chief thing." For this purpose, the Holy One
has revealed Himself to us through the Son and the Holy Spirit. Let
us use the word *holy* with great reverence of God, and then, for
ourselves, with holy desire. Worship the God who says, *"I am the
LORD who sanctifies you"* (Lev. 22:32).

Bow before Him in holy fear and strong desire, and then, in
the fullness of faith, listen to the prayer promise: *"The God of peace
Himself sanctify you completely...who also will do it"* (1 Thess.
5:23–24).

SIN

❧

*And the grace of our Lord was exceedingly abundant, with
faith and love which are in Christ Jesus....Christ Jesus came
into the world to save sinners, of whom I am chief.*
—1 Timothy 1:14–15

Never forget for a moment, as you enter the secret chamber, that your whole relationship to God depends on what you think of sin and of yourself as a redeemed sinner.

It is sin that makes God's holiness so amazing. It is sin that makes God's holiness so glorious, because He has said: *"Be holy, for I am holy"* (Lev. 11:45); *"I am the LORD who sanctifies you"* (Lev. 22:32).

It is sin that called forth the wonderful love of God in not sparing His Son. It was sin that nailed Jesus to the cross and revealed the depth and the power of the love with which He loved. Through all eternity in the glory of heaven, it is our being redeemed sinners that will give music to our praise.

Never forget for a moment that it is sin that has led to the great transaction between you and Christ Jesus. Each day in your fellowship with God, His one aim is to deliver and keep you fully from its power, and to lift you up into His likeness and His infinite love.

It is the thought of sin that will keep you low at His feet and will give the deep undertone to all your adoration. It is the thought of sin, ever surrounding you and seeking to tempt you, that will give fervency to your prayer and urgency to the faith that hides itself in Christ. It is the thought of sin that makes Christ so unspeakably precious, that keeps you every moment dependent on His grace, and that gives you the right to be more than a conqueror *"through Him who loved us"* (Rom. 8:37). It is the thought of sin that calls you to thank God with *"a broken and a contrite heart...[that] God...will not despise"* (Ps. 51:17), and that works in you a contrite and humble spirit in which He delights to dwell.

It is in the inner chamber, in secret with the Father, that sin can be conquered, the holiness of Christ can be imparted, and the Spirit of holiness can take possession of our lives. It is in the inner chamber that we learn to know and experience fully the divine power of these precious words of promise: *"The blood of Jesus Christ His Son cleanses us from all sin"* (1 John 1:7), and *"Whoever abides in Him does not sin"* (1 John 3:6).

THE MERCY OF GOD

Oh, give thanks to the LORD, for He is good!
For His mercy endures forever.
—Psalm 136:1

This Psalm is wholly devoted to the praise of God's mercy. In each of the twenty-six verses, we have the expression, *"His mercy endures forever."* The psalmist was full of this glad thought. Our hearts, too, should be filled with this blessed assurance. The everlasting, unchangeable mercy of God is cause for unceasing praise and thanksgiving.

Read what is said about God's mercy in the well-known Psalm 103: *"Bless the LORD, O my soul, and forget not all His benefits:...who crowns you with lovingkindness and tender mercies"* (vv. 2, 4). Of all God's other attributes, mercy is the crown. May it be a crown upon my head and in my life!

"The LORD is merciful and gracious...and abounding in mercy" (v. 8). As wonderful as God's greatness is, so infinite is His mercy: *"As the heavens are high above the earth, so great is His mercy toward those who fear Him"* (v. 11). What a thought! As high as heaven is above the earth, so immeasurably and inconceivably great is the mercy of God while He waits to bestow His richest blessing.

"The mercy of the LORD is from everlasting to everlasting on those who fear Him" (v. 17). Here again the psalmist spoke of God's boundless lovingkindness and mercy.

How frequently we have read these familiar words without the least thought of their immeasurable greatness! Be still, and meditate until your heart responds in the words of Psalm 36: *"Your mercy, O LORD, is in the heavens"* (v. 5); *"How precious is Your lovingkindness, O God! Therefore the children of men put their trust under the shadow of Your wings"* (v. 7); *"Oh, continue Your lovingkindness to those who know You"* (v. 10).

Take time to thank God with great joy for the wonderful mercy with which He crowns your life, and say: *"Your lovingkindness is better than life"* (Ps. 63:3).

THE WORD OF GOD

The word of God is living and powerful.
—Hebrews 4:12

Both the Word of God and prayer are indispensable for communion with God, and in the inner chamber they should not be separated. In His Word, God speaks to us; in prayer, we speak to God.

The Word teaches us to know the God to whom we pray. It teaches us how He wants us to pray. It gives us precious promises to encourage us in prayer. It often gives us wonderful answers to prayer.

The Word comes from God's heart and brings His thoughts and His love into our hearts. And then, through prayer, the Word goes back from our hearts into His great heart of love. Prayer is the means of fellowship between God's heart and ours.

The Word teaches us God's will—the will of His promises as to what He will do for us, and also the will of His commands. His promises are food for our faith, and to His commands we surrender ourselves in loving obedience.

The more we pray, the more we will feel our need for the Word and will rejoice in it. The more we read God's Word, the more we will have to pray about, and the more power we will have in prayer. One great cause of prayerlessness is that we read God's Word too little, only superficially, or in the light of human wisdom.

The Holy Spirit, through whom the Word has been spoken, is also the Spirit of prayer. He will teach us how to receive the Word and how to approach God.

How blessed the inner chamber would be, what a power and an inspiration in our worship, if we only took God's Word as from Himself, turning it into prayer and definitely expecting an answer! It is in the inner chamber, in God's presence, that by the Holy Spirit God's Word will become our delight and our strength.

When we take God's Word in deepest reverence in our hearts, on our lips, and in our lives, it will be a never failing fountain of strength and blessing to us. Let us believe that God's Word is indeed full of power that will make us strong, able to expect and receive great things from God. Above all, it will give us the daily blessed fellowship with Him as the living God.

"*Blessed is the man...*[whose] *delight is in the law of the LORD, and in His law he meditates day and night*" (Ps. 1:1–2).

THE PSALMS

How sweet are Your words to my taste,
sweeter than honey to my mouth!
—Psalm 119:103

The book of Psalms seeks to help us to worship God. Of the sixty-six books in the Bible, this book was written especially for this purpose. The other books are historical, doctrinal, or practical. But the Psalms take us into the inner sanctuary of God's holy presence, to enjoy the blessedness of fellowship with Him. It is a book of devotions inspired by the Holy Spirit.

If you desire each morning to truly meet God and worship Him in spirit and in truth, then let your heart be filled with the Word of God in the Psalms.

As you read the Psalms, underline the word *Lord* or *God* wherever it occurs, and also the pronouns referring to God—*I, You,* and *He.* This will help to connect the contents of the psalm with God, who is the object of all prayer. When you have taken the trouble to mark the different names of God, you will find that more than one difficult psalm will have light shed upon it. These underlined words will make God the central thought and will lead you to a new worship of Him. Take the psalms upon your lips, and speak them out before Him. Your faith will be strengthened anew to realize how God is your strength and help in all circumstances of life. (See Psalm 46:1.)

Just as the Holy Spirit has taught God's people to pray in years gone by, so the Psalms will, by the power of that Spirit, teach us always to abide in God's presence.

Read Psalm 119. Every time the word *Lord* or *You* or *Your* occurs, underline it. You will be surprised to find that almost every verse contains these words once or more. Meditate on the thought that the God who is found throughout the whole psalm is the same God who gives us His law and will enable us to keep it.

Psalm 119 will soon become one of your most beloved passages of Scripture, and you will find its prayers and its teachings concerning God's Word drawing you continually up to God, in the blessed consciousness of His power and love.

"Oh, how I love Your law! It is my meditation all the day" (Ps. 119:97).

THE GLORY OF GOD

To Him be glory...to all generations.
—Ephesians 3:21

God Himself must reveal His glory to us; only then are we able to know and glorify Him rightly.

There is no more wonderful image of the glory of God in nature than we find in the starry heavens. Telescopes, which are continually made more powerful, have long proclaimed the wonders of God's universe. And by means of photography, the wonders of that glory have been revealed. A photographic plate[1] fixed below the telescope will reveal millions of stars that could never have been seen by the eye through even the best telescope. Man must step aside and allow the glory of the heavens to reveal itself; and the stars, at first wholly invisible, will leave their image upon the plate.

What a lesson for the believer who longs to see the glory of God in His Word! Put aside your own efforts and thoughts. Let your heart be like a photographic plate that waits for God's glory to be revealed. As the plate must be prepared and clean, let your heart be prepared and purified by God's Spirit. *"Blessed are the pure in heart, for they shall see God"* (Matt. 5:8). As the plate must be stationary, let your heart be still before God. As the plate must be exposed up to seven or eight hours in order to obtain the full impression of the farthest stars, let your heart take time in silent waiting upon God, and He will reveal His glory.

If you are silent before God and give Him time, He will put thoughts into your heart that may be of unspeakable blessing to yourself and others. He will create within you desires and dispositions that will indeed be as the rays of His glory shining in you.

Test this principle today. Offer your spirit to God in deep humility, and have faith that He will reveal Himself in His holy love. His glory will descend upon you. You will feel the need of giving Him full time to do His blessed work.

"My soul, wait silently for God alone, for my expectation is from Him" (Ps. 62:5).

"Be still, and know that I am God" (Ps. 46:10).

---

[1] Editor's note: The photographic plates of which Murray writes are rarely used today. Such plates are simply glass squares coated with light-sensitive emulsions. Most astronomers now use common negative film, which does not produce the positive image that can be achieved with plate technology but must be printed onto paper in order to obtain a picture of what was seen through the telescope. Slides, however, are similar to plates and allow one to get a positive image without having to print onto paper.

THE HOLY TRINITY

❧

*Elect according to the foreknowledge of God the
Father, in sanctification of the Spirit, for obedience
and sprinkling of the blood of Jesus Christ.*
—*1 Peter 1:2*

Here is one of the Scriptures in which we see that the great truth of the blessed Trinity lies at the very root of our spiritual lives. In this book, I have written much about the adoration of God the Father and about the need for enough time each day to worship Him in some of His glorious attributes. But we must remind ourselves that, for all our fellowship with God, the presence and power of the Son and the Spirit are absolutely necessary.

What a realm this opens for us in the inner chamber! We need time to realize how all our fellowship with the Father is determined by the active and personal presence and working of the Lord Jesus. It takes time to become fully conscious of how much we need Him every time we approach Him, of what confidence we may have in the work that He is doing for us and in us, and of what the holy and intimate love is in which we may count upon His presence and all-prevailing intercession. But, oh, to learn the lesson that prayer takes time, and that that time will be most blessedly rewarded!

It is the same with the divine and almighty power of the Holy Spirit working in the depths of our hearts as the One who alone is able to reveal the Son within each of us. Through Him alone we have the power to know what and how to pray; above all, through Him we know how to plead the name of Jesus and to receive the assurance that our prayers have been accepted.

Dear reader, have you not felt more than once that it was almost a mockery to speak of spending five minutes alone with God to come under the impression of His glory? And now, does not the thought of the true worship of God in Christ through the Holy Spirit make you feel more than ever that it takes time to enter into such holy alliance with God and to keep the heart and mind in His peace and presence throughout the day? By waiting in the secret of God's presence, you receive grace to abide in Christ and to be led by His Spirit all day long.

Just pause and think: *"Elect according to the foreknowledge of God the Father, in sanctification of the Spirit, for obedience and sprinkling of the blood of Jesus Christ."* What food for thought and worship!

"When You said, 'Seek My face,' my heart said to You, 'Your face, LORD, I will seek'" (Ps. 27:8).

THE LOVE OF GOD

🍂

God is love, and he who abides in love abides
in God, and God in him.
—1 John 4:16

The best and most wonderful word in heaven is *love,* for *"God is love."* And the best and most wonderful word in the inner chamber must also be *love,* for the God who meets us there is love.

What is love? It is the deep desire to give itself for the one who is loved. Love finds its joy in imparting all that it has in order to make the loved one happy. And the heavenly Father, who offers to meet us in the inner chamber—let there be no doubt of this in our minds—has no other aim than to fill our hearts with His love.

All the other attributes of God that have been mentioned find their highest glory in this. The true and full blessing of the inner chamber is nothing less than a life lived in the abundant love of God.

Because of this, our first and chief thought in the inner chamber should be faith in the love of God. As you set yourself to pray, seek to exercise great and unbounded faith in the love of God.

Take time in silence to meditate on the wonderful revelation of God's love in Christ, until you are filled with the spirit of worship and wonder and longing desire. Take time to believe the precious truth: *"The love of God has been poured out in our hearts by the Holy Spirit who was given to us"* (Rom. 5:5).

Let us remember with shame how little we have believed in and sought this love. As we pray, let us be assured that our heavenly Father longs to manifest His love to us. We can say aloud, "I am deeply convinced of the truth. He can and will do it."

"Yes, I have loved you with an everlasting love" (Jer. 31:3).

"That you, being rooted and grounded in love, may be able to comprehend with all the saints what is the width and length and depth and height; to know the love of Christ which passes knowledge" (Eph. 3:17–19).

"Behold what manner of love the Father has bestowed on us" (1 John 3:1).

WAITING ON GOD

🥀

On You I wait all the day.
—Psalm 25:5

Waiting on God—in this expression we find one of the deepest truths of God's Word in regard to the attitude of the soul in its communion with God.

As we wait on God—just think—He will reveal Himself in us, He will teach us all His will, He will do to us what He has promised, and in all things He will be the Infinite God.

Such is the attitude with which each day should begin. In the inner chamber, in quiet meditation, in expressing our ardent desires through prayer, in the course of our daily work, in all our striving after obedience and holiness, in all our struggles against sin and self-will—in everything we must wait on God to receive what He will bestow, to see what He will do, and to allow Him to be the almighty God.

Meditate on these things, and they will help you to truly value the precious promises of God's Word.

"Those who wait on the LORD shall renew their strength; they shall mount up with wings like eagles" (Isa. 40:31). In this we have the secret of heavenly power and joy.

"Wait on the LORD; be of good courage, and He shall strengthen your heart; wait, I say, on the LORD!" (Ps. 27:14).

"Rest in the LORD, and wait patiently for Him" (Ps. 37:7).

The deep root of all scriptural theology is absolute dependence on God. As we exercise this attitude, it will become more natural and blessedly possible to say, *"On You I wait all the day."* Here we have the secret of true, uninterrupted, silent adoration and worship of God.

Has this book helped to teach you the true worship of God? If so, the Lord's name be praised. Or have you only learned how little you know of it? For this, too, let us thank Him.

If you desire a fuller experience of this blessing, read this book again with a deeper insight into what is meant, and a greater knowledge of the absolute need of each day and all day waiting on God. May the God of all grace grant this.

"I wait for the LORD, my soul waits, and in His word I do hope" (Ps. 130:5).

"Rest in the LORD, and wait patiently for Him...and He shall give you the desires of your heart" (Ps. 37:7, 4).

THE PRAISE OF GOD

🦋

Praise from the upright is beautiful.
—Psalm 33:1

Praise will always be a part of adoration. Adoration, when it has entered God's presence and has fellowshipped with Him, will always lead to the praise of His name. Let praise be a part of the incense we bring before God in our quiet time.

When the children of Israel, at their birth as the people of God at the Red Sea, had been delivered from the power of Egypt, their joy of redemption burst forth in the song of Moses, filled with praise: *"Who is like You, O LORD, among the gods? Who is like You, glorious in holiness, fearful in praises, doing wonders?"* (Exod. 15:11).

In the Psalms we see what a large place praise ought to have in the spiritual life. There are more than sixty psalms of praise, becoming more frequent as the book draws to its close. (See Psalm 95–101, 103–107, 111–118, 134–138, 144–150.) The last five are Hallelujah psalms, with the words *"Praise the LORD"* at the beginning and the end. The very last psalm repeats *"Praise Him"* twice in every verse, and it ends with, *"Let everything that has breath praise the LORD"* (Ps. 150:6).

Take time to study this until your heart and life are entirely a continual song of praise: *"I will bless the LORD at all times; His praise shall continually be in my mouth"* (Ps. 34:1); *"Every day I will bless You"* (Ps. 145:2); *"I will sing praises to my God while I have my being"* (Ps. 146:2).

With the coming of Christ into the world, there was a new outburst of praise in the song of the angels, the song of Mary, the song of Zechariah, and the song of Simeon. And then, in *"the song of Moses...and the song of the Lamb"* (Rev. 15:3), we find the praise of God filling creation: *"Great and marvelous are Your works, Lord God Almighty!...Who shall not fear You, O Lord, and glorify Your Name? For You alone are holy"* (vv. 3–4). This song of praise ends with the fourfold *"Alleluia!"* (Rev. 19:1, 3–4, 6). *"For the Lord God Omnipotent reigns!"* (v. 6).

O child of God, let the inner chamber and your quiet time with God always lead your heart to unceasing praise!

Section Four

The Secret of the Faith Life

THE SECRET OF THE FAITH LIFE

The great majority of Christians are content with the initial faith that gives the pardon of sin and the hope of eternal life. But they have little idea of the wonderful promises of God given to a full and strong faith—promises that He will cleanse the heart, so that they will love the Lord with all their hearts and all their souls (Matt. 22:37); promises that He will write the law in their hearts by His Spirit (Jer. 31:33), so that His children can boldly say, *"I delight to do Your will, O my God"* (Ps. 40:8); promises that He will instill fear of Him in their hearts, so that they will never depart from Him; and promises that He will perfect them *"in every good work"* (Heb. 13:21) to do His will.

Such promises are regarded by most as being altogether beyond the sphere of practical religion; they may be beautiful ideals, but it is simply an impossibility to experience them. Those who look on God's promises in this way have never come to know the almighty power with which God is willing to work in their lives. They have never known how completely the Holy Spirit can take possession of a person who is utterly given up to God, how literally Jesus Christ can dwell and live His life in the heart that is fully surrendered to Him.

As I think of such promises, I feel that I have inadequately shown that in every approach to God, we ought to come with an ever larger faith to worship this great and holy Being, who is able to work in us beyond what we can ask or think. (See Ephesians 3:20.) Some who have read this far may feel that this book is not for them; they know they are Christians, but they do not have time for what so evidently appears beyond their reach. They do not have the time to listen as we call them to come and think of an almighty God and what He is able to do in fulfillment of His Word. They do not have the time or courage to enter into a school for the deeper life; they trust in Christ and are willing to do their utmost to serve Him, even though it is on a lower level.

But there are others, I am sure, whose hearts are yearning for something better than what they have known. They earnestly desire to know Jesus Christ, their loving Redeemer, in the power of the Holy Spirit that He has promised—to serve Him with the love that keeps His commandments and always abides in His love. They are eager to know what is the secret cause of their feebleness, of their unbelief, of their inability to influence others around them, of their failure in every attempt to live the prayer life in the joy of daily personal fellowship with Christ Jesus.

It is to such individuals that this section has been written, with the one desire of pointing out the path that leads to the full knowledge of and love for God. The main ideas presented here are very simple and yet very profound. The almighty God, for whom nothing is too difficult, offers to work in them with His omnipotent power every day what they need for the kind of life He wants them to live.

This almighty and most loving God justly claims that they must surrender their entire beings—their lives, their time, and their strength—every day to His keeping and to the fulfillment of His commands. God is to be waited on every day with a childlike confidence that He will reveal Himself as God to work out His will in them. Everything depends on giving the almighty God His place, on yielding our entire lives to His service and His working in us; then we will have the conscious assurance that His mighty power will work in us what we consider impossible.

May every reader be brought under the deep conviction of how such an almighty God, with His wonderful promises, deserves to be met with a strong, wholehearted faith in every approach to Him. He is worthy of it, and nothing less will suffice for our daily lives than a faith that takes possession of and masters our entire selves and always keeps us waiting on God, entirely at His disposal.

The whole God offers Himself to us. Does this blessed and most glorious God not have the right to demand that the whole man, through every moment of his life, be yielded up to Him? Is it not an absolute necessity in the very nature of things?

In this study of what God wants His people to be and what He undertakes to make them, let us beware of only thinking of ourselves. Let each discovery of God's wonderful grace lead us to think of the church of Christ around us, and how little God's children realize what their wonderful privileges in Christ are. As an increasing number of those who are seeking to fully follow the Lord take up the burden of their fellowmen and plead with God for them, we can expect God to visit His people with the revival of the abundant life in Christ, which will make them the power that they are meant to be in the world.

As God's intercessors, we should night and day before Him bear the burden of the low state of the church and of the great majority of believers, and even of many in the ministry. As we forget ourselves and plead for what appears impossible, we will enter more deeply into the fellowship of Christ and His sufferings, as well as that of Christ and His victory. Such prayers will indeed be fruitful for our own souls and for the world around us.

Ever blessed God and Father, how can we praise You for the wonderful salvation that You have prepared for us in Christ Jesus?

We humbly confess that we have so little understood it, believed it, yielded ourselves to its power, and shown forth its beauty to the world around us.

We fervently pray for all saints, that You would give them a vision of the abundant life that is in Christ Jesus. May this stir their hearts to a deep, unquenchable desire to know fully what Christ is meant to be to them. May they feel deeply that all the powerlessness of Your church to bless the world is the result of not giving Christ and His Holy Spirit the place in their hearts that You desire to have.

Above all, grant such an insight into the need, power, and blessedness of a simple wholehearted faith in Jesus Christ, and such an unreserved surrender to His mastery, that their hearts may be prepared to receive Him in all the fullness of His love and of His abiding presence.

Father, we ask You to hear us in the name of Jesus. Give to each reader such a vision of Your power to fulfill in us every promise, and such a humble childlike trust in Your faithfulness, as will be to Your glory. May all the glory be Yours forever. Amen.

THE IMAGE OF GOD

❧

*Then God said, "Let Us make man in Our
image, according to Our likeness."*
—Genesis 1:26

Here we have the first thought of man in the mind of God;
here man's origin and his destiny are shown to be entirely divine.
God undertook the stupendous work of making a creature, who is
not God, to be a perfect likeness of Him in His divine glory. Man
was to live in entire dependence on God and to receive directly and
unceasingly from Him the inflow of all that was holy and blessed in
the Divine Being. God's glory, His holiness, and His love were to
dwell in man and shine through him.

When sin had done its terrible work and had spoiled the image
of God, the promise was given in Paradise of the woman's seed, in
whom the divine purpose would be fulfilled: God's Son, *"the bright-
ness of His glory and the express image of His person"* (Heb. 1:3),
was to become a son of mankind. In Christ, God's plan would be
carried out, His image revealed in human form. The New Testament speaks of those who are *"predestined to be conformed to the
image of His Son"* (Rom. 8:29) and of *"the new man who is renewed
in knowledge according to the image of Him who created him"* (Col.
3:10). We are given the promise: *"We know that when He is revealed, we shall be like Him, for we shall see Him as He is"* (1 John
3:2).

Between God's eternal purpose for man and its eternal realiza-
tion, we have a wonderful promise in regard to life here on earth:
*"We all...beholding...the glory of the Lord, are being transformed
into the same image from glory to glory, just as by the Spirit of the
Lord"* (2 Cor. 3:18). Let us take hold of this promise as the possible
and assured experience of daily life for everyone who gives Christ
His place as the Glorified One. Let us keep our hearts set on the
glory of the image of God in Christ, in the assurance that the Spirit
will change us into that image day by day. Dear reader, take time to
believe firmly and confidently that this promise will be made true
in your Christian life. God Almighty, who created man in His image, seeks now to work out His purpose in changing you into the
image of Christ Jesus by the power of the Holy Spirit.

"Let this mind be in you which was also in Christ Jesus" (Phil.
2:5).

*"I have given you an example, that you should do as I have
done to you"* (John 13:15).

THE OBEDIENCE OF FAITH

❧

The LORD appeared to Abram and said to him, "I am Almighty God; walk before Me and be blameless. And I will...multiply you exceedingly."
—Genesis 17:1–2

In Abraham we see not only how God asks for and rewards faith, but also how He works faith by the gracious training that He gives. When God first called Abraham, He gave the great promise, *"In you all the families of the earth shall be blessed"* (Gen. 12:3). When Abraham reached the land of Canaan, God met him with the promise that the land would belong to him (v. 7). When he returned from battle, God again met him to renew the promise that his descendants would be numbered as the stars. (See Genesis 15:5.)

God sought to strengthen Abraham's faith before the birth of Isaac, so He said, *"Walk before Me and be blameless. And I will...multiply you exceedingly."* Again in the plains of Mamre, God asked, *"Is anything too hard for the LORD?"* (Gen. 18:14). God led Abraham step by step until his faith was perfected for full obedience in the sacrifice of Isaac. As *"by faith Abraham obeyed when he was called to go out"* (Heb. 11:8), so by faith, at the end of forty years, he was able, without any promise, to obey God's will to the very uttermost—even when it appeared to conflict with all His promises.

Children of Abraham, children of God, the Father makes great demands on your faith. If you are to follow in Abraham's footsteps, you, too, must forsake all and live in the land of spiritual promise, separated unto God, with nothing but His Word to depend on. For this you will need a deep and clear insight that the God who is working in you is the Almighty who works according to *"the exceeding greatness of His power toward us who believe"* (Eph. 1:19).

Do not think that it is easy to live the life of faith. It requires a life of abiding in His presence all day long. Bow before God in humble worship, until He speaks to you: *"I am Almighty God; walk before Me and be blameless. And I will...multiply you exceedingly."* When Abraham heard this, he *"fell on his face, and God talked with him"* (Gen. 17:3). In this lies the secret birthplace of the power to trust God for everything that He promises.

We can only go out like Abraham when we are called to a life of true consecration to God. Walk in the footsteps of Abraham. Hide deep in your heart the testimony of God's Word: *"He...was strong in faith...being fully persuaded that, what* [God] *had promised, he was able also to perform"* (Rom. 4:20–21 KJV).

THE LOVE OF GOD

You shall love the LORD your God with all your heart,
with all your soul, and with all your strength.
—Deuteronomy 6:5

God taught Abraham what it was to believe in Him with all his heart; therefore, he *"was strong in faith, giving glory to God"* (Rom. 4:20 KJV). Moses taught Israel what the first and great commandment was: to love God with their whole hearts. This was the first commandment, the fountain out of which the others naturally proceed. It has its foundation in the relationship between God and man—God as the loving Creator, and man made in His image as the object of that love. It could never be otherwise.

Man finds his life, destiny, and happiness in only one thing: loving God with all his heart and all his strength. Moses said, *"The LORD delighted...in your fathers, to love them"* (Deut. 10:15); such a God was infinitely worthy of being loved. All our religion, all our faith in God and obedience to Him, our entire lives are to be inspired by one thought: we are to love God with all our hearts and all our strength. The first duty of the child of God every day is to live out this command.

How seldom Israel was able to obey the command! But before Moses died, after speaking of the judgments God would bring upon His people for their sins, he was able to make known the promise: *"The LORD your God will circumcise your heart...to love the LORD your God with all your heart and with all your soul"* (Deut. 30:6), and He will do it *"with the circumcision made without hands"* (Col. 2:11), by the circumcision of Christ on the cross.

This blessed promise was the first indication of the new covenant. Jeremiah foretold of the law being written in their hearts by the Holy Spirit so that they would no longer depart from God but would walk in His ways (Jer. 31:33). But how little have Christians understood this; how easily they rest content with the thought that it is impossible!

Learn the double lesson. A perfect heart, loving God with all your might, is what God claims, is what God is infinitely worthy of, is what God will Himself give and work in you. Let your whole soul go out in faith to meet, to wait for, and to expect the fulfillment of the promise, that to love God with the whole heart is what God Himself will work in you.

"The love of God has been poured out in our hearts by the Holy Spirit who was given to us" (Rom. 5:5). That makes the grace of loving God with all our hearts most sure and blessed.

THE JOYFUL SOUND

❦

Blessed are the people who know the joyful sound!
They walk, O LORD, in the light of Your countenance.
In Your name they rejoice all day long.
—Psalm 89:15–16

"Good tidings of great joy" (Luke 2:10) was what the angel called the gospel message, which is called *"the joyful sound"* in Psalm 89. Such blessedness consists of God's people walking in the light of God and rejoicing in His name *"all day long."* Undisturbed fellowship and never ending joy are their portion. In the Old Testament, such things were at times the experience of believers. But there was no continuance; the Old Testament could not secure it. Only the New Testament can and does give it.

In every well-ordered family, one finds the father delighting in his children, and the children rejoicing in their father's presence. This mark of a happy home on earth is what the heavenly Father has promised and delights to work in His people—walking in the light of His countenance and rejoicing in His name all day long. It has been promised; it has been made possible in Christ through the Holy Spirit filling the heart with the love of God. It is the heritage of everyone who is indeed seeking to love God with all his heart and with all his strength.

And yet, how many of God's children think it impossible and have even given up the hope and desire for a life of rejoicing in God's presence all day long! But Christ promised it so definitely: *"These things I have spoken to you, that My joy may remain in you, and that your joy may be full"* (John 15:11); *"I will see you again and your heart will rejoice"* (John 16:22).

The Father wants His children to have perfect confidence in and love for Him. He knows their need for His presence every moment of the day for their happiness and strength. Christ maintains this life in us by the power of the Holy Spirit. Let us be content with nothing less than the blessedness of those who know the joyful sound: *"They walk...in the light of Your countenance. In Your name they rejoice all day long....For You are the glory of their strength"* (Ps. 89:15–17).

The deeper we seek to enter into God's will for us, the stronger our faith will be that the Father can be content with nothing less than His child walking in the light of His countenance and rejoicing in His name all day long. We can be assured that what the Father has meant for us will be brought about in us through Christ and the Holy Spirit.

THE THOUGHTS OF GOD

As the heavens are higher than the earth,
so are...My thoughts than your thoughts.
—Isaiah 55:9

In giving us His promises of what He will work in us, God reminds us that, as high as the heavens are above the earth, so high are His thoughts above ours—altogether beyond our power of spiritual understanding.

When He tells us that we are made in His image, that by grace we are actually renewed again into that image, and that as we gaze upon God's glory in Christ we are changed into the same image by the Spirit of the Lord, these are indeed thoughts higher than the heavens. When He told Abraham of all the mighty work He would do in him and his descendants, and through him in all the nations of the earth, this again is a thought higher than the heavens. Our human minds cannot take it in. When God calls us to love Him with all our hearts and promises to renew our hearts so that we will love Him with all our strength, here again is a thought out of the very heights of heaven. And when the Father calls us to a life in the light of His countenance and rejoicing in His name all day long, this is a gift out of the very depths of God's heart of love.

We ought to have deep reverence, humility, and patience while we are waiting for God by His Holy Spirit to impart to our hearts the life and light that can make us feel at home with these thoughts. We need daily, tender, abiding fellowship with God if we are ever to enter into His mind and have His thoughts make their home in us. What great faith is needed to believe that God not only will reveal the beauty and the glory of these thoughts, but also will so mightily work in us that their divine reality and blessing will fill our inmost beings!

Think of what Isaiah said, as quoted by Paul: *"Eye has not seen, nor ear heard, nor have entered into the heart of man the things which God has prepared for those who love Him. But God has revealed them to us through His Spirit"* (1 Cor. 2:9–10). When Christ promised His disciples that the Holy Spirit would come from heaven to dwell with them, He said that the Spirit would fill us with the light and life of the heavenly world. In this way, Christ and the purposes of God—which are higher than the heavens are above the earth—were made their abiding experience. Dear reader, seek to realize that every day the Holy Spirit will fill your heart with the thoughts of God in all their heavenly power and glory.

THE NEW COVENANT IN JEREMIAH 31

❧

I will make a new covenant with the house of Israel....
I will put My law in their minds, and write it on their hearts.
—Jeremiah 31:31, 33

When God made the first covenant with Israel at Sinai, He said, *"If you will indeed obey My voice and keep My covenant, then you shall be a special treasure to Me above all people"* (Exod. 19:5). But Israel, unfortunately, did not have the power to obey. Their whole nature was carnal and sinful. There was no provision in the covenant for the grace that would make them obedient. The law only served to show them their sin.

In Jeremiah 31, God promised to make a new covenant in which provision would be made to enable men to live a life of obedience. In this new covenant, the law was to be put in their minds and written in their hearts, *"not with ink but by the Spirit of the living God"* (2 Cor. 3:3), so that they could say with David, *"I delight to do Your will, O my God, and Your law is within my heart"* (Ps. 40:8). Through the Holy Spirit, the law and the people's delight in it would take possession of their inner lives. Or, as we see in Jeremiah 32:40, God would put His fear in their hearts so that they would not depart from Him.

In contrast to the Old Testament covenant, which made it impossible to remain faithful, this promise ensures a continual, wholehearted obedience as the mark of the believer who takes God at His Word and fully claims what the promise secures.

Learn the lesson well. In the new covenant, God's mighty power is shown in the heart of everyone who believes the promise, *"They will not depart from Me"* (Jer. 32:40). Bow in deep stillness before God, and believe what He says. The measure of our experience of this power of God, which will keep us from departing from Him, will always be in harmony with the law: *"According to your faith let it be to you"* (Matt. 9:29).

We need to make a great effort to keep the contrast between the Old and New Testaments very clear. The Old had a wonderful measure of grace, but not enough for continually abiding in the faith of obedience. But that is the definite promise of the New Testament: the power of the Holy Spirit leading the soul and revealing the fullness of grace to keep us *"blameless in holiness"* (1 Thess. 3:13).

THE NEW COVENANT IN EZEKIEL

℁

*Then I will sprinkle clean water on you, and you
shall be clean; I will cleanse you from all your filthiness....
I will put My Spirit within you and cause you to walk
in My statutes, and you will keep My judgments.*
—*Ezekiel 36:25, 27*

Here we find the same promise as in Jeremiah, the promise of being so cleansed from sin and being so renewed in the heart that there would be no doubt of walking in God's statutes and keeping His law. In Jeremiah God had said, *"I will put My law in their minds"* (Jer. 31:33), and *"I will put My fear in their hearts so that they will not depart from Me"* (Jer. 32:40). Here in Ezekiel He says, *"I will...cause you to walk in My statutes, and you will keep My judgments."* In contrast to the old covenant, in which there was no power to enable them to continue in God's law, the great mark of the new covenant would be a divine power enabling them to walk in His statutes and keep His judgments.

"Where sin abounded, grace abounded much more" (Rom. 5:20), bringing about wholehearted allegiance and obedience. Why is this so seldom experienced? The answer is very simple: the promise is not believed, is not preached; its fulfillment is not expected. Yet how clearly it is laid out for us in a passage like Romans 8:1–4! In this passage, the man who had complained of the power *"bringing* [him] *into captivity to the law of sin"* (Rom. 7:23) thanks God that he is now *"in Christ Jesus"* (Rom. 8:1) and that the *"law of the Spirit of life in Christ Jesus has made* [him] *free from the law of sin and death"* (v. 2), so that the requirement of the law is fulfilled in all who walk after the Spirit (v. 4).

Once again, why are there so few who can give such testimony, and what is to be done to attain it? Just one thing is needed: faith in an omnipotent God who will, by His wonderful power, do what He has promised. *"I, the LORD, have spoken, and will do it"* (Ezek. 22:14). Oh, let us begin to believe that the promise will come true: *"You shall be clean; I will cleanse you from all your filthiness....I will...cause you to walk in My statutes, and you will keep My judgments."* Let us believe all that God promises here, and God will do it. Beyond all power of thought, God has made His great and glorious promises dependent on our faith. And the promises will bring about more of that faith as we believe them. *"According to your faith let it be to you"* (Matt. 9:29). Let us put this truth to the test even now.

THE NEW COVENANT AND PRAYER

🦋

*Call to Me, and I will answer you, and show you
great and mighty things, which you do not know.*
—*Jeremiah 33:3*

*I, the LORD, have spoken it, and I will do it....I will
also let the house of Israel inquire of Me to do this for them.*
—*Ezekiel 36:36–37*

The fulfillment of the great promises of the new covenant is dependent on prayer. In answer to the prayer of Jeremiah, God had said, *"I will put My fear in their hearts so that they will not depart from Me"* (Jer. 32:40). And to Ezekiel He had spoken, *"I will... cause you to walk in My statutes, and you will keep My judgments"* (Ezek. 36:27). Because we are unbelieving and we judge the meaning of God's Word according to human thought and experience, there is no expectation of these promises being truly fulfilled. We do not believe that God means them to be literally true. We do not have the faith in the mighty power of God that is waiting to make His promise true in our experience.

And God has said that without such faith, our lives will be very partial and limited. He has graciously pointed out the way in which such faith can be found; it is in the path of much prayer: *"Call to Me, and I will answer you, and show you great and mighty things, which you do not know."* Moreover, *"I will also let the house of Israel inquire of Me to do this for them."* When individual men and women turn to God with their whole hearts to plead these promises, He will fulfill them. It is in the exercise of intense, persevering prayer that faith will be strengthened to take hold of God and will surrender itself to His omnipotent working. Then, as one and another can testify of what God has done and will do, believers will help each other and will take their place as the church of the living God, pleading for and firmly expecting His promises to be fulfilled in larger measure. Then power will be given to them for the great work of preaching Christ in the fullness of His redemption to perishing men.

The state of the church, its members, our ministers, and our own hearts calls for unceasing prayer. We need to pray intensely and persistently that the need for the power of the Holy Spirit may be deeply felt and that a strong faith may be roused in the hearts of many to claim and to expect His mighty working. *"I, the LORD, have spoken, and will do it"* (Ezek. 22:14).

"Lord, I believe; help my unbelief!" (Mark 9:24).

THE NEW COVENANT IN HEBREWS

❧

*For I will be merciful to their unrighteousness, and their
sins and their lawless deeds I will remember no more.*
—Hebrews 8:12

In the book of Hebrews, Christ is called the *"Mediator of a better covenant, which was established on better promises"* (v. 6). In
Him the two parts of the covenant find their complete fulfillment.

First of all, He came to atone for sin, so that its power over
man was destroyed and free access to God's presence and favor was
secured. With that came the fuller blessing: the new heart, freed
from the power of sin, with God's Holy Spirit breathing into it the
delight in God's law and the power to obey it.

These two parts of the covenant can never be separated. And
yet, unfortunately, many people put their trust in Christ for the
forgiveness of sin but never think of claiming the fullness of the
promise of being God's people and knowing Him as their God. They
do not allow God to bring into their experience a new heart
cleansed from sin, with the Holy Spirit breathing into it such love
and delight in God's law, and such power to obey, that they have
access to the full blessing of the new covenant.

Jesus Christ is *"the Mediator of the new covenant"* (Heb. 9:15),
in which the forgiveness of sin is in the power of His blood, and in
which the law is written in hearts by the power of His Spirit. Oh, if
only we could understand that, just as surely as the complete pardon of sin is assured, so the complete fulfillment of the promises
may be expected, too: *"I will put My fear in their hearts so that they
will not depart from Me"* (Jer. 32:40); *"I will...cause you to walk in
My statutes, and you will keep My judgments"* (Ezek. 36:27).

But God has said, *"Behold, I am the LORD, the God of all flesh.
Is there anything too hard for Me?"* (Jer. 32:27). He spoke these
words to Jeremiah in regard to the new covenant. The new covenant requires strong, wholehearted desire for a life wholly given up
to God. It means we must set aside all our preconceived opinions,
and in faith believe in the mighty power of God. It means a surrender to Jesus Christ as *"the Mediator of the new covenant"* (Heb.
9:15), a willingness to accept our place with Him, crucified to the
world, to sin, and to self. It means a readiness to follow Him at any
cost. Succinctly, the new covenant means a simple, wholehearted
acceptance of Christ as Lord and Master—heart and life wholly His.
God has said it and will do it. *"I, the LORD, have spoken, and will
do it"* (Ezek. 22:14).

THE TRIAL OF FAITH

🦚

And [Naaman's] *servants came near and spoke to him, and
said, "My father, if the prophet had told you to do something
great, would you not have done it? How much more then,
when he says to you, 'Wash, and be clean'?"*
—2 Kings 5:13

In Naaman we have a striking illustration of the place faith
holds in God's dealings with man. It gives us a wonderful revelation
of what faith really is. Think first of how intense Naaman's desire
was for healing. He would do anything, even appeal to the King of
Syria and the King of Israel. He would undertake a long journey and
humble himself before the prophet, who did not even come out and
see him. In this intensity of desire for blessing, we have the root and
first mark of a strong faith. And it is just this seeking for God and
His blessing that is too much lacking in our religion.

A second mark of faith is that it has given up all its preconceived opinions and bows before the Word of God. This was more
than Naaman was willing to do, and he turned away in rage. It was
well for him that a wise and faithful servant gave him better advice. Faith is often held back by the thought that such a simple
thing as accepting God's Word can bring about a mighty revolution
in the heart.

Faith, thirdly, submits implicitly to the Word of God: *"Wash,
and be clean."* At first it might appear futile, but faith proves itself
in obedience. It does not obey only once or twice, but *"seven times"*
(2 Kings 5:10), in the assurance that the mighty wonder will be
brought about. Taking hold of the simple word, *"Wash, and be
clean,"* it finds itself renewed as with the life of a little child, *"completely clean"* (John 13:10). The mighty deed is done.

When God's Word brings us to the promise, *"I will sprinkle
clean water on you, and you shall be clean; I will cleanse you from
all your filthiness"* (Ezek. 36:25), it is nothing but unbelief that
holds us back. Let us believe that a simple, determined surrender of
the whole will to God's promise will indeed bring the heart-
cleansing we need. *"There is a river whose streams shall make glad
the city of God"* (Ps. 46:4). It flows from under the throne of God
and the Lamb, through the channels of a thousand precious promises, and at each step the word is heard: *"Wash, and be clean."*
Christ cleanses *"with the washing of water by the word"* (Eph.
5:26), and He says to you, *"You are already clean because of the
word which I have spoken to you"* (John 15:3)—*"completely clean"*
(John 13:10).

FAITH IN CHRIST

🦋

You believe in God, believe also in Me.
—John 14:1

In the Farewell Discourse (John 14–17), when Christ was about to leave His disciples, He taught them that they were to believe in Him with the same perfect confidence with which they had rested in God. *"You believe in God, believe also in Me"*; *"Believe Me that I am in the Father"* (John 14:11); *"He who believes in Me, the works that I do he will do also"* (v. 12). Here on earth, He had not been able to make Himself fully known to His disciples. But in heaven, the fullness of God's power would be His; and He would, in and through His disciples, do greater things than He had ever done upon earth.

This faith must first of all focus itself on the person of Christ in His union with the Father. The disciples were to have perfect confidence that all that God had done could now be done by Jesus, too. The deity of Christ is the rock on which our faith depends. Christ as man, partaker of our nature, is indeed true God. As the divine power has worked in Christ even to the resurrection from the dead, so Christ can also, in His divine omnipotence, work in us all that we need.

Dear Christian, do you not see of what deep importance it is that you take time to worship Jesus in His divine omnipotence as one with the Father? That will teach you to depend on Him in His sufficiency to work in you all that you can desire. This faith must so possess you that every thought of Christ will be filled with the consciousness of His presence as an almighty Redeemer, able to save, sanctify, and empower you to the uttermost.

Child of God, bow in deep humility before this blessed Lord Jesus, and worship Him—*"My Lord and my God!"* (John 20:28). Take time until you become fully conscious of an assured faith that Christ, as the almighty God, will work for you, in you, and through you all that God desires and all that you need. Let the Savior you have known and loved become as never before the Mighty God. Let Him be your confidence and your strength.

In His farewell charge on the last night, the Savior began by telling His disciples that everything in their lives would depend on simply believing Him. By this, they would do greater things than He had ever done. At the close of His address He repeated again, *"Be of good cheer, I have overcome the world"* (John 16:33). Our one need is a direct, definite, unceasing faith in the mighty power of Christ working in us.

CHRIST'S LIFE IN US

Because I live, you will live also.
—John 14:19

There is a great difference between the first three gospels and that of John. John was the beloved friend of Jesus. He understood the Master better than the others. John 13–17 is considered by many to be the inmost sanctuary of the New Testament. The other gospel writers spoke of repentance and the pardon of sin as the first great gift of the New Testament. But they said little of the new life that the new covenant was to bring, with the new heart in which the law had been put as a living power. John recorded what Christ taught about His life really becoming ours and our being united with Him just as He was with the Father. The other gospel writers spoke of Christ as the Shepherd seeking and saving the lost; John spoke of Him as the Shepherd who so gives His life for the sheep that His very life becomes theirs. *"I came that they may have life, and may have it abundantly"* (John 10:10 RV).

And so in John 14 Christ said, *"Because I live, you will live also."* The disciples were to receive from Him, not the life He then had, but the resurrection life in the power of its victory over death and of His exaltation to the right hand of God. He would from then on always dwell in them; a new, heavenly, eternal life—the life of Jesus Himself—would fill them. And this promise is to all who will accept it in faith.

Unfortunately, so many people are content with the beginnings of the Christian life but never desire to have it in its fullness—the more abundant life. They do not believe in it; they are not ready for the sacrifice implied in being wholly filled with the life of Jesus. Child of God, the message comes again to you: *"The things which are impossible with men are possible with God"* (Luke 18:27). Take time and let Christ's wonderful promise possess your heart. Be content with nothing less than a full salvation, Christ living in you, and you living in Christ. Be assured that it is meant for everyone who will take time to listen to Christ's promises and will believe that the almighty power of God will work in him the mighty wonder of His grace—Christ dwelling in the heart by faith.

THE OBEDIENCE OF LOVE

If you keep My commandments, you will abide in My love.
—John 15:10

Believers often ask, "How can I come to abide in Christ always, to live wholly for Him? Such is my desire and fervent prayer." In the above verse, the Lord gave the simple but far-reaching answer: *"Keep My commandments."* This is the only sure way, the blessed way, of abiding in Him. *"If you keep My commandments, you will abide in My love, just as I have kept My Father's commandments and abide in His love"* (v. 10). Loving obedience is the way to the enjoyment of His love.

The Lord spoke of this relationship between love and obedience on His last night. In John 14 we find it three times: *"If you love Me, keep My commandments,"* (v. 15); *"He who has My commandments and keeps them, it is he who loves Me. And he who loves Me will be loved by My Father, and I will love him"* (v. 21); *"If anyone loves Me, he will keep My word; and My Father will love him, and We will come to him and make Our home with him"* (v. 23). And chapter fifteen contains three more instances: *"If...My words abide in you, you will ask what you desire, and it shall be done for you"* (v. 7); *"If you keep My commandments, you will abide in My love"*; and *"You are My friends if you do whatever I command you"* (v. 14). All six times the Lord connected the keeping of the commandments with the promise of the great blessing that accompanies loving obedience—the indwelling of the Father and the Son in the heart. The love that keeps His commandments is the only way to abide in His love. In our relationship with Christ, love is everything—Christ's love for us, our love for Him, proved in our love for our fellow Christians.

How seldom believers have accepted this teaching! Many are content to think that it is impossible. They do not believe that through the grace of God, we can be kept from sin. They do not believe in the promise of the new covenant: *"I will put My Spirit within you and cause you to walk in My statutes, and you will keep My judgments"* (Ezek. 36:27). They have no concept how, to a heart fully surrendered and given over to Him, Christ will make possible what otherwise appears beyond our reach: loving Him, keeping His commandments, and abiding in His love.

The wonderful promise of the Holy Spirit as the power of Christ's life in us is the pledge that we will indeed love Him and keep His words. This is the great secret of abiding in Christ, of having the indwelling of Christ and of God, and of the effectiveness of our prayers to bring God's blessing on all our work.

THE PROMISE OF THE SPIRIT

❧

If I depart, I will send Him [the Holy Spirit] *to you....He will*
glorify Me, for He will take of what is Mine and declare it to you.
—John 16:7, 14

The crucified Christ was to be glorified on the throne of
heaven. Out of that glory He would send down the Holy Spirit into
the hearts of His disciples to glorify Him in them. The Spirit of the
crucified and glorified Christ would be their life in fellowship with
Him, and their power for His service. The Spirit comes to us as the
Spirit of divine glory; as such we are to welcome Him and yield ourselves absolutely to His leading.

Yes, the Spirit who *"searches...the deep things of God"* (1 Cor.
2:10), who dwells in the very roots of the Divine Being, who had
been with Christ through His life and in His death upon the cross—
this Spirit of the Father and the Son was to come and dwell in the
disciples and make them the conscious possessors of the presence of
the glorified Christ. It was this blessed Spirit who was to be their
power for a life of loving obedience, to be their Teacher and Leader
in praying down from heaven the blessing that they needed. And it
was in His power that they were to conquer God's enemies and
carry the Gospel to the ends of the world.

It is this Spirit that the church lacks so sadly; it is this Spirit
she grieves so unceasingly. It is owing to this spiritual poverty that
her work is so often feeble and fruitless.

The Spirit is God. As God, He claims possession of our entire
beings. We have too often thought of Him as our help in the Christian life, while we have not known that our hearts and lives are to
be entirely and unceasingly under His control. Indeed, we are to be
led by the Spirit every day and every hour. In His power, we are to
directly and continually abide in the love and fellowship of Jesus.
No wonder we have not believed in the great promise that, in a love
that keeps the commandments, we can always abide in Christ's
love! No wonder we do not have the courage to believe that Christ's
mighty power will work in us and through us! No wonder His divine prayer-promises are beyond our reach! The Spirit who
"searches...the deep things of God" claims the very depths of our
beings, so that He may there reveal Christ as Lord and Ruler.

The promise waits for its fulfillment in our lives: *"He will glo-*
rify Me, for He will take of what is Mine and declare it to you." Let
us yield ourselves today to believe the promise at once and with our
whole hearts. Christ waits to make it true.

IN CHRIST

&🙐

At that day you will know that I am in My
Father, and you in Me, and I in you.
—John 14:20

Our Lord spoke of His life in the Father: *"Believe Me that I am in the Father and the Father in Me"* (v. 11). He and the Father were not two individuals next to each other; they were in each other. Though Christ was on earth as a man, He lived in the Father. Everything He did was what the Father did in Him.

This divine life of heaven, of Christ in God and of God in Christ, is the picture and the pledge of what our life in Christ is to be here on earth. It is in the very nature of the divine life that the Son is in the Father. Even so, we must know and ever live in the faith that we are in Christ. Then we will learn that, even as the Father worked in Christ, so Christ will also work in us if we only believe that we are in Him and yield ourselves to His power.

And even as the Son waited on the Father and as the Father worked through Him, so the disciples would make known to Him in prayer what they wanted done on earth, and He would do it. Their life in Him was to be the reflection of His life in the Father. As the Father worked in Him, because He lived in the Father, so Christ would work in them as they lived in Him.

But this would not be fulfilled until the Holy Spirit came. They had to wait until they were filled with the power from on high. For this they abided in Him by daily fellowship and prayer, so that He might do in them the greater works He had promised.

How little the church understands that the secret of her power is to be found in nothing less than where Christ found it, abiding in the Father and His love! Ministers, too, seldom understand that this should be their one great goal, daily and hourly to abide in Christ as the only possible way of being equipped and used by Him in the great work of winning souls to Him. If anyone asks what the lost secret of the pulpit is, we have it here: *"At that day"*—when the Spirit fills your heart—*"At that day you will know that I am in My Father, and you in Me."*

Blessed Lord, teach us to surrender ourselves unreservedly to the Holy Spirit. Teach us, above everything, to wait daily for His teaching, so that we, too, may know the blessed secret, that as You are in the Father, so we are in You, and You work through us.

Gracious Lord, pour down upon all Your children who are seeking to work for You, such a spirit of grace and of supplication that we may not rest until we, too, are filled with the Holy Spirit.

ABIDING IN CHRIST

Abide in Me, and I in you.
—John 15:4

Using the Parable of the Vine and the Branch, our Lord sought to enforce and illustrate what He had taught in John 14 concerning our union with Him and His union with the Father. He did this all for the sake of bringing home to the apostles and to all His servants in the Gospel the absolute necessity of a life in daily full communion with Him. *"Abide in Me."*

On the one hand, He pointed to Himself and to the Father and indicated, "Just as truly and fully as I am in the Father, so you are in Me." Then, pointing to the vine, He essentially said, "Just as truly as the branch is in the vine, you are in Me. Just as the Father abides in Me and works in Me; just as I work out what He works in Me; just as as the branch abides in the vine, the vine gives its life and strength to the branch, and the branch receives it and puts it forth in fruit—even so do you abide in Me and receive My strength. With an almighty power I will work My work in you and through you. *'Abide in Me.'*"

Dear child of God, you have often meditated on this blessed passage. But do you not feel that you still have much to learn in order to have Christ's almighty power working in you as He desires? The great need is to take time in waiting on the Lord Jesus in the power of His Spirit, until the two great truths get complete mastery of your being: Christ is in God, and you are in Christ.

"He who abides in Me, and I in him, bears much fruit" (v. 5), said our Lord. Fruit is what Christ seeks, is what He works, is what He will assuredly give to the person who trusts Him.

To the feeblest of God's children, Christ says, "You are in Me. Abide in Me, and you will bear much fruit." To the strongest of His messengers, He still says, "Abide in Me, and you will bear much fruit." To one and all the message comes: daily, continuous, unbroken abiding in Christ Jesus is the one condition of a life of power and blessing. Take time, and let the Holy Spirit so renew in you the secret abiding in Him that you may understand the meaning of His words: *"These things I have spoken to you, that My joy may remain in you, and that your joy may be full"* (v. 11).

The Lord says to us, "Do you believe that I can do this, that I can keep you abiding in My love?" And when we answer Him, "Yes, Lord," He tells us, *"Do not be afraid; only believe"* (Mark 5:36).

THE POWER OF PRAYER

*If ye abide in me, and my words abide in you, ask
whatsoever ye will, and it shall be done unto you.*
—John 15:7 RV

Before our Lord went up to heaven, He taught His disciples
two great lessons in regard to their relationship with Him in the
great work they had to do. The one was that in heaven, He would
have much more power than He had upon earth, and He would use
that power for the salvation of men, solely through them, their
words, and their work. The other lesson was that, without Him,
they could do nothing, but they could depend on Him to work in
them and through them, and so carry out His purpose. Their first
and chief work would therefore be to bring everything they wanted
done to Him in prayer. They knew and depended on His promise:
"Ask whatsoever ye will, and it shall be done unto you."

With these two truths written in their hearts, He sent them
out into the world. They could confidently undertake their work.
The almighty, glorified Jesus was ready to do in and with and
through them greater things than He Himself had ever done upon
earth. The helpless disciples on earth unceasingly looked up to Him
in prayer, with the full confidence that He would hear those prayers—but only on the condition that they have an unflinching confidence in the power of His promise. The chief thing in their lives
and in their ministry was to be the maintenance of a spirit of
prayer and supplication.

But how little the church has understood and believed this!
Why? Simply because believers live so little in the daily abiding in
Christ that they are powerless in believing His *"great and precious
promises"* (2 Pet. 1:4). Let us learn the lesson, both for our lives
and our work, that as the members of Christ's body, the chief thing
every day must be a close abiding fellowship with Christ that is
based in deep dependence and unceasing supplication. Only then
can we do our work in the full assurance that He has heard our
prayers and will be faithful in doing His part—in giving the power
from on high as the source of strength and abundant blessing. Take
time, you *"servants of the LORD"* (Ps. 113:1), and with your whole
hearts believe the word Christ has spoken. Christ asks, *"Do you
believe this?...Yes, Lord, I believe"* (John 11:26–27). *"If ye abide in
me, and my words abide in you, ask whatsoever ye will, and it shall
be done unto you."*

"Abide in My love" (John 15:9).

THE MYSTERY OF LOVE

🐾

*That they all may be one, as You, Father, are in Me, and I in
You....that they may be one just as We
are one: I in them, and You in Me.
—John 17:21–23*

During His last evening on earth, Christ especially pressed the
thought of the disciples being in Him and abiding in Him. He also
mentioned His being in them, but He did not emphasize this as
much as their being in Him. But in His prayer as High Priest, He
gave greater place to the thought of His being in them, just as the
Father was in Him: *"That they may be one just as We are one: I in
them, and You in Me; that they may be made perfect in one, and that
the world may know that You have sent Me, and have loved them as
You have loved Me"* (vv. 22–23).

The power to convince the world that God loved the disciples
as He loved His Son, could only come as believers lived their lives
with Christ in them and proved it by loving their fellowmen as
Christ loved them. The feebleness of the church is owing to the fact
that we have not, by our example, proved to the world that our
lives are in Christ and His life is in us. What is needed? Nothing
less than a complete indwelling of Christ in the heart, and a binding together of believers because they know each other as those
who have Christ dwelling in them. The last words of Christ's
prayer in John 17 read, *"I have declared to them Your name, and
will declare it, that the love with which You loved Me may be in
them, and I in them"* (v. 26). The divine indwelling has its chief glory
in that it is the manifestation of divine love. It is the Father's love
for Christ, brought by Christ to us, flowing out from us to all men.

Christ gave this great promise to every loving, obedient disciple: *"My Father will love him, and We will come to him and make
Our home with him"* (John 14:23). It is to live this life of love for
Christ and one's fellowmen, that the Holy Spirit, in whom the Father and the Son are one, desires to live in our hearts. Let nothing
less than this be what you seek, what you believe, what you claim
with your whole heart and strength—the indwelling of the Lord
Jesus in the love *"which passes knowledge"* (Eph. 3:19), with which
He can fill your heart. In this way the world will be constrained by
the love God's children have for each other to acknowledge that
Christ's words are being fulfilled: *"That the love with which You
loved Me may be in them, and I in them"* (John 17:26).

"Do you believe this?...Yes, Lord" (John 11:26–27).

CHRIST OUR RIGHTEOUSNESS

❧

Justified freely by His grace through the
redemption that is in Christ Jesus.
—Romans 3:24

The first three gospel writers spoke of redemption as a pardon of sin, or justification. John spoke of it as a life that Christ is to live in us—a regeneration. In Paul's letters, however, we find both truths in beautiful harmony.

Paul first spoke of justification in Romans 3:21–5:11. Then he went on from 5:12 to 8:39 to speak of the life that is lived in union with Christ. In Romans 4 he told us that we find both these things in Abraham: *"Abraham believed God....To him who...believes on Him who justifies the ungodly, his faith is accounted for righteousness"* (v. 3, 5). Then, in verse 17, Abraham *"believed...God, who gives life to the dead."* Just as God considered Abraham's faith as righteousness and then led him on to believe in Him as the God who can give life to the dead, so it is with every believer.

Justification comes when the eye of faith is fixed on Christ. But that is only the beginning. Gradually the believer begins to understand that he was at the same time born again, that he has Christ in him, and that his calling now is to abide in Christ and let Christ abide and live and work in him.

Most Christians strive, by holding on to their faith in justification, to stir themselves up and strengthen themselves for a life of gratitude and obedience. But they fail sadly because they do not know, do not in full faith yield themselves to Christ, to maintain His life in them. They have learned from Abraham the first lesson: to believe in God *"who justifies the ungodly."* But they have not gone on to the second great lesson: to believe in God *"who gives life to the dead"* and daily renews that life through Christ, who lives in them and in whose life alone there is strength and fullness of blessing. The Christian life must be *"from faith to faith"* (Rom. 1:17). The grace of pardon is only the beginning; growing in grace leads on to the fuller insight and experience of what it means to be in Christ, to live in Him, and to *"grow up in all things into Him who is the head"* (Eph. 4:15).

CHRIST OUR LIFE

🦙

*Much more those who receive abundance of grace and of the gift
of righteousness will reign in life through the One, Jesus Christ.*
—Romans 5:17

*Reckon yourselves to be dead indeed to sin,
but alive to God in Christ Jesus our Lord.*
—Romans 6:11

Paul taught us that our faith in Christ as our righteousness is
to be followed by our faith in Him as our life from the dead. He
asked, *"Do you not know that as many of us as were baptized into
Christ Jesus were baptized into His death?"* (Rom. 6:3). We were
buried with Him and were raised from the dead with Him. Just as
all of mankind died in Adam, so all believers in Christ actually died
in Him. *"Our old man was crucified with Him"* (v. 6); with Him we
were raised from the dead (Col. 2:12); and now we are to consider
ourselves as *"dead indeed to sin, but alive to God."*

Truly, just as the new life in us is a participation in and experience of the risen life of Christ, so our death to sin in Christ is also
a spiritual reality. When we, by the power of the Holy Spirit, are
enabled to see how we were really one with Christ in His death and
in His resurrection, we will understand that in Him sin has no
power over us. We present ourselves unto God *"as being alive from
the dead"* (Rom. 6:13).

The man who knows that he died in Christ and is now alive in
Him can confidently depend on it that *"sin shall not have dominion
over* [him]*"* (v. 14), not even for a single moment. *"Reckon yourselves to be dead indeed to sin, but alive to God in Christ Jesus."*
This is the true life of faith.

Just as we can only live in Christ and have Him live in us as
we experience the full power of the Holy Spirit, so it is here. Paul
said, *"The law of the Spirit of life in Christ Jesus has made me free
from the law of sin and death"* (Rom. 8:2), which, he had complained, had kept him in captivity. Then he added, *"That the righteous requirement of the law might be fulfilled in us who do not walk
according to the flesh but according to the Spirit"* (v. 4). Through
the Spirit we enter into the glorious liberty of the children of God.

Oh, that God might open the eyes of His children to see what
the power is of Christ living in them for a life of holiness and fruitfulness, when they consider themselves *"dead indeed to sin, but
alive to God in Christ Jesus"*!

CRUCIFIED WITH CHRIST

*I have been crucified with Christ; it is no longer I
who live, but Christ lives in me.*
—Galatians 2:20

As in Adam we died and went out of the life and will of God
into sin and corruption, so in Christ we are made partakers of a
new spiritual death—a death out of sin and into the will and life of
God. Such was the death Christ died; such is the death we are made
partakers of in Him. To Paul, this was such a reality that he was
able to say, *"I have been crucified with Christ; it is no longer I who
live, but Christ lives in me."* Dying with Christ had had such power
that he no longer lived his own life; instead, Christ lived His life in
him. He had indeed died to the old nature and to sin and had been
raised up into the power of the living Christ dwelling in him.

It was the crucified Christ who lived in Paul and made him a
partaker of all that the cross had meant to Christ Himself. The
very mind that was in Christ—who emptied Himself and took *"the
form of a bondservant"* (Phil. 2:7) and who *"humbled Himself and
became obedient to the point of death"* (v. 8)—was at work in him
because the crucified Christ lived in him. He lived as a crucified
man.

Christ's death on the cross was His highest display of His holiness and victory over sin. The believer who receives Christ is made
a partaker of all the power and blessing that the crucified Lord has
won. As the believer learns to accept this by faith, he yields himself
as crucified to the world and dead to its pleasure and pride, its lusts
and self-pleasing. He learns that the mystery of the cross, as the
crucified Lord reveals its power in him, opens the door into the
fullest fellowship with Christ and the conformity to His sufferings.
And so he learns, in the full depth of its meaning, what the Word
has said: *"Christ crucified...the power of God and the wisdom of
God"* (1 Cor. 1:23–24). He grows into a fuller understanding of the
blessedness of daring to say, *"I have been crucified with Christ; it is
no longer I who live, but Christ lives in me."*

Oh, the blessedness and power of the God-given faith that enables a man to live all day yielding himself to God and considering
himself as *"dead indeed to sin, but alive to God in Christ Jesus"*
(Rom. 6:11).

THE FAITH LIFE

🙊

*The life which I now live in the flesh I live by faith in
the Son of God, who loved me and gave Himself for me.*
—*Galatians 2:20*

If we were able to ask Paul, "What is your part in living life, if
you no longer live but Christ lives in you?" he would answer, *"The
life which I now live in the flesh I live by faith in the Son of God,
who loved me and gave Himself for me."* His whole life, day by day
and all day long, was one of unceasing faith in the wonderful Love
that had given itself for him. Faith was the power that possessed
and permeated Paul's whole being and his every action.

Here we have the simple but full statement of the secret of the
true Christian life. It is not faith that rests only in certain promises
of God or in certain blessings that we receive from Christ. It is a
faith that sees how entirely Christ gives Himself to the soul to be
his entire life and all that that implies for every moment of the day.
Just as continuous breathing is essential to the support of our
physical life, so is the unceasing faith in which the soul trusts
Christ and depends on Him to maintain the life of the Spirit within
us. Faith always rests on the infinite love in which Christ gave
Himself wholly for us to be entirely ours and to live His life over
again in us. By virtue of His divine omnipresence, by which He
"fills all in all" (Eph. 1:23), He can be to each what He is to all—a
complete and perfect Savior, an abiding Guest, taking charge and
maintaining our life in us and for us—as if each of us were the only
one in whom He lives. Just as truly as the Father lived in Him and
worked in Him all that He was to work out, so will Christ live and
work in each one of us.

When our faith is led and taught by God's Holy Spirit, we obtain such a confidence in the omnipotence and omnipresence of
Christ that we carry all day in the depths of our hearts this unbroken assurance: "He who loved me and gave Himself for me, He
lives in me; He is my life and my all." *"I can do all things through
Christ who strengthens me"* (Phil. 4:13). May God reveal to us the
inseparable union between Christ and us, in which the consciousness of Christ's presence may become as natural to us as the consciousness of our existence.

FULL CONSECRATION

❧

*Indeed I also count all things loss for the excellence
of the knowledge of Christ Jesus my Lord.*
—Philippians 3:8

In studying the promises Jesus gave to His disciples during His last night, the question arises: What was it that made these men worthy of the high honor of being baptized with the Holy Spirit from heaven? The answer is simple. When Christ called them, they forsook all and followed Him. They denied themselves, even to the hating of their own lives, and gave themselves to obey His commands. They followed Him to Calvary, and amid its suffering and death, their hearts clung to Him alone. It was this that prepared them for receiving a share in His resurrection life, and so they were made ready to be filled with the Spirit, even as Christ received the fullness of the Spirit from the Father in glory.

Just as Jesus had to sacrifice all to be wholly an offering to God, so all His people—from Abraham, Jacob, and Joseph to His twelve disciples to today's believers—have had to give up all to follow the divine leading, and have lived separated unto God, before the divine power could fulfill God's purposes through them.

It was this way with Paul, too. To *"count all things loss for the excellence of the knowledge of Christ Jesus my Lord"* was the keynote of his life, as it must be in ours if we are to share fully in the power of His resurrection. But how little the church understands that we have been entirely redeemed from the world, to live wholly and only for God and His love! As the merchant who found the treasure in the field had to sell all he had to purchase it, Christ claims the whole heart, the whole life, and the whole strength if we are indeed to share with Him in His victory through the power of the Holy Spirit. The law of God's kingdom is unchangeable—*"all things loss for the excellence of the knowledge of Christ Jesus my Lord."*

The disciples had to spend years with Christ in order to be prepared for Pentecost. Christ calls us to walk every day in the closest union with Himself, to abide in Him without ceasing, and so to live as those who are not their own, but wholly His. In this life of full surrender, we will find the path to the fullness of the Spirit.

In faith, boldly believe that such a life is meant for you. Let your heart's fervent desire reach out for nothing less than this. Love the Lord and Christ your Savior with your whole heart. You will be *"more than conquerors through Him who loved us"* (Rom. 8:37).

ENTIRE SANCTIFICATION

❧

Now may the God of peace Himself sanctify you completely; and may...[you be] blameless at the coming of our Lord Jesus Christ. He who calls you is faithful, who also will do it.
—1 Thessalonians 5:23–24

What a promise! One would expect to see all God's children clinging to it, claiming its fulfillment. But, unfortunately, unbelief does not know what to think of it, and only a few people consider it their treasure and joy.

"The God of peace"—the peace that He made by the blood of the cross, the peace that passes all understanding and keeps our hearts and thoughts in Christ Jesus (Phil. 4:7)—alone can and will do it. This God of peace Himself promises to sanctify us, to *"sanctify [us] completely,"* in Christ our sanctification, in the sanctification of the Spirit. It is God who is doing the work. It is in close, personal fellowship with God Himself that we become holy.

Should not all of us rejoice with exceeding joy at the prospect? But it is as if the promise is too great for many of us, and so it is repeated and amplified. May your spirit (the inmost part of your being, created for fellowship with God), your soul (the seat of the life and all its powers), and your body (through which sin entered and in which sin proved its power even unto death, but which has been redeemed in Christ)—may these be preserved whole, without blame, at the coming of our Lord Jesus Christ (1 Thess. 5:23).

To prevent the possibility of any misunderstanding, as if it is too great to be literally true, these words are added to our text verse: *"He who calls you is faithful, who also will do it."* Yes, God has said, *"I, the LORD, have spoken it, and I, [in Christ and through the Holy Spirit] will do it"* (Ezek. 36:36). He asks only that we come and abide in close fellowship with Him every day. As the heat of the sun shines on the body and warms it, so the fire of His holiness will burn in us and make us holy.

Child of God, beware of unbelief. It dishonors God, it robs your soul of its heritage. Take refuge in this: *"He who calls you is faithful, who also will do it."* Let every thought of your high and holy calling elicit the response: *"He who calls you is faithful, who also will do it."* Yes, He will do it, and He will give you grace to abide in His nearness so that you can always be under the cover of His perfect peace and of the holiness that He alone can give.

"All things are possible to him who believes....Lord, I believe; help my unbelief!" (Mark 9:23–24).

THE EXCEEDING GREATNESS OF HIS POWER

[I] do not cease to...[make] *mention of you in my prayers:*
that the God of our Lord Jesus Christ, the Father of glory,
may give to you the spirit of wisdom and revelation...the
eyes of your understanding being enlightened; that you may know
...what is the exceeding greatness of His power toward us who
believe, according to the working of His mighty power which
He worked in Christ when He raised Him from the dead.
—Ephesians 1:16–20

Here is one of the great Scriptures that will make our faith large and strong and bold. Paul was writing to those who had been sealed with the Holy Spirit. And yet he felt the need for unceasing prayer for the enlightening of the Spirit, so that they might truly know the mighty power of God that was working in them. It was nothing less than this very same power, the strength of His might, by which He raised Christ from the dead.

Christ died on the tree, weighed down by the sin of the world and its curse. When He descended into the grave, it was under the weight of all that sin and under the power of the death that had apparently mastered Him. What a mighty working of the power of God, to raise that Man out of the grave to the power and the glory of His throne! And now it is that same power, in its *"exceeding greatness...toward us who believe,"* that we, by the teaching of the Holy Spirit, are to know as working in us every day of our lives. The Lord, who said to Abraham, "I am God Almighty, nothing is too hard for Me" (see Jeremiah 32:27), comes to us with the message that what He did not only in Abraham, but also in Christ Jesus, is the pledge of what He is doing every moment in our hearts and will complete if we learn to trust Him.

It is by that almighty power that the risen and exalted Christ can be revealed in our hearts as our life and our strength. How rarely Christians believe this! Oh, let us cry to God; let us trust God for His Holy Spirit to enable us to claim nothing less every day than the *"exceeding greatness"* of this resurrection power working in us!

Let us especially pray for all believers around us and throughout the church, that they may have their eyes opened to the wonderful vision of God's almighty resurrection power working in them. And let ministers, like Paul, make this a matter of continual intercession for those among whom they labor. What a difference it would make in their ministry—the unceasing prayer for the Spirit to reveal the power that dwells and works in them!

THE INDWELLING CHRIST

*For this reason I bow my knees to the Father of our
Lord Jesus Christ...that He would grant you, according to the
riches of His glory, to be strengthened with might through His
Spirit in the inner man, that Christ may dwell in your hearts
through faith; that you, being rooted and grounded in love...
may be filled with all the fullness of God.*
—Ephesians 3:14, 16–17, 19

The great privilege that separated Israel from other nations was this: they had God dwelling in their midst; His home was in *"the Holiest of All"* (Heb. 9:3).

The New Testament is the dispensation of the indwelling God in the hearts of His people. Christ said, *"If anyone loves Me, he will keep My word; and My Father will love him, and We will come to him and make Our home with him"* (John 14:23). This is what Paul referred to as *"the riches of the glory of this mystery among the Gentiles: which is Christ in you, the hope of glory"* (Col. 1:27). Or, as he said of himself, *"Christ lives in me"* (Gal. 2:20). How few Christians experience this! Let us study Paul's teaching on the way to experience this crowning blessing of the Christian life.

1. *"I BOW MY KNEES TO THE FATHER."* The blessing must come from the Father. It is to be found in much prayer.

2. *"THAT HE WOULD GRANT YOU, ACCORDING TO THE RICHES OF HIS GLORY"*—SOMETHING VERY SPECIAL AND DIVINE—*"TO BE STRENGTHENED WITH MIGHT THROUGH HIS SPIRIT IN THE INNER MAN."* God gives us the strength to be separate from sin and the world, to yield to Christ as Lord and Master, and to live the life of love for Christ and keeping His commandments to which the promise has been given: *"We will come to him and make Our home with him"* (John 14:23).

3. *"THAT CHRIST MAY DWELL IN YOUR HEARTS THROUGH FAITH."* Christ, in His divine omnipresence and love, longs for hearts to dwell in. As a believer sees this by faith, bows his knee, and asks God for this great blessing, he receives grace to believe that the prayer is answered. And through that faith, he accepts the wonderful gift desired for so long—Christ dwelling in the heart by faith.

4. *"THAT YOU, BEING ROOTED AND GROUNDED IN LOVE...MAY BE FILLED WITH ALL THE FULLNESS OF GOD,"* as far as it is possible for man to experience it.

Feed on the words the Holy Spirit has given here, and hold fast to the confident assurance that God will do *"abundantly above all that we ask or think"* (Eph. 3:20).

CHRISTIAN PERFECTION

☙

*May the God of peace...make you complete in every good
work to do His will, working in you what is well
pleasing in His sight, through Jesus Christ.*
—Hebrews 13:20–21

Prepare your heart, my reader, for a large and strong faith—a faith that takes hold of one of God's promises that are as high above all our thoughts as the heaven is above the earth (Isa. 55:9).

In the epistle to the Hebrews, we have a wonderful presentation of the eternal redemption that Christ our great High Priest, *"the Mediator of the new covenant"* (Heb. 9:15), worked out for us through the shedding of His precious blood. The writer of the epistle closed his whole argument and all its deep spiritual teaching with the benediction, *"May the God of peace...make you complete in every good work to do His will."* Does that not include everything? Can we desire more? Yes, *"working in you what is well pleasing in His sight,"* and that through Jesus Christ.

The great thought here is that all that Christ had accomplished for our redemption, and all that God had done in raising Him from the dead, was done just with the one aim that He might now have more room to work in us the everlasting redemption that Christ brought in. He Himself, as God the Omnipotent, will make us *"complete in every good work."* And if we want to know in what way, we have the answer: by His working within us *"what is well pleasing in His sight, through Jesus Christ."*

All that we have been taught about the completeness of the salvation in Christ and our call to follow Him, here finds its consummation: we may be assured that God Himself takes such an entire charge of the man who really trusts Him, that He Himself will through Jesus Christ work all that *"is well pleasing in His sight."*

The thought is too high; the promise is too large; we cannot attain it. And yet there it is, claiming, stimulating our faith. It calls us to take hold of the one truth that the everlasting God works in us every hour of the day *"through Jesus Christ."* We have just one thing to do: yield ourselves into God's hands for Him to work—not to hinder Him by our working, but in a silent adoring faith to be assured that He Himself through Jesus Christ will work in us all that *"is well pleasing in His sight."*

Lord, *"increase our faith"* (Luke 17:5)!

THE GOD OF ALL GRACE

❧

*May the God of all grace, who called us to His eternal
glory by Christ Jesus, after you have suffered a while,
perfect, establish, strengthen, and settle you.*
—1 Peter 5:10

The book of Hebrews gathers up all its teaching in the wonderful promise, *"The God of peace...make you complete in every good work"* (Heb. 13:20–21). Peter did the same thing here: *"The God of all grace...perfect, establish, strengthen, and settle you."* God Himself is to be the one object of our trust every day; as we think of our work, our needs, our lives, and all our hearts' desires, God Himself must be the one object of our hope and trust.

Just as God is the center of the universe, the one source of its strength, the one Guide who orders and controls its movements, so God must have the same place in the life of the believer. With every new day, the first and chief thought ought to be, "God, God alone, can help me to live today as He wants me to live."

And what is to be our position toward this God? Should not our first thought every day be to humbly place ourselves in His hands, to confess our absolute helplessness, and to yield ourselves in childlike surrender to receive from Him the fulfillment of His promises—promises such as *"the God of peace...make you complete in every good work"* (Heb. 13:20–21); *"The God of all grace... perfect, establish, strengthen, and settle you"*?

In the earlier section of this book entitled "The Secret of Adoration," you saw how absolutely indispensable it is to meet God every morning, to give Him time to reveal Himself and take charge of your life for the day. Do we not have to do the same with these wonderful words of Peter? Yes, it must be understood between God and ourselves that our hearts are resting on Him, that our hope is in His Word: *"The God of peace...make you complete in every good work"* (Heb. 13:20–21); *"The God of all grace...perfect, establish, strengthen, and settle you."*

By His grace, may this henceforth be the spirit in which we awake every morning to go out to our work, humbly trusting in the promise that God Himself will perfect us: *"The LORD will perfect that which concerns me"* (Ps. 138:8).

Ever blessed Father, open the eyes of Your children to the vision that, even as Your Son was perfected forevermore, so You are waiting to work in each of us that work of perfecting Your saints in which Your glory will be seen.

NOT SINNING

🦜

You know that He was manifested to take away our sins, and in Him there is no sin. Whoever abides in Him does not sin.
—*1 John 3:5–6*

John had taken deep into his heart and life the words that Christ had spoken on the last night—words about abiding in Him. He always remembered how the Lord had spoken six times of loving Him and keeping His commandments as the way to abide in His love and to receive the indwelling of the Father and the Son. And so, abiding in Christ is one of the key promises in this epistle that he wrote in his old age. (See 1 John 2:6, 24, 28; 3:6, 24; 4:13, 16.)

In the text verse above, John taught how we can be kept from sinning. *"Whoever abides in Him does not sin."* Though there is sin in our nature, the abiding in Christ, in whom there is no sin, does indeed free us from the power of sin and enable us to live daily so as to please God. The Scriptures record that Christ had said of the Father, *"I always do those things that please Him"* (John 8:29). And so John wrote later in his epistle, *"Beloved, if our heart does not condemn us, we have confidence toward God. And whatever we ask we receive from Him, because we keep His commandments and do those things that are pleasing in His sight"* (1 John 3:21–22).

Let the soul who longs to be free from the power of sin take hold of these simple but far-reaching words: *"In Him there is no sin"* (v. 5), and *"He who establishes us...in Christ...is God"* (2 Cor. 1:21). As you seek to abide in Him in whom there is no sin, Christ will indeed live out His own life in you in the power of the Holy Spirit and will equip you for a life in which you always do the things that are pleasing in His sight.

Dear child of God, you are called to a life in which faith—great faith, strong, continuous, and unbroken—in the almighty power of God is your one hope. As you daily take time and yield yourself to the God of peace, who perfects you *"in every good work"* (Heb. 13:21) to do His will, you will experience that God indeed works in those who wait for Him. (See Lamentations 3:25.)

"Whoever abides in Him does not sin." The promise is sure: God Almighty has pledged that He will work in you what is well pleasing in His sight, through Christ Jesus (Heb. 13:20–21). In that faith, abide in Him.

"Did I not say to you that if you would believe you would see the glory of God?" (John 11:40).

OVERCOMING THE WORLD

🦋

*Who is he who overcomes the world, but he who
believes that Jesus is the Son of God?*
—1 John 5:5

Christ had spoken strongly about the world hating Him. His
kingdom and the kingdom of this world were in deadly hostility.
John had understood the lesson and summed it up in these words:
*"We know that we are of God, and the whole world lies under the
sway of the wicked one"* (v. 19); *"Do not love the world or the things
in the world. If anyone loves the world, the love of the Father is not
in him"* (1 John 2:15).

John also taught us what the real nature and power of the
world is: *"the lust of the flesh"* (v. 16), with its self-pleasing; *"the
lust of the eyes"* (v. 16), which sees and seeks the glory of the world;
"and the pride of life" (v. 16), with its self-exaltation. Eve in Paradise had these three marks of the world. She *"saw that the tree was
good for food, that it was pleasant to the eyes, and a tree desirable to
make one wise"* (Gen. 3:6). Through the body, the eyes, and the
pride of wisdom, the world acquired mastery over her and over us.

The world still exerts a terrible influence over the Christian
who does not know that, in Christ, he has been crucified to the
world. (See Galatians 6:14.) The power of this world proves itself in
the pleasure of eating and drinking, in the enjoyment of what is to
be seen of its glory, and in all that constitutes the pride of life. Most
Christians are either utterly ignorant of the danger of a worldly
spirit, or they feel themselves utterly powerless to conquer it.

Christ left us with the great far-reaching promise: *"Be of good
cheer, I have overcome the world"* (John 16:33). As the child of God
abides in Christ and seeks to live the heavenly life in the power of
the Holy Spirit, he may confidently depend on the power given him
to overcome the world. *"Who is he who overcomes the world, but he
who believes that Jesus is the Son of God?"* This is the secret of
daily, hourly victory over the world and all its secret, subtle temptations: *"I live by faith in the Son of God, who loved me and gave
Himself for me"* (Gal. 2:20). But it needs a heart and a life entirely
possessed by the faith of Jesus Christ to maintain the victor's attitude at all times. My fellow believer, take time to ask whether you
believe with your whole heart in the victory that faith gives over the
world. Put your trust in the mighty power of God, in the abiding
presence of Jesus, as the only pledge of certain, continual victory.

"Do you believe this?...Yes, Lord, I believe" (John 11:26–27).

JESUS: THE AUTHOR AND FINISHER OF OUR FAITH

Lord, I believe; help my unbelief!
—Mark 9:24

What a treasure of encouragement these words contain! Our Lord had said to the father of the possessed child, who had asked for His help, *"If you can believe, all things are possible to him who believes"* (v. 23). The father felt that Christ was throwing the responsibility on him. If he believed, the child could be healed. But he felt as if he did not have such faith. As he looked in the face of Christ, he felt assured that the love that was willing to heal would also be ready to help with his faith and graciously accept even its feeble beginnings. And so he cried with tears, *"Lord, I believe; help my unbelief!"* Christ heard the prayer, and the child was healed.

What a lesson for us who have so often felt, as we listened to the wonderful promises of God, that our faith was too feeble to grasp the precious gift! Here we receive the assurance that the Christ who waits for our faith to do its work is the same Savior who will care for our faith. However feeble our faith may be, and though it comes with tears, let us cry, *"Lord, I believe; help my unbelief!"* Christ will accept the prayer that puts its trust in Him. Let us do this, even though our faith is *"as a mustard seed"* (Matt. 17:20). In contact with Christ, the feeblest faith is made strong and bold. Jesus Christ is *"the author and finisher of our faith"* (Heb. 12:2).

Dear Christian, as you read God's wonderful promises and long to have them fulfilled, remember the mustard seed. However small it may be, if it is put into the ground and allowed to grow, it becomes a great tree. Take the hidden, feeble seed of the little faith you have, and with the Word of promise on which you are resting, plant it in your heart. As it makes contact with Christ through fervent prayer to Him, He will accept the feeble, trembling faith that clings to Him without letting Him go. A feeble faith in an almighty Christ will become the great faith that can move mountains.

With Abraham, God took charge of his faith and trained him to become *"strong in faith, giving glory to God"* (Rom. 4:20 KJV). You can confidently depend on Christ's desire to strengthen your faith. And when the question comes again, *"Do you believe this?"* (John 11:26), let your heart confidently say, *"Yes, Lord, I believe"* (v. 27). Praise God! Christ not only waits to give us the fullness of the heavenly life and the blessings of the covenant, but He also secretly works in us the faith that can claim it all.

Section Five

The Secret of United Prayer

THE LOST SECRET

❧

*Wait for the Promise of the Father....You shall be
baptized with the Holy Spirit not many days from now.
—Acts 1:4–5*

After our Lord had given the great command, *"Go into all the world and preach the gospel to every creature"* (Mark 16:15), He added His very last command: *"Tarry in the city of Jerusalem until you are endued with power from on high"* (Luke 24:49); *"Wait for the Promise of the Father....You shall be baptized with the Holy Spirit not many days from now."*

All Christians agree that the great command to preach the Gospel to every creature was not only for the disciples, but is our obligation as well. But not everyone appears to believe that Christ's very last command—not to preach until they had received the power from on high—is as binding on us as it was on the disciples. The church seems to have lost possession of what ought to be her secret of secrets—the daily, abiding consciousness that only as she lives in the power of the Holy Spirit can she preach the Gospel with Spirit and power. Therefore, there is much preaching and working with little spiritual result. It is owing to nothing but this that the universal complaint is heard that there is too little prayer, especially that much-availing prayer that brings down the power from on high. Without the baptism of the Holy Spirit, prayer is not likely to produce results.

In this section, I desire to study the secret of Pentecost as it is revealed in the words and deeds of our blessed Master, and in the words and deeds of His disciples as they took Him at His word and continued with one accord in prayer and supplication until the promise was fulfilled. As the disciples were filled with the Holy Spirit, they proved what the mighty power of their God could do through them.

Let us seek earnestly the grace of the Holy Spirit, who alone can reveal to us what *"eye has not seen, nor ear heard, nor have entered into the heart of man,"* that is, *"the things which God has prepared for those who love Him"* (1 Cor. 2:9). Let us pray that the lost secret may be found—the sure promise that in answer to fervent prayer, the power of the Holy Spirit will indeed be given.

THE KINGDOM OF GOD

🦋

*[Jesus] presented Himself alive [to His disciples]...being
seen by them during forty days and speaking of the
things pertaining to the kingdom of God.*
—Acts 1:3

When Christ began to preach, He took up the message of John:
"The kingdom of heaven is at hand" (Matt. 4:17). Later on He said,
*"There are some standing here who will not taste death till they see
the kingdom of God present with power"* (Mark 9:1). This could not
be until the King had ascended His throne. Then He and His disciples would be ready to receive the great gift of the Holy Spirit,
bringing down the kingdom of God into their hearts.

Acts 1:3 tells us that all the teaching of Jesus during the forty
days after the Resurrection dealt with the kingdom of God. It is
remarkable how Luke, in the last verses of Acts, summed up all the
teaching of Paul at Rome, who *"testified of the kingdom of God"*
(Acts 28:23) and was *"preaching the kingdom of God"* (v. 31).

Christ, seated upon the throne of God, was now King and Lord
of all. To His disciples He had entrusted the announcement of the
kingdom, which is *"righteousness and peace and joy in the Holy
Spirit"* (Rom. 14:17). The prayer He had taught them—*"Our Father in heaven...Your kingdom come"* (Luke 11:2)—now had a new
meaning for them. The reign of God in heaven came down in the
power of the Spirit, and the disciples were full of this one thought:
to preach the coming of the Spirit into the hearts of men. There
were now on earth good tidings of the kingdom of God—a kingdom
of God ruling and dwelling with men, even as in heaven.

When Jesus spoke about the kingdom of God in Acts 1, He implied all the essential characteristics of a kingdom. Throughout this
section, I will expound upon these six marks of the kingdom of God.
The first two characteristics of every kingdom are the king and his
subjects. We know the King of God's government to be the crucified
Christ, and the disciples His faithful followers. Acts 1:8 tells us of a
power that enabled the disciples to serve their King, and that was
the Holy Spirit, the third mark of a kingdom. Their work was to testify of Christ as His witnesses, and their aim was to reach the ends of
the earth—the fourth and fifth marks of a kingdom. But before they
could begin, their first duty was to wait on God in united, unceasing
prayer, and so we have the sixth mark of a kingdom.

If we are to take up and continue the prayer of the disciples, it
is essential to have a clear and full impression of all that Christ
spoke to them in that last moment, and what it meant for their inner lives and all their service.

CHRIST AS KING

🦋

And He said to them, "Assuredly, I say to you that
there are some standing here who will not taste death till
they see the kingdom of God present with power."
—Mark 9:1

The first mark of the kingdom of God, the church, is that Christ is King. Christ and John had both preached that the kingdom of God was *"at hand"* (Matt. 3:2; 4:17). In Mark 9:1 Christ said that the kingdom would come in power during the lifetimes of some who heard Him. That could mean nothing else but that when He, as King, had ascended the throne of the Father, the kingdom would be revealed in the hearts of His disciples by the power of the Holy Spirit. In the kingdom of heaven, God's will was always being done; in the power of the Holy Spirit, Christ's disciples would do His will on earth as it was done in heaven.

The characteristics of a kingdom can be seen in its king. Christ now reigns on the throne of the Father. There is no external manifestation of the kingdom on earth; rather, its power is seen in the lives of those in whom it rules. It is only in the church, the members of Christ, that the united body can be seen and known. Christ lives and dwells and rules in their hearts. Our Lord Himself taught how close the relationship would be: *"At that day you will know that I am in My Father, and you in Me, and I in you"* (John 14:20). The faith of His oneness with God and His omnipotent power would be next to the knowledge that they lived in Him and He in them.

This must be our first lesson if we are to follow in the steps of the disciples and share their blessing. We must know that Christ, as King, dwells and rules in our hearts. We must know that we live in Him and by His power are able to accomplish all that He wants us to do. Our lives are to be entirely devoted to our King and the service of His kingdom.

This blessed relationship to Christ means, above all, a daily fellowship with Him in prayer. The prayer life is to be a continuous and unbroken exercise. It is in this way that His people can rejoice in their King and can be *"more than conquerors"* (Rom. 8:37) in Him.

THE CRUCIFIED JESUS

❧

God has made this Jesus, whom you
crucified, both Lord and Christ.
—Acts 2:36

The King of the kingdom of heaven is none other than the crucified Jesus. All that we have to say of Him, of His divine power, His abiding presence, and His wonderful love, does not teach us to know Him fully unless we maintain the deep awareness that our King is the crucified Jesus. God has placed Him *"in the midst of* [His] *throne"* as a Lamb, *"as though it had been slain"* (Rev. 5:6), and it is thus that the hosts of heaven adore Him. It is thus that we worship Him as a King.

Christ's cross is His highest glory. It is through this that He has conquered every enemy and gained His place on the throne of God. And it is this that He will impart to us, too, if we are to know fully the meaning of victory over sin. When Paul wrote, *"I have been crucified with Christ...Christ lives in me"* (Gal. 2:20), he taught us that Christ ruled on the throne of his heart as the Crucified One, and that the spirit of the cross would triumph over us as it did in Him.

This was true of the disciples. This was their deepest preparation for receiving the Holy Spirit. With their Lord, they had been crucified to the world. The *"old man"* (Rom. 6:6) had been crucified; in Him they were *"dead indeed to sin"* (v. 11), and their lives were *"hidden with Christ in God"* (Col. 3:3). Each one of us needs to experience this fellowship with Christ in His cross if the Spirit of Pentecost is really to take possession of us. It was through the eternal Spirit that Christ gave Himself as a sacrifice and became the King on the throne of God. As we become *"conformed to His death"* (Phil. 3:10) in the entire surrender of our wills, and in the entire self-denial of our old natures, in the entire separation from the spirit of this world, we can become the worthy servants of a crucified King, and our hearts the worthy temples of His glory.

THE APOSTLES

❧

Being assembled together with them, he charged them not to depart from Jerusalem, but to wait for the promise of the Father.
—*Acts 1:4 RV*

The second mark of the church is found in the disciples whom the Lord had prepared to receive His Spirit and to be His witnesses. If we want to understand fully the outpouring of the Spirit in answer to the prayer of the disciples, we must above all ask, "What was in these men that enabled them to speak forth such powerful, effective prayer, and to receive the wonderful fulfillment of the promise that came to them?" They were simple, uneducated men with many faults whom the Lord had called to forsake all and follow Him. They had done this as far as they could; they followed Him in the life He led and the work He did. Though there was much sin in them and they had as yet no power to deny themselves fully, their hearts clung to Him in deep sincerity. In the midst of much stumbling, they followed Him to the cross. They shared with Him His death; unconsciously, but in truth, they died with Him to sin and were raised with Him in the power of a new life. It was this that prepared them for power in prayer and for being clothed with the *"power from on high"* (Luke 24:49).

Let this be the test by which we examine ourselves: have we indeed surrendered to the fellowship of Christ's sufferings and death? Have we hated our own lives and crucified them? And have we received the power of Christ's life in us? It is this that will give us liberty to believe that God will hear our prayers. It is this that will assure us that God will give us His Holy Spirit to work in us what we and He desire. Let us indeed with one accord take up the disciples' prayer and share in the answer. We must, like them, be willing learners in the school of Jesus, and we must seek, above everything, the intimate fellowship with Him that will prepare us for praying the prayer of Pentecost and receiving its answer.

NOT OF THIS WORLD

❧

They are not of the world, just as I am not of the world.
—John 17:14

During His last night, our Lord took great effort to make clear to His disciples the impassable gulf between Him and the world, and between them and the world. He had said of the Spirit, *"The world cannot receive* [Him], *because it neither sees Him nor knows Him"* (John 14:17). *"Because you are not of the world...therefore the world hates you"* (John 15:19).

One great characteristic of the disciples was that they were to be as separated from the world as Christ had been. They and Christ had become united in the Cross and the Resurrection; they both belonged to another world, the kingdom of heaven. This separation from the world is to be the mark of all believers who long to be filled with the Spirit.

Why is faith in the Holy Spirit so seldom preached and practiced in Christendom? The world rules too much in the lives of Christians. Christians rarely live the heavenly life to which they are called in Christ Jesus. The love of the world—*"the lust of the flesh* [pleasure in eating, drinking, ease, and comfort], *the lust of the eyes* [delight in all that the world offers of beauty and possession], *and the pride of life* [the self-exaltation in what the wisdom and power of man has accomplished]" (1 John 2:16)—robs the heart of its desire for the true self-denial that enables a man to receive the Holy Spirit.

If you wish to pray the Pentecostal prayer for the power of the Holy Spirit, examine yourself. Is the spirit of the world the reason that you do not love to pray the prayer that is absolutely necessary to receive the promise of the Father? May the Lord write this thought deep in every heart: the world cannot receive the Holy Spirit!

"[You] *are not of the world, just as I am not of the world."*

OBEDIENCE

🍃

If you love Me, keep My commandments. And I will pray
the Father, and He will give you another Helper.
—John 14:15–16

We have learned to know the disciples in their preparation for the baptism of the Spirit, and we have seen what was needed for their continuing *"with one accord"* (Acts 1:14) in prayer for the power of the Spirit. Christ was everything to them. Even before the Cross, He was literally their life, their one thought, their only desire. But He was much more so after the Cross, and with the Resurrection.

Was such devotion to Christ something particular to the disciples, not to be expected of everyone? Or was it indeed something that the Lord asked from all who desired to be filled with the Spirit? God expects it of all His children. The Lord needs such individuals now, as much as He did then, to receive His Spirit and His power, to show them forth here on earth, and, as intercessors, to link the world to the throne of God.

Is Christ something, nothing, or everything to us? For the unconverted, Christ is nothing. For the half-converted, the average Christian, Christ is something. But for the true Christian, Christ is everything. Each one who prays for the power of the Spirit must be ready to say, "Today I yield myself with my whole heart to the leading of the Spirit." A full surrender is the question of life or death, an absolute necessity.

My brother or sister in Christ, you have read the words of John 14:15: *"If you love Me, keep My commandments."* The surrender to live every day, all day long, abiding in Christ and keeping His commandments, is to be the one sign of your discipleship. Only when the heart longs in everything to do God's will can the Father's love and Spirit rest upon the child of God. This was the disposition in which the disciples continued with one accord in prayer, and this will be the secret of power in our intercession as we plead for the church and the world.

THE HOLY SPIRIT

⅌

You shall be baptized with the Holy Spirit....You shall
receive power when the Holy Spirit has come upon you.
—Acts 1:5, 8

The third mark of the church is the power for service through the Holy Spirit. Since the time of Adam's fall, when he lost the spirit that God had breathed into him, God's Spirit had striven with men and had worked in some with power, but He had never been able to find His permanent home in them. Only when Christ had come, had broken the power of sin by His death, and had won in the Resurrection a new life for men to live in Himself, could the Spirit of God come and take possession of the whole heart and make it a dwelling place for Christ and for God.

Nothing less than this is the power in us by which sin can be overcome and the prisoners be set free. This power is the Holy Spirit. In the Old Testament He was called *"the Spirit of God"* (Gen. 1:2). But now that the holiness of God had been magnified in the cross of Christ, and now that Christ has sanctified us so that we might be like Him, the Spirit of God's holiness descends to dwell in men and take possession of them as God's holy temple.

He is also the Spirit of the Son. On earth He led the Son first into the desert to be tempted by Satan, then to the synagogue in Nazareth to proclaim Himself as the fulfillment of what the prophet had spoken in Isaiah 61:1. (See Luke 4:18.) And so on the cross, Christ yielded Himself implicitly to the leading of the Spirit.

The Spirit now reveals Christ in us as our Life, our Strength for a perfect obedience, and the Word that is preached in the power of God.

Amazing mystery—the Spirit of God, our Life; the Spirit of Christ, our Light and Strength! As we become men and women who are led by this Spirit of the first disciples, we will have the power to pray *"the effective, fervent prayer of a righteous man* [that] *avails much"* (James 5:16).

THE POWER FROM ON HIGH

❧

Tarry in the city of Jerusalem until you are
endued with power from on high.
—Luke 24:49

The Lord had said to the disciples, *"Without Me you can do nothing"* (John 15:5). Why, then, did He choose these powerless, helpless men to go out to conquer the world for Him? So that in their feebleness they might yield themselves and give Him, as Lord on His throne, the opportunity to show His power working through them. As the Father had done all the work in Christ when He was on earth, so Christ in heaven would now be the Great Worker, proving in them that all power had been given to Him *"in heaven and on earth"* (Matt. 28:18). Their place would be to pray, to believe, and to yield themselves to the mighty power of Christ.

The Holy Spirit would not live in them as a power of which they could have possession. But He would possess them, and their work would indeed be the work of the almighty Christ. Their whole attitude each day would be that of unceasing dependence and prayer, and of confident expectation.

The apostles had learned to know Christ intimately. They had seen all His mighty works; they had received His teaching; they had gone with Him through all His sufferings, even to His death on the cross. They had not only seen Him, but they had also known Him in the power of His resurrection and the experience of that resurrection life in their own hearts. Yet they were not capable of fully making Him known, until He Himself, from the throne of heaven, had taken possession of them by His Spirit dwelling in them.

Every minister of the Gospel is called to rest content with nothing less than the indwelling life and power of the Holy Spirit. This is to be his only preparation for preaching the Gospel in power. Nothing less than having Christ speaking through us in the power of His omnipotence will make us able ministers of the New Testament, bringing salvation to all who hear us.

MY WITNESSES

❧

You shall be [My] *witnesses.*
—Acts 1:8

The fourth mark of Christ's church is that His servants are to be witnesses for Him, continually testifying of His wonderful love, His power to redeem, His continual abiding presence, and His wonderful power to work in them.

This is the only weapon that the King allows His redeemed ones to use. Without claiming authority or power, without wisdom or eloquence, without influence or position, each one is called, not only by his words, but also by his life and actions, to be a living proof and witness of what Jesus can do.

This is the only weapon they are to use in conquering men and bringing them to the feet of Christ. This is what the first disciples did. When they were filled with the Spirit, they began to speak of the mighty things that Christ had done.

It was in this power that those who were scattered abroad by persecution went forth, even as far as Antioch, preaching in the name of Jesus, so that a multitude of the unsaved believed. They had no commission from the apostles; they had no special gifts or training, but out of the fullness of their hearts they spoke of Jesus Christ. They could not be silent; they were filled with the life and love of Christ and could not help but witness for Him. It was this that gave the Gospel its power to increase; every new convert became a witness for Christ.

One non-Christian writer wrote, in regard to the persecutions, that if the Christians had only been content to keep the worship of Jesus to themselves, they would not have had to suffer. But in their zeal, they had wanted Christ to rule over all.

This is the secret of a flourishing church: every believer a witness for Jesus. And here we see that the cause of the weakness of the church is that so few are willing in daily life to testify that Jesus is Lord.

What a call to prayer! Lord, teach Your disciples the blessedness of knowing Jesus and the power of His love in such a way that they may find their highest joy in testifying of what He is and has done for them.

THE GOSPEL MINISTRY

🍂

You shall be [My] *witnesses.*
—Acts 1:8

The Spirit of truth...will testify of Me. And you also will
bear witness, because you have been with Me from the beginning.
—John 15:26–27

When Christ said the words, "[My] *witnesses,"* He not only re-
ferred to all believers, but especially to all ministers of the Gospel.
This is the high calling and the only power of the preacher of the
Gospel—in everything to be a witness for Jesus.

This gives us two great truths. The first is that the preacher
must place the preaching of Christ Himself above everything he
teaches from the Word of God. This is what the first disciples did:
"In every house, they did not cease teaching and preaching Jesus as
the Christ" (Acts 5:42). This was what Philip did at Samaria: he
"preached Christ to them" (Acts 8:5). And so Paul wrote, *"For I de-*
termined not to know anything among you except Jesus Christ and
Him crucified" (1 Cor. 2:2).

The minister of the Gospel must never forget that it is especially for this that he has been set apart: to be, along with the Holy
Spirit, a witness for Christ. As he does this, sinners will find salvation, and God's children will be sanctified and equipped for His
service. Only in this way can Christ have His place in the hearts of
His people and in the world around.

But there is a second thought of equal importance. And that is
that the preacher's teaching must always be a personal testimony
from his own experience of what Christ is and can do. As this note
is sounded, the Holy Spirit carries the message as a living reality to
the listeners' hearts. This is what will build up believers so that
they can walk in such fellowship with Jesus Christ that He can reveal Himself through them. And this is what will lead them to the
knowledge of the indispensable secret of spiritual health—the
prayer life in daily fellowship, in childlike love, and true consecration with the Father and the Son.

Such thoughts will bring much unity in prayer and will cultivate among believers and ministers the joy of the Holy Spirit, in
which the mouth speaks out of the abundance of the heart (see
Matthew 12:34), to the praise and glory of our ever blessed Redeemer, Jesus Christ our Lord.

THE WHOLE WORLD

❧

> [My] *witnesses...to the end of the earth.*
> —Acts 1:8

Here we have the fifth mark of Christ's church: reaching the whole world. These must have seemed remarkable words from the Man who, in what appeared to be absolute powerlessness, had been crucified by His enemies. How could He speak of the ends of the earth as His dominion? How could it have entered the mind of any writer to venture the prophecy that a Jew who had been crucified, whose whole life had seemingly been proved by that cross to be an utter failure and whose disciples had utterly forsaken Him in the end—that He would conquer the world by them?

But what foolishness it is on the part of those who speak of Christ as being nothing but a man! No human mind could have formed such an idea. It is the thought of God; He alone could plan and execute such a purpose.

The words that Jesus spoke to His disciples, *"You shall receive power when the Holy Spirit has come upon you"* (Acts 1:8), gave them the assurance that the Holy Spirit would maintain Christ's divine power in them. As Christ did His works only because the Father worked in Him, so Christ assured His disciples that He Himself from the throne of heaven would work all their works in them. They might ask what they desired and it would be done for them (John 15:7). In the strength of that promise, the church of Christ can make the ends of the earth its one aim.

Oh, that Christian people might understand that the extension of God's kingdom can only be brought about by the united, continued prayer of men and women who give their hearts wholly to wait on Christ in the assurance that what they desire He will do for them!

Oh, that God would grant that His children prove their faith in Christ by making His aim their aim, and by yielding themselves to be His witnesses in united, persevering prayer, waiting upon Him in the full assurance that He will most surely and most gloriously give all that they can ask.

My reader, become one of those intercessors who really believe that in answer to their prayers the crucified Jesus will do far more than they can ask or think (Eph. 3:20).

THE WHOLE EARTH FILLED WITH HIS GLORY

🐾

*Blessed be His glorious name forever! And let the whole
earth be filled with His glory. Amen and Amen.*
—*Psalm 72:19*

What a prospect—this earth, now under the power of the Evil One, renewed and filled with the glory of God's new earth in which righteousness will dwell! Though we believe it so little, it will surely come to pass; God's Word is the pledge of it. God's Son by His blood and death conquered the power of sin, and through the eternal Spirit the power of God is working out His purpose. What a vision—the whole earth *"filled with His glory"*!

But what a great and difficult work. It is nearly two thousand years since Christ gave the promise and ascended the throne, and yet more than half of the human race have never learned to know even the name of Jesus. And in the other half, millions are called by His name yet do not know Him. This great work of bringing the knowledge of Christ to every creature has been entrusted to a church that hardly thinks of her responsibility and of what the consequence of her neglect will be. We may indeed ask, "Will the work ever be done?" Blessed be His name, His power and His faithfulness are pledges that one day we will see it—the whole earth filled with the glory of God.

What a wonderful prayer our text contains: *"Let the whole earth be filled with His glory. Amen and Amen!"* It is to this prayer that every believer is called, and he can depend on the Holy Spirit to inspire and strengthen him. It is to this prayer that we desire to strengthen each other, so that every day of our lives, with all the power there is in us, we desire with one accord to pray continually in the faith of the name of Jesus and the power of His Spirit.

What blessedness to know that true prayer will indeed help and be answered! What blessedness every day of our lives to seek God's face, and with confidence to lay hold of Him and give Him no rest until the earth is full of His glory! Once again, what blessedness to unite with all God's willing children who are seeking to prepare the way for our King in this the day of His power!

THE FIRST PRAYER MEETING

✺

These all continued with one accord in prayer
and supplication, with the women.
—Acts 1:14

The sixth mark of the early church is that they waited on the promise of the Father in united prayer. It is difficult to form a correct idea of the unspeakable importance of this first prayer meeting in the history of the kingdom—a prayer meeting that was the simple fulfillment of the command of Christ. It was to be for all time the indication of the one condition on which His presence and Spirit would be known in power. In it we have the secret key that opens the storehouse of heaven with all its blessings.

Christ had prayed that the disciples might be one, just as He and the Father were one (John 17:22). He prayed *"that they may be made perfect in one, and that the world may know that You have sent Me, and have loved them as You have loved Me"* (v. 23). We see, in the strife that was among them at the Lord's Table as to who would be chief, how far the disciples were from such a state when Christ prayed the prayer. It was only after the Resurrection and after Christ had gone to heaven that they were brought, in the ten days of united supplication, to that holy unity of love and purpose that would make them the one body of Christ prepared to receive the Spirit in all His power.

What a prayer meeting! It was the fruit of Christ's training during His three years of fellowship with them. Adam's body was created before God breathed His Spirit into him; likewise, the body of Christ had to be formed before the Spirit could take possession.

This prayer meeting gave us the law of the kingdom for all time. Where Christ's disciples are linked to each other in love and yield themselves wholly to Him in undivided consecration, the Spirit will be given from heaven as the seal of God's approval, and Christ will show His mighty power. One of the great marks of the new dispensation is the united, unceasing prayer that *"avails much"* (James 5:16) and is crowned with the power of the Holy Spirit. Do we not have here the reason why, if our prayers are confined in great measure to our own church or interests, the answer cannot come in such power as we expected?

THE UNITY OF THE SPIRIT

🐦

Endeavoring to keep the unity of the Spirit....
There is one body and one Spirit.
—Ephesians 4:3–4

From Paul we learn how the Christian communities in different places ought to remember each other in the fellowship of prayer. He pointed out how God is glorified in such prayer. So he wrote more than once about how the ministry of intercession abounds to the glory of God. (See 2 Corinthians 1:11; 4:15; 9:12–13.)

In today's church, there is a great need for the children of God throughout the world to be drawn close together in the knowledge of having been chosen by God to be a holy priesthood (see 1 Peter 2:9), ministering continually the *"sacrifice of praise"* (Jer. 33:11) and prayer. There is too little distinction between the world and the body of Christ; in the lives of many of God's children there is very little difference from what the world is. It is a question of the deepest importance: What can be done to foster the unity of the Spirit?

Nothing will help so much as the separation to a life of more prayer, interceding that God's people may prove their unity in a life of holiness and love. That will be a living testimony to the world of what it means to live for God. When Paul wrote, *"Praying always with all prayer and supplication in the Spirit, being watchful to this end with all perseverance and supplication for all the saints"* (Eph. 6:18), he named one of the essential differences between God's people and the world.

You say you desire to bear this mark of the children of God, and to be able to pray for them so that you may prove to yourself and to others that you are indeed not of the world. Resolve in your life to carry about with you this one great distinctive feature of the true Christian—a life of prayer and intercession. Join with God's children who are unceasingly seeking God with one accord to maintain the *"unity of the Spirit"* and the body of Christ, to *"be strong in the Lord and in the power of His might"* (Eph. 6:10), and to pray down a blessing upon His church. Let none of us think it too much to give fifteen minutes every day for meditation on some word of God connected with His promises to His church, and then to plead with Him for its fulfillment. Slowly yet surely, you will taste the blessedness of being one, heart and soul, with God's people, and you will receive the power to pray *"the effective, fervent prayer...*
[that] avails much" (James 5:16).

UNION IS STRENGTH

❧

*And when they had prayed...they were all filled
with the Holy Spirit, and they spoke the word of God with
boldness. Now the multitude of those who believed were
of one heart and one soul.*
—Acts 4:31–32

We see the power of union everywhere in nature. How feeble is a drop of rain as it falls to earth! But when the many drops are united in one stream and become one body, the power is soon irresistible. Such is the power of true union in prayer. Some translations of Psalm 34:5, rather than saying, *"They looked to Him,"* read instead, "They flowed to Him," or even, "They rushed toward Him like a stream of water." Such was the prayer in the Upper Room. And so can our prayer be if we unite all our forces in pleading the promise of the Father. Then, when the world *"comes in like a flood"* (Isa. 59:19), it can be overcome in the power of united prayer.

In Natal, South Africa, owing to the many mountains, the streams often flow down with great force. The Zulus, who live there, are accustomed to joining hands when they wish to pass through a stream. The leader will have a strong stick in his right hand, and he will give his left hand to the man who comes behind him. And so they form a chain of men and help each other to cross the current. Let us believe that when God's people reach out their hands to each other in spirit, there will be power to resist the terrible influence that the world can exert. And in that unity, God's children, when they have overcome the power of the world and the flesh, will have power to prevail with God.

It was in the Upper Room that the disciples spent the ten days until they had truly become one heart and one soul. When the Spirit of God descended, He not only filled each individual, but He also took possession of the whole company as the body of Christ.

Dear reader, in this twentieth century the prayer of our Lord Jesus is still being offered: "Father, *'that they may be one just as We are one'* (John 17:22)." In the fellowship of loving and believing prayer, our hearts can be melted into one, and we will become strong in faith to believe and accept what God has promised us.

PRAYER IN THE NAME OF CHRIST

✇

*Whatever you ask in My name, that I will do, that
the Father may be glorified in the Son.
—John 14:13*

How wonderful is the link between our prayers and Christ's glorifying the Father in heaven! Much prayer on earth brings Him much glory in heaven. What an incentive to pray much, to intercede incessantly! Our prayer is indispensable to the glorifying of the Father.

During His last night on earth, Christ's desire was so deep for His disciples to learn to believe in the power of His name, and to take hold of His promise of a sure and abundant answer, that we find the promise repeated seven times. He knew how slow men are to believe in the wonderful promise of answer to prayer in His name. He desires to rouse a large and confident faith, to free our prayers from every shadow of doubt, and to teach us to look upon intercession as the most certain and most blessed way of bringing glory to God, joy to our own souls, and blessing to the perishing world around us.

If the thought comes to us that such prayer is not easy to attain, we only need to remember what Christ told His disciples. It was when the Holy Spirit came that they would have power to pray in power. In order to draw us on to yield ourselves fully to the control of the blessed Spirit, He holds out to us the precious promise: *"Ask, and you will receive, that your joy may be full"* (John 16:24). As we believe in the power of the Spirit working in us in full measure, intercession will become to us the joy and the strength of all our service.

When Paul wrote, *"And whatever you do in word or deed, do all in the name of the Lord Jesus"* (Col. 3:17), he reminded us how, in daily life, everything is to bear the signature of the name of Jesus. As we learn to do this, we will have the confidence to say to the Father, "As we live in Your name before men, we come to You with the full confidence that our prayers in Your name will be answered." Our lives lived among men are to be lived in communion with God. When the name of Jesus rules everything in our lives, it will give power to our prayers, too.

OUR HEAVENLY FATHER

❧

Our Father in heaven.
—Luke 11:2

How simple, how beautiful, is this invocation that Christ puts on our lips! And yet how inconceivably rich is its meaning, in the fullness of the love and blessing it contains!

Just think of the book that could be written of all the memories that there have been on earth of wise and loving fathers. Just think of what this world owes to the fathers who have made their children strong and happy to give their lives for the welfare of their fellowmen. Then think how all this is only a shadow of exquisite beauty, and only a shadow of what the Father in heaven is to His children on earth.

Christ bestowed a great gift on us when He gave us the right to say "Father" to the God of the universe. We have the privilege of calling upon Him as "The Father of Christ," "Our Father," and "My Father."

We call Him *"our Father in heaven,"* our heavenly Father. We consider it a great privilege as we bow in worship to know that the Father comes near to us where we are upon earth. But we soon begin to feel the need to rise up to enter into His holy presence in heaven, to breathe its atmosphere, to drink in its spirit, and to become truly heavenly minded. And as our thoughts leave earth behind, and in the power of the Holy Spirit we enter the Holiest of All, where the seraphim worship, the words *heavenly Father* take on a new meaning, and our hearts come under an influence that can abide all day long.

As we then gather up our thoughts of what fatherhood on earth has meant, and as we hear the voice of Christ saying, *"How much more"* (Luke 11:13), we feel the distance between the earthly picture and the heavenly reality. And we can only bow in lowly, loving adoration, saying, "Father, our Father, my Father." Only in this way can full joy and power come to us as we rest rejoicingly in this Scripture: *"How much more will your heavenly Father give the Holy Spirit to those who ask Him!"* (v. 13).

Oh, for grace to cultivate a heavenly spirit, to prove daily that we are children who have a Father in heaven and who love to dwell in His holy presence every day!

THE POWER OF PRAYER

❧

The effective, fervent prayer of a righteous man avails much.
—James 5:16

Prayer *"avails much."* It *"avails much"* with God. It *"avails much"* in the history of His church and people. Prayer is the one great power that the church can exercise in securing the working of God's omnipotence in the world.

The *"prayer of a righteous man avails much."* That is, a man who has the righteousness of Christ, not only as a garment covering him, but also as a life-power inspiring him, is a *"new man which was created...in true righteousness and holiness"* (Eph. 4:24), a man who lives *"as [a slave] of righteousness"* (Rom. 6:19). These are the righteous whom the Lord loves and whose prayers have power. (See Psalm 66:18–19; 1 John 3:22.)

When Christ gave His great prayer promises during His last night, it was to those who keep His commandments: *"If you love Me, keep My commandments. And I will pray the Father, and He will give you another Helper"* (John 14:15–16); *"If you keep My commandments, you will abide in My love...[and] you will ask what you desire, and it shall be done for you"* (John 15:10, 7).

"The effective, fervent prayer of a righteous man avails much." It is only when the righteous man stirs up himself and rouses his whole being to take hold of God that the prayer *"avails much."* As Jacob said, *"I will not let You go"* (Gen. 32:26); as the importunate widow gave the just judge no rest, so does the *"effective, fervent prayer"* bring about great things.

And then comes the *"effective, fervent prayer"* of many righteous people. When two or three agree, there is the promise of an answer (Matt. 18:19). How much more when hundreds and thousands unite with one accord to cry to God to display His mighty power on behalf of His people!

Let us join those who have united themselves to call upon God for the mighty power of His Holy Spirit in His church. What a great and blessed work, and what a sure prospect, in God's time, of an abundant answer! Let us ask God individually and unitedly for the grace of the *"effective, fervent prayer [that] avails much."*

PRAYER AND SACRIFICE

❦

I want you to know what a great conflict I have for you.
—Colossians 2:1

Just as men who are undertaking a great thing in the world have to prepare themselves and use all their natural abilities to succeed, so Christians need to prepare themselves to pray with their whole hearts and strength. This is the law of the kingdom. Prayer requires the Christian to sacrifice his ease, his time, and his self. The secret of powerful prayer is sacrifice. It was the same with Christ Jesus, the Great Intercessor. It is written of Him, *"When You make His soul an offering for sin, He shall see His seed....He shall see the labor of His soul....He shall divide the spoil with the strong, because He poured out His soul unto death"* (Isa. 53:10–12). In Gethsemane, *"He had offered up prayers and supplications, with vehement cries and tears"* (Heb. 5:7). Prayer is sacrifice. The psalmist said, *"Let my prayer be set before You as incense, the lifting up of my hands as the evening sacrifice"* (Ps. 141:2).

Prayer is sacrifice. Our prayers have worth only from being rooted in the sacrifice of Jesus Christ. Just as He gave up everything in His prayer, *"Your will be done"* (Matt. 6:10), so our posture and disposition must ever be the offering up of everything to God and His service.

A pious miner had a relative whom the doctor ordered to go to a nearby state in order to get well. But there was no money. The miner resolved to take the little money that he had and ventured to use it all. He procured a comfortable lodging at a few dollars per day for the invalid. He was content with a small shack for himself and lived on only a few pennies a day for an entire month. He spent much time in prayer until he got the assurance that the invalid would recover. On the last day of the month, the sick one was well. When the miner reached home, he said that he had now learned more than ever that the secret law and hidden power of prayer lay in self-sacrifice.

Do we need to ask why we lack power in our prayers when there is so much reluctance to make the necessary sacrifice in waiting upon God? Christ, the Christ we trust in, the Christ who lives in us, offered Himself as a sacrifice to God. As this attitude lives and rules in us, we will receive power from Him as intercessors to pray the *"effective, fervent prayer* [that] *avails much"* (James 5:16).

THE INTERCESSION OF THE SPIRIT FOR BELIEVERS

🦋

*He who searches the hearts knows what the mind of
the Spirit is, because He makes intercession for
the saints according to the will of God.*
—*Romans 8:27*

What a light these words cast upon the prayer life in the hearts of the saints! *"For we do not know what we should pray for as we ought"* (v. 26). How often this hinders our prayer or hinders the faith that is essential to its success! But here we are told for our encouragement that the Holy Spirit *"makes intercession for us with groanings which cannot be uttered"* (v. 26). *"He makes intercession for the saints according to the will of God."*

What a prospect is opened up to us here! Where and how does the Spirit make intercession for all believers? In the heart that does not know what to pray, He secretly and effectively prays what is according to the will of God. This of course implies that we trust Him to do His work in us, and that we wait before God even when we know what to pray, in the assurance that the Holy Spirit is praying in us. This further implies that we take time to wait in God's presence, that we exercise an unbounded dependence on the Holy Spirit who has been given to cry *"Abba Father"* (v. 15) within us, even when we have nothing to offer but *"groanings which cannot be uttered."*

What a difference it would make in the lives of many of God's children if they realized this! They have not only Jesus the Son of God, the great High Priest, *"always liv*[ing] *to make intercession for them"* (Heb. 7:25); they have not only the liberty of asking in faith what they desire, and the promise that it will be given them; but they have actually the Holy Spirit, *"the Spirit of grace and supplication"* (Zech. 12:10), to carry on, in the depths of their beings, His work of interceding for them according to the will of God.

What a call to separate ourselves from the world, to yield ourselves wholeheartedly to the leading and praying of the Spirit within us, deeper than all our thoughts or expectations! What a call to surrender ourselves in stillness of soul, resting in the Lord and waiting patiently for Him, as the Holy Spirit prays within us not only for ourselves, but especially for all believers according to the will of God!

THAT THEY MAY BE ONE

🦚

*Holy Father, keep through Your name those whom You have
given Me, that they may be one as We are....I do not pray for these
alone, but also for those who will believe in Me through their
word; that they all may be one, as You, Father, are in Me, and
I in You; that they also may be one in Us....And the glory which
You gave Me I have given them, that they may be one just as We
are one: I in them, and You in Me; that they may be made perfect
in one, and that the world may know that You have sent Me.*
—John 17:11, 20–23

Notice carefully how the Lord used the expression, *"that they
may be one,"* five times. It is as if He felt the need of strongly plac-
ing the emphasis on these words if we are going to realize the chief
thought of His high-priestly prayer. He desires that the words and
the thought will indeed have the same place in our hearts that they
have in His.

As He was on the way to go to the Father through the cross,
He wanted us to understand that He took the thought and the desire with Him to heaven, to make it the object of His unceasing intercession there. And He entrusted the words to us, so that we
would take them into the world with us and make them the object
of our unceasing intercession, too. This alone would enable us to
fulfill the new commandment to love our fellowmen as He loves us,
so that our joy might be full (John 15:11–12).

How little the church has understood this! How little its different branches are marked by a fervent, affectionate love toward all
believers of whatever name or denomination. Will we not heartily
welcome the invitation to make this prayer, *"That they may be
one,"* a chief part of our daily fellowship with God? How simple it
would be once we connected the words *our Father* with all the children of God throughout the world. Each time we used these sacred
words, we would only have to expand the little word *our* into all the
largeness and riches of God's fatherly love, and our hearts would
soon learn to say "our" with a childlike affection for all the saints of
God, whoever and wherever they may be. We would do this as
naturally as we say "Father" with the thought of His infinite love
and our love for Him. The prayer *"that they may be one"* would
then become a joy and a strength, a deeper bond of fellowship with
Christ Jesus and all His saints, and an offer of a sweet savor to the
Father of love.

THE DISCIPLES' PRAYER

🦋

These all continued with one accord in prayer and supplication.
—Acts 1:14

And they continued steadfastly in...fellowship...and in prayers.
—Acts 2:42

What a lesson it would be to us in the school of prayer to have a clear understanding of what this continuing *"with one accord in prayer"* meant to the disciples!

Just think of the object of their desire. However defective the thoughts were that they had of the Blessed Spirit, this they knew from the words of Jesus: *"It is to your advantage that I go away"* (John 16:7), so that the Spirit would give the glorified Christ into their very hearts in a way they had never known Him before. And it would be He Himself, in the mighty power of God's Spirit, who would be their strength for the work to which He had called them.

With what confidence they expected the fulfillment of the promise! Had not the Master, who had loved them so well, given them the assurance of what He would send to them from the throne of the Father in heaven?

And with what intensity and persistency they pleaded! In the midst of the praise and thanksgiving that filled their hearts as they worshipped their Lord in heaven, remembering all He had taught them about importunity, they had the full assurance that He would fulfill their desires, however long the answer might be delayed. Let us nourish our hearts with thoughts such as these, until we see that the very same promise that was given to the disciples is given to us, and that we, too, even though we have to cry day and night to God, can count upon the Father to answer our prayers.

Lastly—and this is not the least—let us believe that as they continued *"with one accord in prayer,"* we also may unite in presenting our petitions even though we cannot be together in one place. In the love with which His Spirit makes us one, and in the experience of our Lord's presence with each one who joins with his fellow believers in pleading the blessed name, we can claim the promise that we, too, will be filled with the Holy Spirit.

PAUL'S CALL TO PRAYER

*With all prayer and supplication praying at all seasons
in the Spirit, and watching thereunto in all perseverance and
supplication for all the saints, and on my behalf.
—Ephesians 6:18–19 RV*

Paul had a deep sense of the divine unity of the whole body of Christ and of the need for unceasing prayer for all the members of the body by all who belong to it. It is evident from the words he used that he did not mean this to be an occasional thing, but the unceasing exercise of the life union in which they were bound together. *"With all prayer and supplication praying at all seasons in the Spirit, and watching thereunto in all perseverance and supplication for all the saints."*

Paul expected believers to be so filled with the consciousness of living in Christ, and through Him being united so consciously to the whole body, that in their daily lives and activities, their highest aim would always be the welfare of the body of Christ of which they had become members. He counted on their being filled with the Spirit, so that it would be perfectly natural to them—not ever a burden or constraint to them—to pray for all who belong to the body of Jesus Christ. As natural as it is for each member of my body to be ready every moment to do what is necessary for the welfare of the whole, even so, where the Holy Spirit has entire possession, the consciousness of union with Christ will always be accompanied by consciousness of the union, joy, and love of all the members.

Is this not what we need in our daily lives, that every believer who has yielded himself undividedly to Christ Jesus will daily and continually live in the consciousness that he is one with Christ and His body? Just as a war will bring to light the intensity and the readiness with which millions of the subjects of the king sacrifice their all for the king and his service, so the saints of God will live for Christ their King, and also for all the members of the body of which He is the Head. May God's people be willing for this sacrifice of prayer and intercession at all times and for all believers!

PAUL'S REQUEST FOR PRAYER

🕉

*And for me, that utterance may be given to me, that I may open
my mouth boldly to make known the mystery of the gospel...
that in it I may speak boldly, as I ought to speak.*
—Ephesians 6:19–20

"*And for me*"—what light these words cast on the deep reality
of Paul's faith in the absolute necessity and the wonderful power of
prayer! What did he ask the Ephesians to pray for? "*That utterance
may be given to me, that I may open my mouth boldly...that in it I
may speak boldly, as I ought to speak.*" By this time, Paul had been
a minister of the Gospel for more than twenty years. One might
think that he had such experience in preaching that it would come
naturally to him to "*speak boldly, as* [he] *ought to speak.*" But so
deep was his conviction of his own insufficiency and weakness, so
absolute was his dependence on divine teaching and power, that he
felt that he could not do the work as it should have been done without the direct help of God. The sense of his total and unalterable
dependence on God, who was with him, teaching him what and how
to speak, was the basis for all his confidence and the keynote of his
whole life.

But there is more. In his twenty years of ministry, there were
innumerable times when his circumstances were so bad that he was
left to throw himself upon God alone, with no one to help him in
prayer. And yet, such was his deep spiritual insight into the unity
of the body of Christ, and into his own actual dependence on the
prayers of others, that he pleaded with them to pray "*with all
prayer and supplication in the Spirit, being watchful to this end
with all perseverance and supplication*" (v. 18), and he asked them
not to forget to pray for him. Just as a wrestler cannot afford to
dispense with the help of the weakest members of his body in the
struggle in which he is engaged, so Paul could not do without the
prayers of the believers.

What a call to us in this twentieth century, to awake to the
consciousness that Christ our Intercessor in heaven, and all believers here upon earth, are engaged in one mighty battle! It is our
duty to call out and cultivate the gift of unceasing supplication for
the power of God's Spirit in all His servants, so that all may be
given divine utterance and all "*may speak boldly, as* [they] *ought to
speak.*"

PRAYER FOR ALL BELIEVERS

❧

*To the saints and faithful brethren in Christ who are in
Colosse....We give thanks to God...praying always for you,
since we heard of...your love for all the saints.*
—Colossians 1:2–4

*Continue earnestly in prayer, being vigilant in it with
thanksgiving; meanwhile praying also for us.*
—Colossians 4:2–3

Prayer for all believers—it will take much time, thought, and
love to see all that is included in this simple expression. Think of
your own neighborhood and the believers you know. Think of your
whole country, and praise God for all who are His children. Think
of all the Christian nations of the world, and the believers to be
found in each of these. Think of all the unsaved nations and the
children of God to be found among them in ever increasing num-
bers.

Think of all the different circumstances and conditions in
which these are to be found, and all the varying needs that call for
God's grace and help. Think of many—oh, so many—who are God's
children, and yet through ignorance or sloth, through worldly-
mindedness or an evil heart of unbelief, are walking in the dark
and are bringing no honor to God. Think of so many who are in
earnest and yet are conscious of a life of failure, with little or no
power to please God or to bless man. Then think again of those who
are to be found everywhere, in solitary places or among company,
whose one aim is to serve the Lord who bought them and to be the
light of those around them. Think of them especially as joining, often unaware of their relationship to the whole body of Christ, in
pleading for the great promise of the Holy Spirit and the love and
oneness of heart that He alone can give.

This is not the work of one day or one night. It needs a heart
that will set itself to do serious thinking in regard to the condition
of the body of Christ to which we belong. But once we begin, we
will find what abundant reason there is for our persevering and
yielding to God's Spirit, so that He may prepare us for the great
and blessed work of daily praying the twofold prayer: for the love of
God and Christ to fill the hearts of His people, and for the power of
the Holy Spirit to come down and accomplish God's work in this
sinful world.

PRAYER BY ALL BELIEVERS

🎙

We trust that He will still deliver us, you also
helping together in prayer for us.
—2 Corinthians 1:10–11

[Some] *preach Christ from selfish ambition...supposing*
to add affliction to my chains....For I know that this will
turn out for my deliverance through your prayer and
the supply of the Spirit of Jesus Christ.
—Philippians 1:16, 19

This subject calls us once again to think of all believers throughout the world, but leads us to view them from a different standpoint. If we ask God to increase the number and the power of those who do pray, we will be led to form some impression of the hope that our circle of intercessors may gradually increase in number and power.

Our first thoughts will naturally turn to the multitude of believers who know very little about the duty or the blessedness of pleading for the body of Christ, or for all the work that has to be done to perfect its members. We then have to remember how many people do intercede for the power of His Spirit—and we thank God for them—but whose thoughts are chiefly limited to spheres of work with which they are acquainted or in which they are directly interested.

That leaves us with what is, comparatively speaking, a very limited number of people who will be ready to take part in the prayer that ought to be sent up by the whole church for the unity of the body and the power of the Spirit. And even then, the number may be small who really feel drawn to take part in this daily prayer for the outpouring of the Spirit on all God's people.

And yet many may be feeling that the proposal meets a longfelt need, and that it is an unspeakable privilege, whether with few or many, to make Christ's last prayer, *"That they may be one"* (John 17:11), the daily supplication of our faith and love. In time, believers might join together in small circles or throughout wider districts, helping to rouse those around them to take part in the great work of making prayer for all believers become one prayer prayed by all believers.

This message is sent out to all who desire to be in touch with it and who seek to prove their consecration to their Lord in the unceasing, daily supplication for the power of His love and Spirit to be revealed to all His people.

PRAYER FOR ALL THE FULLNESS OF THE SPIRIT

✺

*"Bring all the tithes into the storehouse...and try Me now in
this," says the LORD of hosts, "if I will not open for you the
windows of heaven and pour out for you such blessing
that there will not be room enough to receive it."*
—Malachi 3:10

This last promise in the Old Testament tells us how abundant
the blessing is to be. Pentecost was only the beginning of what God
is willing to do. The promise of the Father, as Christ presented it,
still waits for its perfect fulfillment. Let us try to realize the liberty
that we possess to ask and expect great things.

Just as the great command to *"go...and preach the gospel"*
(Mark 16:15) was meant not only for the disciples, but also for us,
so the very last command—*"Tarry...until you are endued with
power from on high"* (Luke 24:49); *"Wait for the Promise of the Father....You shall be baptized with the Holy Spirit"* (Acts 1:4–5)—is
also for us and is the basis for the confident assurance that our
prayers with one accord will be heard.

Take time to think of the cry of need that can be heard
throughout the whole church and throughout all our mission fields.
Let us realize that the only remedy that can be found for ineffec-
tiveness or powerlessness, to enable us to gain the victory over the
powers of this world and of darkness, is in the manifested presence
of our Lord in the midst of His hosts and in the power of His Spirit.
Let us take time to think of the state of all the churches throughout
Christendom, until we are brought deeper than ever to believe that
nothing except the supernatural, almighty intervention of our Lord
Himself will rouse His hosts for the great battle against evil. Can
anyone imagine or suggest any other matter for prayer that can
compete with this: for the power of God on the ministers of the
Gospel, and on all His people, to fill them *"with power from on
high"* (Luke 24:49) that will make the Gospel the power of God
unto salvation?

As we connect the prayer for the whole church on earth with
the prayer for the whole power of God in heaven, we will feel that
the greatest truths of the heavenly world and the kingdom of God
have possession of us, and that we are indeed asking what God is
longing to give, as soon as He finds hearts utterly yielded to Him in
faith and obedience.

EVERY DAY

🙠

Give us day by day our daily bread.
—Luke 11:3

Some Christians are afraid that a promise to pray every day is altogether beyond them. They could not undertake it, and yet they pray to God to give them their bread *"day by day."* Surely if a child of God has once yielded himself with his whole life to God's love and service, he should consider it a privilege to take advantage of any invitation that would help him every day to come into God's presence with the great need of His church and kingdom.

Many confess that they desire to live wholly for God. They acknowledge that Christ gave Himself for them and that His love now watches over them and works in them without ceasing. They acknowledge the claim that nothing less than the measure of Christ's love for us is to be the measure of our love for Him. They feel that if this is indeed to be the standard of their lives, they surely ought to welcome every opportunity for proving each day that they are devoting their hearts' strength to the interests of Christ's kingdom and to the prayer that can bring down God's blessings.

Our invitation to daily, united prayer may come to some as a new and perhaps unexpected opportunity of becoming God's remembrancers who *"cry out day and night"* (Luke 18:7) for His power and blessing on His people and on this needy world. Think of the privilege of being allowed to plead every day with God on behalf of His children, for the outpouring of His Spirit, and for the coming of His kingdom that His will may indeed be done on earth as it is in heaven (Matt. 6:10). To those who have to confess that they have scarcely understood the high privilege and the solemn duty of waiting on God in prayer for His blessing on the world, the invitation ought to be most welcome. And even to those who already have their special circles for which to pray, the thought that their vision and their hearts can be enlarged to include all God's children, all the work of His kingdom, and all the promise of an abundant outpouring of His Spirit, should urge them to take part in a ministry by which their other work will not suffer, but their hearts will be strengthened with a joy, a love, and a faith that they have never known before.

WITH ONE ACCORD

They were all with one accord in one place....And they
were all filled with the Holy Spirit.
—Acts 2:1, 4

Several of the previous chapters have opened to us wonderful thoughts of the unity of the whole body of Christ, and the need for deliberately cultivating the slumbering or buried talents of intercession. We may indeed thank God, for we know of the tens of thousands of His children who in daily prayer are pleading for some portion of the work of God's kingdom in which they are personally interested. But in many cases in which they take an interest, there is a lack of the largehearted and universal love that embraces all the children of God and their service. The people do not have the boldness and strength that come from the consciousness of being part of a large and conquering army under the leadership of our conquering King.

I have said that a wrestler must gather up all his strength and depend on every member of his body to do its very utmost. In an army with millions of soldiers at war, each detachment not only throws its whole heart into the work that it has to do, but it is also ready to rejoice and take new courage from every report of bravery and enthusiasm of the far-distant members of the same army. Is this not what we need in the church of Christ—such an enthusiasm for the King and His kingdom that His name will be made known to every human being? Do we not need such a faith in His purpose that our prayers will rise up every day with a largehearted love that grasps the whole body of Christ and pleads daily for the power of the Holy Spirit on all its members, even to the very weakest?

The strength that unity gives is something inconceivable. The power of each individual member is increased greatly by the inspiration of fellowshipping with a large and conquering multitude. Nothing can so help believers to an ever larger faith as the consciousness of being one body and one spirit in Christ Jesus. Only as the disciples were all *"with one accord in one place"* on the Day of Pentecost *"were [they] all filled with the Holy Spirit."* United prayer brings the answer to prayer.

A PERSONAL CALL

–

We should not trust in ourselves but in God...who
delivered us...and...will still deliver us.
—2 Corinthians 1:9–10

[Some] *preach Christ from selfish ambition...supposing*
to add affliction to my chains....For I know that this will
turn out for my deliverance through your prayer and
the supply of the Spirit of Jesus Christ.
—Philippians 1:16, 19

Scriptures like these prove that there were still Christians in the churches under the full power of the Holy Spirit, on whom Paul could depend for *"effective, fervent prayer"* (James 5:16). When we plead with Christians to *"pray without ceasing"* (1 Thess. 5:17), there are many who quietly decide that such a life is not possible for them. They do not have any special gift for prayer; they do not have that intense desire for glorifying Christ in the salvation of souls; they have not yet learned what it is, under the power of the love of Christ, to live not for themselves, but for Him who died for them and rose again (2 Cor. 5:15).

And yet we bring to them the call to offer themselves in wholehearted surrender to live entirely for Christ. We ask them whether they are not ashamed of the selfish life that simply uses Christ as a convenience to escape from hell and to secure a place in heaven. We come to them with the assurance that God can change their lives and fill their hearts with Christ and His Holy Spirit. We plead with them to believe that *"with God all things are possible"* (Matt. 19:26). He is able and willing; He is anxious to restore them to the Father's house, to the joy of His presence and service.

In order to attain this, they must listen to the call for men and women who will daily and continually, in the power of Christ's abiding presence, live in the spirit of unceasing intercession for all believers. They must receive the power of the Holy Spirit and acknowledge that this is nothing less than a duty, a sacrifice that Christ's love has a right to claim, and that He by His Spirit will indeed work in them. The person who accepts the call as coming from Christ and draws near to God in humble prayer for the needed grace, however far he may have come short, will have taken the first step on the path that leads to fellowship with God, to a new faith and life in Christ Jesus, and to the surrender of his whole being to the intercession of the Spirit that will help to bring Pentecost again into the hearts of God's people.

Section Six

❧

The Secret of the Cross

Jesus now has many lovers of His heavenly kingdom, but few bearers of His cross. He has many who desire consolation, but few who desire tribulation. He finds many companions of His table, but few of His abstinence. All desire to rejoice with Him, but few are willing to endure anything for Him or with Him. Many follow Jesus to the breaking of bread, but few to the drinking of the cup of His passion. Many revere His miracles, but few follow the humiliation of His cross.

—THOMAS Á KEMPIS

THE SECRET OF THE CROSS

The question often arises why, with so much churchgoing, Bible reading, and prayer, the Christian fails to live the life of entire sanctification and lacks the love and joy of the Lord. One of the most important answers undoubtedly is that he does not know what it is to die to himself and to the world. Without this, God's love and holiness cannot have their dwelling place in his heart. He has repented of some sins, but he does not know what it is to turn both from sin and from his old nature and self-will.

Yet this is what the Lord Jesus taught. He said to the disciples that if any man would follow Him, he must hate and lose his own life. (See Matthew 16:24–25; Luke 14:26.) He taught them each to take up his cross. That meant they were to consider their lives as sinful and under penalty of death. They were to give up themselves, their own wills and powers, and any goodness of their own. When their Lord had died on the cross, they would learn what it was to die to themselves and the world, and to live their lives in the fullness of God.

Our Lord used the apostle Paul to make this still clearer to us. Paul did not know Christ in the flesh, but through the Holy Spirit Christ was revealed in his heart. Therefore, he could testify, *"I have been crucified with Christ; it is no longer I who live, but Christ lives in me"* (Gal. 2:20). In more than one of his epistles, the truth is made clear that we are dead to sin with Christ, and we receive and experience the power of the new life through the continual working of God's Spirit in us each day.

As the Easter season approaches each year, our thoughts are occupied with the sufferings and death of our Lord. Sermons once again emphasize Christ's death for us on the cross as the foundation of our salvation. But less is said about our death with Christ. The subject is a deep and difficult one, yet every Christian needs to consider it. It is my earnest desire to help those Christians who are considering this great truth, that death to self and to the world is necessary for a life in the love and joy of Christ.

I have sought to explain the words of our Lord and of His disciples on this subject. Allow me to point out two more things. First, take time to read over what you do not immediately understand. Spiritual truth is not easy to grasp. But experience has taught me that God's words, taken into the heart and meditated on with prayer, gradually help the soul to understand the truth. Secondly, be assured that only through the continual teaching of the Holy Spirit in your heart will you be able to take hold of spiritual truths. The great work of the Holy Spirit is to reveal Christ in our hearts and lives as the Crucified One, who dwells within us. Let this be the chief aim of all your devotion: complete dependence on God, and an expectation of continually receiving all goodness and salvation from Him alone. In this way you will learn to die to yourself and to the world; you will receive Christ, the Crucified and Glorified One, into your heart; and you will be kept by the continual working of the Holy Spirit.

Let us pray fervently for each other, that God may teach us what it is to die with Christ—a death to ourselves and to the world, and a life in Christ Jesus.

A PRAYER

Heavenly Father, how can I thank You for the unspeakable gift of Your Son on the cross? How can I thank You for our eternal salvation, worked out by that death on the cross? He died for me so that I might live eternally. Through His death on the cross, I am dead to sin and live in the power of His life.

Father in heaven, teach me what it means that I am dead with Christ and can live my life in Him. Teach me to realize that my sinful flesh is wholly corrupt and nailed to the cross to be destroyed, so that the life of Christ may be manifested in me.

Teach me, above all, to believe that I cannot either understand or experience this except through the continual working of the Holy Spirit dwelling within me. Father, for Christ's sake, I ask it. Amen.

THE REDEMPTION OF THE CROSS

*Christ has redeemed us from the curse of the law,
having become a curse for us.*
—*Galatians 3:13*

Scripture teaches us that there are two points of view from which we may regard Christ's death upon the cross. The one is the redemption of the cross: Christ dying for us as our complete deliverance from the curse of sin. The other is the fellowship of the cross: Christ taking us up to die with Him and making us partakers of the fellowship of His death.

In the above verse, we find three great unsearchable thoughts. First, the law of God has pronounced a curse on all sin and on all that is sinful. Second, Christ took our curse upon Him and even became a curse, thereby destroying its power. Third, in the cross we now have the everlasting redemption from sin and all its power. The cross reveals to us that man's sin is under the curse, that Christ became a curse and overcame it, and that He is our full and everlasting deliverance from the curse.

In these thoughts, the most lost and hopeless sinner may find a sure ground of confidence and hope. In Paradise, God had indeed pronounced a curse on this earth and all that belongs to it. (See Genesis 3:17–19.) On Mount Ebal, in connection with giving the law, half of the people of Israel were twelve times over to pronounce a curse on all sin. (See Deuteronomy 27:11–26.) And there was to be in their midst a continual reminder of it: *"He who is hanged is accursed of God"* (Deut. 21:23). And yet, who could ever have thought that the Son of God Himself would die on the accursed tree and become a curse for us? But such is the Gospel of God's love, and the penitent sinner can now rejoice in the confident assurance that the curse is forever put away from all who believe in Christ Jesus.

The preaching of the redemption of the cross is the foundation and center of the salvation the Gospel brings us. To those who believe its full truth, it is a cause of unceasing thanksgiving. It gives us boldness to rejoice in God. There is nothing else that will keep the heart more tender toward God, enabling us to live in His love and to make Him known to those who have never yet found Him. God be praised for the redemption of the cross!

THE FELLOWSHIP OF THE CROSS

Let this mind be in you which was also in Christ Jesus.
—Philippians 2:5

Paul told us here of the mind that was in Christ: He emptied Himself; He took the form of a servant; He humbled Himself, *"even* [to] *the death of the cross"* (v. 8). It is this mind that was in Christ—the deep humility that gave up His life to the very death—that is to be the spirit that animates us. In this way, we will prove and enjoy the blessed fellowship of His cross.

Paul had said to the Philippians, *"If there is any consolation in Christ"* (v. 1)—the Comforter had come to reveal His real presence in them—*"if any fellowship of the Spirit"* (v. 1)—it was in this power of the Spirit that they were to breathe the Spirit of the crucified Christ and manifest His disposition in the fellowship of the cross in their lives.

As they strove to do this, they would feel the need of a deeper insight into their real oneness with Christ. They would learn to appreciate the truth that they had been crucified with Christ, that their *"old man"* (Rom. 6:6) had been crucified, and that they had died to sin in Christ's death and were now living to God in His life. They would learn to know what it meant that the crucified Christ lived in them, and that they had *"crucified the flesh with its passions and desires"* (Gal. 5:24). Because the crucified Jesus lived in them, they could live crucified to the world.

And so they would gradually enter more deeply into the meaning and power of their high calling to live as those who were dead to sin, the world, and self. Each in his own measure would bear the marks of the cross, with its sentence of death on the flesh, with its hating of the self-life and its entire denial of self, and with its growing conformity to the crucified Redeemer in His deep humility and entire surrender of His will to the life of God.

This is a difficult thing to learn; there is no quick lesson in this school of the cross. But the personal experience of the fellowship of the cross will lead to a deeper understanding and a higher appreciation of the redemption of the cross.

CRUCIFIED WITH CHRIST

*I have been crucified with Christ; it is no longer I
who live, but Christ lives in me.*
—Galatians 2:20

The thought of fellowship with Christ in bearing His cross has often led to the futile attempt to follow Him and bear His image in our own power. But this is impossible for man until he first learns to know what it means to say, *"I have been crucified with Christ."*

Let us try to understand this. When Adam died, all his descendants died with him and in him. In his sin in Paradise, and in the spiritual death into which he fell, you and I had a share; we died in him. And the power of that sin and death, in which all his descendants share, works in every child of Adam every day.

Christ came as the Second Adam. All who believe in Him have a share in His death on the cross. Each one may say in truth, *"I have been crucified with Christ."* As the Representative of His people, He took them up with Him on the cross. This includes you and me. The life that He gives is the crucified life in which He entered heaven and was exalted to the throne, standing as *"a Lamb as though it had been slain"* (Rev. 5:6). The power of His death and life does its work in us. As we hold fast the truth that we have been crucified with Him, and that now we no longer live, but Christ lives in us, we receive power to conquer sin. The life that we have received from Him is a life that has been crucified and made free from the power of sin.

This is a deep and very precious truth. Most Christians have little knowledge of it. This knowledge is not gained easily or speedily. It requires a great desire to be dead to all sin. It requires a strong faith, given by the Holy Spirit, so that the union with the crucified Christ and the fellowship of His cross can each day become our life. The life that He lives in heaven has its strength and its glory in the fact that it is a crucified life. And the life that He imparts to the believing disciple is a crucified life with its victory over sin and its power of access into God's presence.

It is indeed true that *"it is no longer I who live, but Christ lives in me."* As we realize this by faith and hold fast the fact that the crucified Christ lives in us, life in the fellowship of the cross becomes a possibility and a blessed experience.

CRUCIFIED TO THE WORLD

*But God forbid that I should boast except in the cross
of our Lord Jesus Christ, by whom the world has
been crucified to me, and I to the world.
—Galatians 6:14*

What Paul had written in Galatians 2 is here confirmed at the end of the epistle and is expressed even more strongly. He insisted that his only glory was that, in Christ, he had been crucified to the world and entirely delivered from its power. When he said, *"I have been crucified with Christ"* (Gal. 2:20), it was not only an inner spiritual truth, but also an actual, practical experience in relation to the world and its temptations.

Christ had spoken about the world hating Him and about His having overcome the world. Paul knew that the world that had nailed Christ to the cross had in that deed done the same to him. He boasted that he lived as one who had been crucified to the world, and that the world as a powerless enemy was now crucified to him. It was this that made him glory in the cross of Christ. It had brought him complete deliverance from the world.

How very different is the relationship of Christians to the world today! They acknowledge that they must not commit the sins that the world allows. But still they are good friends with the world, and they feel free to enjoy as much of it as they can, if they only stay away from "open sin." They do not know that the most dangerous source of sin is the love of the world with its lusts and pleasures.

Dear Christian, when the world crucified Christ, it crucified you with Him. When Christ overcame the world on the cross, He made you an overcomer, too. He calls you now, at whatever cost of self-denial, to regard the world, in its hostility to God and His kingdom, as a crucified enemy over whom the cross can ever keep you a conqueror.

The Christian who has learned to say by the Holy Spirit, *"I have been crucified with Christ...*[the crucified] *Christ lives in me"* (Gal. 2:20), has a very different relationship to the pleasures and attractions of the world. Let us ask God fervently that the Holy Spirit, through whom Christ offered Himself on the cross, may reveal to us in power what it means to *"boast...in the cross of our Lord Jesus Christ, by whom the world has been crucified to me."*

THE FLESH CRUCIFIED

🙌

*Those who are Christ's have crucified the flesh
with its passions and desires.*
—Galatians 5:24

Concerning the flesh Paul taught us, *"In me (that is, in my flesh) nothing good dwells"* (Rom. 7:18). And again he said, *"The carnal mind* [the mind of the flesh] *is enmity against God; for it is not subject to the law of God, nor indeed can be"* (Rom. 8:7). When Adam lost the Spirit of God, he became ruled by the flesh. "The flesh" is the expression for the evil, corrupt nature that we inherit from Adam. Of this flesh it is written, *"Our old man was crucified with Him"* (Rom. 6:6). And here Paul put it even more strongly: *"Those who are Christ's have crucified the flesh."*

When the disciples heard and obeyed the call of Jesus to follow Him, they honestly meant to do so; but, as He later taught them what that would imply, they were far from being ready to yield immediate obedience. Likewise, those who are Christ's and have accepted Him as the Crucified One scarcely understand what that includes. By their act of surrender, they actually have crucified the flesh and consented to regard it as an accursed thing, nailed to the cross of Christ.

But unfortunately, many Christians have never for a moment thought of such a thing! It may be that the preaching of Christ crucified has been defective. It may be that the truth of our being crucified with Christ has not been taught. They shrink back from the self-denial that it implies, and as a result, where the flesh is allowed in any measure to have its way, the Spirit of Christ cannot exert His power.

Paul taught the Galatians, *"Walk in the Spirit, and you shall not fulfill the lust of the flesh"* (Gal. 5:16); *"As many as are led by the Spirit of God, these are sons of God"* (Rom. 8:14). The Spirit alone can guide us as the flesh, in living faith and fellowship with Christ Jesus, is kept in the place of crucifixion.

Blessed Lord, how little I understood when I accepted You in faith that I once and for all *"crucified the flesh with its passions and desires"*! I humbly ask You, teach me to believe and to live in You, the Crucified One, in such a way that, like Paul, I may always glory in the cross on which the world and the flesh are crucified.

BEARING THE CROSS

❧

He who does not take his cross and follow after Me is not worthy
of Me....He who loses his life for My sake will find it.
—Matthew 10:38–39

Thus far we have looked at some of Paul's words to the Galatians about the cross and our being crucified with Christ. Let us now turn to the Master Himself to see what He has to teach us. We find that what Paul could teach openly and fully after the crucifixion was given by the Master in words that could at first hardly be understood and yet contained the seed of the full truth.

It was when Christ sent forth His disciples that He first used the expression that the disciple must take up his cross and follow Him. The only meaning the disciples could attach to these words was from what they had often seen, when an evildoer who had been sentenced to death by the cross was led out, bearing his cross, to the place of execution. In bearing the cross, the criminal acknowledged the sentence of death that was on him.

Christ wanted His disciples to understand that their natures were so evil and corrupt that only by losing their natural lives could they find true life. Of Himself it was true: all His life He bore His cross, the sentence of death that He knew was resting upon Him on account of our sins. And so He wants each of His disciples to bear his own cross, the sentence of death that is on himself and on his evil, carnal nature.

The disciples could not understand all this right away. But Christ gave them words that, like seeds, would germinate in their hearts and later begin to reveal their full meaning. Each disciple of Christ was not only to carry the sentence of death in himself, but also to learn that in following the Master to His cross, he would find the power to lose his life and to receive instead of it the life that would come through the cross of Christ.

Christ asks His disciples to forsake all and take up their crosses, to give up their whole wills and lives, and to follow Him. The call comes to us, too, to give up the self-life with its self-pleasing and self-exaltation, and to bear the cross in fellowship with Him. In this way, we will be made partakers of His victory.

SELF-DENIAL

*If anyone desires to come after Me, let him deny himself,
and take up his cross, and follow Me.*
—*Matthew 16:24*

For the first time, Christ had definitely announced that He would have to suffer much and be killed and be raised again. *"Peter took Him aside and began to rebuke Him, saying, 'Far be it from You, Lord; this shall not happen to You!'"* (v. 22). Christ's answer was, *"Get behind Me, Satan!"* (v. 23). The spirit of Peter, seeking to turn Him away from the cross and its suffering, was nothing but Satan tempting Him to turn aside from the path that God had appointed as our way of salvation.

Christ then added the words of our text verse, in which He used for the second time the words *"take up his cross."* But with these words, He used a very significant expression revealing what is implied: *"If anyone desires to come after Me, let him deny himself."* When Adam sinned, he fell out of the life of heaven and of God into the life of the world and of self. Self-pleasing, self-sufficiency, and self-exaltation became the laws of his life. When Jesus Christ came to restore man to his original place, *"He humbled Himself and became obedient to the point of death, even the death of the cross"* (Phil. 2:8). What He has done Himself He asks of all who desire to follow Him: *"If anyone desires to come after Me, let him deny himself."*

Instead of denying himself, Peter denied his Lord: *"I do not know the Man!"* (Matt. 26:72). When a man learns to obey Christ's commands, he says of himself, *"I do not know the* [man]!*"* The secret of true discipleship is to bear the cross, to acknowledge the death sentence that has been passed on self, and to deny any right that self has to rule over us.

Death to self—such is to be the Christian's watchword. The surrender to Christ is to be so entire, the surrender to live for those around us so complete, that self is never allowed to come down from the cross to which it has been nailed, but is always kept in the place of death.

Listen to the voice of Jesus: "Deny self." Let us ask God that we, as the disciples of Christ, who denied Himself for us, may by the grace of the Holy Spirit always live as those in whom self has been crucified with Christ, and in whom the crucified Christ now lives as Lord and Master.

HE CANNOT BE MY DISCIPLE

🕸

*If anyone comes to Me and does not hate...his own life...he
cannot be My disciple. And whoever does not bear his cross and
come after Me cannot be My disciple....So likewise, whoever
of you does not forsake all that he has cannot be My disciple.*
—Luke 14:26–27, 33

For the third time, Christ spoke here about bearing the cross.
He gave new meaning to it when He said that a man must hate his
own life and forsake all that he has. Three times He solemnly repeated the words that without this a man cannot be His disciple.

If a man *"does not hate...his own life"*—why does Christ make
such an exacting demand the condition of discipleship? Because the
sinful nature we have inherited from Adam is indeed so vile and
full of sin that if our eyes were only opened to see it in its true nature, we would flee from it as loathsome and incurably evil. The
flesh is *"enmity against God"* (Rom. 8:7); the soul that seeks to love
God cannot help hating the *"old man"* (Rom. 6:6) that is corrupt
through its whole being. Nothing less than this, the hating of our
own lives, will make us willing to bear the cross and carry within us
the sentence of death on our evil natures. Not until we hate this life
with a deadly hatred will we be ready to give up the old nature to
die the death that is its due.

Christ added one more thing: *"Whoever of you does not forsake
all that he has"*—whether in property or character—*"cannot be My
disciple."* Christ claims all. Christ undertakes to satisfy every need
and to give a hundredfold more than we give up. When we by faith
become conscious of what it means to know Christ, to love Him,
and to receive from Him what can enrich and satisfy our immortal
spirits, then we will regard as our highest privilege the surrender
that at first appeared so difficult. As we learn what it means that
Christ is our life, we will *"count all things loss for the excellence of
the knowledge of Christ Jesus* [our] *Lord"* (Phil. 3:8). In the path of
following Him and always learning to know and love Him better,
we will willingly sacrifice all—including self with all its life—to
make room for Him who is more than all.

FOLLOW ME

Then Jesus, looking at him, loved him, and said to him,
"One thing you lack: Go your way, sell whatever you have…
and come, take up the cross, and follow Me."
—Mark 10:21

When Christ spoke these words to the young ruler, he went away grieved. Jesus said, *"How hard it is for those who have riches to enter the kingdom of God!"* (v. 23). The disciples were astonished at His words. When Christ repeated once again what He had said, they were astonished beyond measure. *"'Who then can be saved?' But Jesus looked at them and said, 'With men it is impossible, but not with God; for with God all things are possible'"* (vv. 26–27).

Christ had spoken about bearing the cross as the one condition of discipleship. This is the human side. Here with the rich young ruler, He revealed from the side of God what is needed to give men the will and the power to sacrifice all in order to enter the kingdom. He said to Peter, when he had confessed Him as Christ, the Son of God, that *"flesh and blood"* (Matt. 16:17) had not revealed it to him, but his Father in heaven. This was to remind Peter and the other disciples that it was only by divine teaching that he could make the confession. With the young ruler, likewise, He unveiled the great mystery that it is only by divine power that a man can take up his cross, can lose his life, can deny himself, and can hate the life to which he is by nature so attached.

Multitudes have sought to follow Christ and obey His command yet have found that they have utterly failed. Multitudes have felt that Christ's claims were beyond their reach and have sought to be Christians without any attempt at the wholehearted devotion and the entire self-denial that Christ asks for.

In our study of what the fellowship of the cross means, let us take today's lesson to heart. Let us believe that only by putting our trust in the living God and the mighty power in which He is willing to work in the heart can we attempt to be disciples who forsake all and follow Christ in the fellowship of His cross.

A GRAIN OF WHEAT

Verily, verily, I say unto you, Except a grain of wheat fall into the earth and die, it abideth by itself alone; but if it die, it beareth much fruit. He that loveth his life loseth it; and he that hateth his life in this world shall keep it unto life eternal.
—John 12:24–25 RV

All nature is the parable of how the losing of a life can be the way of securing a truer and a higher life. Every grain of wheat, every seed throughout the world, teaches the lesson that through death lies the path to beautiful and fruitful life.

It was so with the Son of God. He had to pass through death in all its bitterness and suffering before He could rise to heaven and impart His life to His redeemed people. And here, under the shadow of the approaching cross, He called His disciples: "If any man will serve Me, let him follow Me." (See Matthew 16:24.) He repeated the words: *"He that hateth his life in this world shall keep it unto life eternal."*

One might have thought that Christ did not need to lose His holy life before He could find it again. But so it was: God had *"laid on Him the iniquity of us all"* (Isa. 53:6), and He yielded to the inexorable law that through death comes life and fruit.

How much more should we, in the consciousness of that evil nature and the death that we inherited in Adam, be most grateful that there is a way open to us by which, in the fellowship of Christ and His cross, we can die to this accursed self! With what gratitude we should listen to the call to bear our cross, to yield our *"old man"* (Rom. 6:6) as crucified with Christ daily to the death that he deserves! Surely the thought that the power of eternal life is working in us ought to make us willing and glad to die the death that brings us into the fellowship and the power of life in a risen Christ.

Unfortunately, this is rarely understood. Let us believe that what is impossible to man is possible to God (Matt. 19:26). Let us believe that the law of the Spirit of Christ Jesus, the Risen Lord, can indeed make His death and His life the daily experience of our souls.

YOUR WILL BE DONE

🖕

O my Father, if it be possible, let this cup pass away from me:
nevertheless, not as I will, but as thou wilt.
—Matthew 26:39 RV

The death of Christ on the cross is the highest and holiest thing that can be known of Him even in the glory of heaven. And the highest and holiest thing that the Holy Spirit can work in us is to take us up and keep us in the fellowship of the cross of Christ. We need to enter deeply into the truth that Christ, the beloved Son of the Father, could not return to the glory of heaven until He had first given Himself over to death. As this great truth opens up to us, it will help us to understand how in our lives and in our fellowship with Christ, it is impossible for us to share His life until we have first surrendered ourselves every day to die to sin and the world, and so to abide in unbroken fellowship with our crucified Lord.

From Christ alone we can learn what it means to have fellowship with His sufferings and to be *"conformed to His death"* (Phil. 3:10). In the agony of Gethsemane, when He looked toward what a death on the cross would be, He got such a vision of what it meant to die the accursed death under the power of sin, with God's face turned from Him so that not a single ray of its light could penetrate the darkness, that He prayed that the cup might pass from Him. But when no answer came and He understood that the Father could not allow the cup to pass by, He yielded up His whole will and life: *"Your will be done"* (Matt. 26:42).

Dear Christian, in these words of your Lord in His agony, you can enter into fellowship with Him. In His strength, your heart will be made strong to believe most confidently that God in His omnipotence will enable you to yield up everything, because you have been crucified with Him.

"Your will be done" (v. 42). Let this be the deepest and highest word in your life. In the power of Christ, with whom you have been crucified, and in the power of His Spirit, the definite daily surrender to the ever blessed will of God will become the joy and strength of your life.

THE LOVE OF THE CROSS

Then Jesus said, "Father, forgive them, for they
do not know what they do."
—Luke 23:34

The seven words on the cross, *"They do not know what they do,"* reveal the mind of Christ and show what the minds of His disciples should be. Three words express Christ's wonderful love: *"Father, forgive them."* Christ prayed for His enemies. In the hour of their triumph over Him, in the hour of shame and suffering that they delighted in showering on Him, He poured out His love in prayer for them. The call to everyone who believes in a crucified Christ is to go and do likewise, even as He said, *"Love your enemies, bless those who curse you, do good to those who hate you, and pray for those who...persecute you"* (Matt. 5:44). The law of the Master is the law for every disciple; the love of the crucified Jesus is the only rule for those who believe in Him.

The love that cared for His enemies also cared for His friends. Jesus felt what the anguish must be in the heart of His widowed mother and so committed her to the care of the beloved disciple: *"Woman, behold your son!...Behold your mother!"* (John 19:26–27). Jesus knew that for John there could be no higher privilege and no more blessed service than that of taking His place in the care of Mary. Similarly, we who are the disciples of Christ must not only pray for His enemies, but must also prove our love to Him and to all who belong to Him by making sure that every person is comforted and that every loving heart has some work to do in caring for those who belong to the blessed Master.

"Assuredly, I say to you, today you will be with Me in Paradise" (Luke 23:43). The penitent thief had appealed to Christ's mercy to remember him. With what readiness of joy and love Christ gave the immediate answer to his prayer! Whether it was the love that prayed for His enemies, the love that cared for His friends, or the love that rejoiced over the penitent sinner who was being cast out by man—in all these Christ proved that the cross is a cross of love, that the Crucified One is the embodiment of a love that *"passes knowledge"* (Eph. 3:19).

With every thought of what we owe to that love, with every act of faith in which we rejoice in its redemption, let us prove that the mind of the crucified Christ is our mind, and that His love is not only what we trust in for ourselves, but also what guides us in our loving fellowship with the world around us.

THE SACRIFICE OF THE CROSS

My God, My God, why have You forsaken Me?
—*Matthew 27:46*

I thirst....It is finished!
—*John 19:28, 30*

These words spoken on the cross reveal love in its outflow to men, and in the tremendous sacrifice that it brought to deliver us from our sins and give the victory over every foe. They reveal the mind that was in Christ, which is to be the disposition of our whole lives.

"My God, My God, why have You forsaken Me?" How deep must have been the darkness that overshadowed Him, when not one ray of light from the Father shone upon Him and He could not say, "My Father"! It was this awful desertion, breaking in upon that life of childlike fellowship with the Father in which He had always walked, that caused Him the agony and the bloody sweat in Gethsemane. *"O My Father...let this cup pass from Me"* (Matt. 26:39). But He knew it could not pass away, and He bowed His head in submission: *"Your will be done"* (v. 42). His love for God and for man caused Him to yield Himself to the very uttermost. As we learn to believe and to worship that love, we, too, will learn to say, *"Your will be done."*

"I thirst." The body of Christ here gave expression to the terrible experience of what it passed through when the fire of God's wrath against sin came upon Him in the hour of His desertion. He had spoken of the rich man crying out, *"I am tormented in this flame"* (Luke 16:24). Likewise, Christ uttered His complaint of what He had suffered. Physicians tell us that in crucifixion, the whole body is in agony with terrible fever and pain. Our Lord endured it all and cried, *"I thirst."* He sacrificed both soul and body to the Father.

And now comes the great word: *"It is finished!"* All that there was to suffer and endure had been suffered and endured. He had finished the work the Father gave Him to do. His love held nothing back. He gave Himself as an offering and a sacrifice. Such was the mind of Christ, and such must be the attitude of everyone who owes himself and his life to that sacrifice. The mind that was in Christ must be in us, ready to say, "I have come *'to do the will of Him who sent Me, and to finish His work'* (John 4:34)." And every day that our confidence grows fuller in Christ's finished work, our hearts must more entirely yield themselves as burnt offerings in the service of God and His love.

THE DEATH OF THE CROSS

"Father, 'into Your hands I commit My spirit.'"
Having said this, He breathed His last.
—Luke 23:46

Like David, Christ had often committed His spirit into the hands of the Father for His daily life and needs. (See Psalm 31:5.) But here is something new and very special. He gave up His spirit into the power of death, gave up all control over it, and sank down into the darkness and death of the grave, where He could neither think, pray, nor will. He surrendered Himself completely into the Father's hands, trusting Him to care for Him in the dark, and in due time to raise Him up again.

If we have indeed died in Christ and are now to carry about with us the death of our Lord Jesus in faith every day (2 Cor. 4:10), this word is the one that we need. Just think once again what Christ meant when He said that we must hate and lose our lives (John 12:24–25).

We died in Adam; the life we receive from him is death; there is nothing good or heavenly in us by nature. It is to this inward evil nature, to all the life that we have from this world, that we must die. There cannot be any thought of any real holiness without totally dying to this self, this *"old man"* (Rom. 6:6). Many people deceive themselves because they seek to be alive in God before they are dead to their own natures—something as impossible as a grain of wheat being alive before it dies. This total dying to self lies at the root of all true piety. Spiritual life must grow out of death.

And if you ask how you can do this, you will find the answer in the mind in which Christ died. Like Him, you may cast yourself upon God, without knowing how the new life is to be attained. But as you say in fellowship with Jesus, *"Father, 'into Your hands I commit My spirit,'"* and as you depend simply and absolutely on God to raise you up into the new life, the wonderful promise of God's Word will be fulfilled in you. You will know *"what is the exceeding greatness of His power toward us who believe, according to the working of His mighty power which He worked in Christ when He raised Him from the dead"* (Eph. 1:19–20).

This is indeed the true rest of faith: living every day and every hour in absolute dependence on the continual and immediate quickening of the divine life in us by God Himself through the Holy Spirit.

IT IS FINISHED

🦚

When Jesus had received the sour wine,
He said, "It is finished!"
—John 19:30

Once again, these words of our Lord on the cross reveal to us His mind and disposition. At the beginning of His ministry, He said, *"My food is to do the will of Him who sent Me, and to finish His work"* (John 4:34). In all things, the small as well as the great, He would accomplish God's work. In His high-priestly prayer at the end of the three years' ministry, He could say, *"I have glorified You on the earth. I have finished the work which You have given Me to do"* (John 17:4). He sacrificed all, and in dying on the cross could in truth say, *"It is finished!"*

With these words to the Father, Christ laid down His life. With these words, He was strengthened, after the terrible agony on the cross, in the knowledge that all was now fulfilled. And with these words, He uttered the truth of the Gospel of our redemption, that all that was needed for man's salvation had been accomplished on the cross.

This disposition should characterize every follower of Christ. The mind that was in Him must be in us (Phil. 2:5)—it must be our food, the strength of our lives, to do the will of God in all things and to finish His work. There may be small things about which we are not aware that bring harm to ourselves and to God's work. Or we might draw back before some great thing that demands too much sacrifice. No matter what happens, however, we may find strength to perform our duty in Christ's words: *"It is finished!"* His finished work secured the victory over every foe. By faith we may take hold of these dying words of Christ on the cross and may find the power for daily living and daily dying in the fellowship of the crucified Christ.

Child of God, study the inexhaustible treasure contained in this Scripture: *"It is finished!"* Faith in what Christ accomplished on the cross will enable you to manifest in daily life the spirit of the cross.

DEAD TO SIN

🙶

How shall we who died to sin live any longer in it?
—Romans 6:2

In the first section of the epistle to the Romans, Paul had expounded the great doctrine of justification by faith. (See Romans 1:16–5:11.) After having done this, Paul proceeded in the second section to unfold the related doctrine of the new life by faith in Christ. (See Romans 5:12–8:39.) Using Adam as an illustration of Christ, Paul taught that, just as we all died in Adam and his death reigns in our natures, so those who believe in Christ actually died to sin in Him, were set free from it, and became partakers of the new holy life of Christ.

Paul asked, *"How shall we who died to sin live any longer in it?"* In these words we have the deep spiritual truth that our death to sin in Christ delivers us from its power, so that we no longer can or need to live in it. The secret of true and full holiness is to live, by faith and in the power of the Holy Spirit, with the knowledge that you are dead to sin.

In expounding this truth, Paul reminded the Romans that they were baptized into the death of Christ. *"We were buried with Him through baptism into death....We have been united together* [with Him] *in the likeness of His death....Our old man was crucified with Him, that the body of sin might be done away with"* (Rom. 6:4–6)— rendered void and powerless. Take time to quietly ask for the teaching of the Holy Spirit. Ponder these words until this truth masters you: you are indeed dead to sin in Christ Jesus. As you grow in the consciousness of your union with the crucified Christ, you will experience that the power of His life in you has made you free from the power of sin.

Romans 6 is one of the most blessed portions of the New Testament of our Lord Jesus, teaching us that our *"old man"* (v. 6)— the old nature that is in us—was actually crucified with Him, so that we no longer need to be in bondage to sin. But remember, only as the Holy Spirit makes Christ's death a reality within us will we know—not by force of argument or conviction, but in the reality of the power of a divine life—that we are indeed dead to sin. It only requires the continual living in Christ Jesus.

THE RIGHTEOUSNESS OF GOD

Abraham believed God, and it was accounted to him for righteousness....He believed...God, who gives life to the dead.
—Romans 4:3, 17

Now that we have studied the words of our Lord Jesus about our fellowship with Him in the cross, let us turn to Paul to see how, through the Holy Spirit, he gave deeper insight into what our death in Christ means.

As I said before, the first section of Romans is devoted to the doctrine of justification by faith in Christ. After writing about the awful sin of the heathen (see Romans 1:18–32) and then about the sins of the Jews (see Romans 2:1–29), he pointed out how both Jew and Gentile are *"guilty before God"* (Rom. 3:19). *"All have sinned and fall short"* (v. 23). And then Paul set forth the free grace that gave the redemption that is in Christ Jesus (vv. 21–31). In chapter 4, he pointed to Abraham, who, when he believed, understood that God justified him freely by His grace, and not for anything that he had done.

Abraham had believed not only this, but also something more. *"Abraham believed God...who gives life to the dead and calls those things which do not exist as though they did"* (Rom. 4:3, 17). This is significant because it indicates the two essential needs in the redemption of man in Christ Jesus. There is the need for justification by faith, to restore man to the favor of God. But something more is needed. Man must also be quickened to a new life. Just as justification is by faith alone, so is regeneration. Christ died for our sins; He was raised again out of, or through, our justification.

In the first section of Romans (1:1–5:11), Paul dealt exclusively with the great thought of our justification. But in the second section (Romans 5:12–8:39), he expounded the wonderful union with Christ through faith, by which we died with Him, by which we live in Him, and by which we are made free through the Holy Spirit. We are free not only from the punishment, but also from the power of sin, and we are enabled to live the life of righteousness, obedience, and sanctification.

DEAD WITH CHRIST

*If we died with Christ, we believe that we
shall also live with Him.*
—Romans 6:8

The reason God's children live so little in the power of the resurrection life of Christ is that they have so little understanding of or faith in their death with Christ. How clearly this appears from what Paul said: *"If we died with Christ, we believe that we shall also live with Him."* Such is the knowledge and experience that give us the assurance of His resurrection power in us. *"He died to sin once for all; but the life that He lives, He lives to God"* (v. 10). Only as we know that we are dead with Him can we live with Him.

On the strength of this, Paul pleaded earnestly with his readers: *"Likewise you also, reckon yourselves to be dead indeed to sin, but alive to God in Christ Jesus"* (v. 11). The words *"likewise you also, reckon yourselves"* are a call to bold and confident faith. *"Reckon yourselves to be dead indeed to sin"* as much as Christ is, *"but alive to God in Christ Jesus."* These words give us a divine assurance of what we actually are and have in Christ—not as a truth that our minds can master and take hold of, but as a reality that the Holy Spirit will reveal within us. In His power, we accept our death with Christ on the cross as the power of our daily lives.

Then we are able to accept and obey the command: *"Do not let sin reign in your mortal body...but present yourselves to God as being alive from the dead...for sin shall not have dominion over you"* (vv. 12–14). *"Having been set free from sin, you became slaves of righteousness....Present your members as slaves of righteousness for holiness....Having been set free from sin...you have your fruit to holiness"* (vv. 18–19, 22).

All of Romans 6 is a wonderful revelation of the deep meaning of its opening words: *"How shall we who died to sin live any longer in it?"* (v. 2). Everything depends on our acceptance of the divine assurance that if we died with Christ, we have the power to live for God, just as Christ who died now lives for God.

DEAD TO THE LAW

*You also have become dead to the law through the body
of Christ....Having died to what we were held by, so that
we should serve in the newness of the Spirit.*
—*Romans 7:4, 6*

The believer is not only dead to sin, but also dead to the law. This is a deeper truth, giving us deliverance from the thought of a life of effort and failure, and opening the way to life in the power of the Holy Spirit. "Thou shalt" is done away with; the power of the Spirit takes its place.

In the remainder of Romans 7, we find a description of the Christian as he still tries to obey the law but utterly fails. His experience is such that he says, *"In me (that is, in my flesh) nothing good dwells"* (v. 18). He discovers that the law of sin, notwithstanding his greatest efforts, continually brings him into captivity and causes him to cry out, *"O wretched man that I am! Who will deliver me from this body of death?"* (v. 24). In the whole passage, "I" is everywhere, without any thought of the Spirit's help. Only when he has cried out in despair is he brought to see that he is no longer under the law, but under the rule of the Holy Spirit. *"There is therefore now no condemnation"*—such as he had experienced in his attempt to obey the law—*"to those who are in Christ Jesus.... For the law of the Spirit of life in Christ Jesus has made me free from the law of sin and death"* (Rom. 8:1–2).

As chapter 7 gives us the experience that leads to being a captive under the power of sin, chapter 8 reveals the experience of a man in Christ Jesus who has now been made free from the law of sin and death. In the former, we have the life of the ordinary Christian doing his utmost to keep the commandments of the law and to walk in God's ways, but always ending in failure and shortcoming. In the latter, we have the man who knows that he is in Christ Jesus, dead to sin and alive to God, and by the Spirit has been made free and is kept free from the bondage of sin and of death.

Oh, that men understood the deep meaning of Romans 7, where a man learns that in him, in his flesh, there is no good thing, and that there is no deliverance from this condition except by yielding to the power of the Spirit! Only in this way can men be free from the bondage of the flesh and can fulfill the righteousness of the law in the power of Christ.

THE FLESH CONDEMNED ON THE CROSS

❧

*What the law could not do in that it was weak through the flesh,
God did by sending His own Son in the likeness of sinful
flesh, on account of sin: He condemned sin in the flesh.*
—Romans 8:3

In Romans 8:7 Paul wrote, *"The carnal mind* [the mind of the flesh] *is enmity against God; for it is not subject to the law of God, nor indeed can be."* Here Paul opened up the depth of sin that is in the flesh. In chapter 7 he had said that *"in my flesh, nothing good dwells"* (v. 18). Here he went deeper and told us that the flesh is *"enmity against God"*; it hates God and His law. It was on this account that God condemned sin in the flesh on the cross; all the curse that is on sin is on the flesh in which sin dwells. As the believer understands this, he will cease from any attempt at seeking to perfect in the flesh what is begun in the Spirit. (See Galatians 3:3.) The two are at deadly, irreconcilable enmity.

This lies at the very root of the true Christian life: *"God... condemned sin in the flesh, that the righteous requirement of the law might be fulfilled in us who do not walk according to the flesh but according to the Spirit"* (Rom. 8:3–4). All the requirements of God's law will be fulfilled, not in those who strive to keep and fulfill that law (a thing that is utterly impossible), but in those who walk by the Spirit and, in His power, live out the life that Christ won for us on the cross and imparted to us in the Resurrection.

May God's children learn the double lesson here. In me, that is in my flesh, in the old nature that I have from Adam, there dwells literally no good thing that can satisfy the eye of a holy God. And that flesh can never by any process of discipline, struggling, or prayer be made better than it is. But the Son of God, in the likeness of sinful flesh and in the form of a man, condemned sin on the cross. *"There is therefore now no condemnation to those who are in Christ Jesus, who do not walk according to the flesh, but according to the Spirit"* (v. 1).

JESUS CHRIST AND HIM CRUCIFIED

*I determined not to know anything among you except Jesus
Christ and Him crucified....And my speech and my preaching
were...in demonstration of the Spirit and of power.*
—*1 Corinthians 2:2, 4*

This passage of Scripture is very often understood to mean
that Paul's purpose in his preaching was to know nothing but Jesus
Christ and Him crucified. But it contains a far deeper meaning.
Paul spoke of his purpose, not only in the matter of his preaching,
but also in his whole spirit and life, in order to prove how he in everything sought to act in conformity to the crucified Christ. Thus he
wrote, "[Christ] *was crucified in weakness, yet He lives by the power
of God. For we also are weak in Him, but we shall live with Him by
the power of God toward you"* (2 Cor. 13:4).

His whole ministry and all his actions bore the mark of
Christ's likeness; he was crucified through weakness, yet he lived
by the power of God. Just before the words of our text, Paul had
written, *"For the message of the cross is foolishness to those who are
perishing, but to us who are being saved it is the power of God"* (1
Cor. 1:18). Not only in his preaching, but also in all his activities
and behavior, he sought to act in harmony with the weakness in
which Christ was crucified. He had so identified himself with the
weakness of the cross and its shame that, in his whole life and con-
duct, he proved that he sought to show forth the likeness and the
spirit of the crucified Jesus in everything. Hence he said, *"I was
with you in weakness, in fear, and in much trembling"* (1 Cor. 2:3).

It is on this account that he spoke so strongly and said,
"Christ...[sent me] *to preach the gospel, not with wisdom of words,
lest the cross of Christ should be made of no effect"* (1 Cor. 1:17);
*"My speech and my preaching were not with persuasive words of
human wisdom, but in demonstration of the Spirit and of power"* (1
Cor. 2:4). Is this not the great reason why the power of God is so
little manifested in the preaching of the Gospel? Christ the Crucified One may be the subject of the preaching, and yet, because of
men's confidence in human learning and eloquence, there may be
none of the likeness of the crucified Jesus that alone gives preaching its supernatural, divine power.

God help us to understand how the life of every minister and of
every believer must bear the stamp of the sanctuary—nothing but
Jesus Christ and Him crucified.

TEMPERATE IN ALL THINGS

❧

Everyone who competes for the prize is temperate in all things....I discipline my body and bring it into subjection.
—*1 Corinthians 9:25, 27*

Here Paul reminded us of the well-known principle that anyone competing for a prize is *"temperate in all things."* Everything, however attractive, that might be a hindrance in the race is given up or set aside. And this is done in order to obtain an earthly prize. We who strive for an *"imperishable crown"* (v. 25) and strive so that Christ may be Lord of all—will we not be *"temperate in all things"* that could in the very least prevent our following the Lord Jesus with an undivided heart?

Paul said, *"I discipline my body and bring it into subjection."* He would allow nothing to hinder him. He told us, *"One thing I do...I press toward the goal for the prize"* (Phil. 3:13–14). No self-pleasing in eating and drinking, no comfort or ease, would for a moment have kept him from showing the spirit of the cross in his daily life, or from sacrificing all, like his Master. Read the following four passages that comprise Paul's life history: 1 Corinthians 4:11–13; 2 Corinthians 4:8–12; 2 Corinthians 6:4–10; and 2 Corinthians 11:23–27. The cross was not only the theme of his preaching, but also the rule of his life in all its details.

We need to ask God that this disposition may be found in all Christians and preachers of the Gospel, through the power of the Holy Spirit. When the death of Christ works with power in the preacher, then Christ's life will be known among the people. Let us pray that the fellowship of the cross may regain its old place, and that God's children may obey the command: *"Let this mind be in you which was also in Christ Jesus"* (Phil. 2:5). *"He humbled Himself and became obedient to the point of death, even the death of the cross"* (v. 8). *"For if we have been united together in the likeness of His death, certainly we also shall be in the likeness of His resurrection"* (Rom. 6:5).

THE DYING OF THE LORD JESUS

☙

*Always carrying about in the body the dying of the Lord
Jesus, that the life of Jesus also may be manifested in our
body....So then death is working in us, but life in you.*
—2 Corinthians 4:10, 12

Paul was very bold in speaking of the intimate union that was
between the life of Christ in him and the life he lived in the flesh
with all its suffering. In Galatians 2:20, he had spoken of being crucified with Christ and of Christ living in him. Here he talked about
how he was *"carrying about in the body the dying of the Lord Jesus"*; it was through this that the life of Jesus was also manifested
in his body. And he told the Corinthians that because the death of
Christ was thus working in and through him, Christ's life could
work in them.

We often speak of abiding in Christ, but we forget that this
means abiding in a crucified Christ. Many believers seem to think
that, once they have claimed Christ's death in the fellowship of the
cross and have considered themselves as crucified with Him, they
may now consider it as over and done with. They do not understand
that it is in the crucified Christ, and in the fellowship of His death,
that they are to abide daily and unceasingly. The fellowship of the
cross is to be a daily experience. The self-emptying of our Lord, His
taking the form of a servant, His humbling Himself and becoming
"obedient to the point of death, even the death of the cross" (Phil.
2:8)—this mind that was in Christ is to be the disposition that
marks our daily lives.

*"Always carrying about in the body the dying of the Lord Je-
sus."* This is what we are called to as much as Paul was. If we are
indeed to live for the welfare of others around us, if we are to sacrifice our ease and pleasure to win souls for our Lord, it will be true
of us as of Paul, that we are able to say, *"Death is working in us,
but life in* [those for whom we pray and labor]*.*" It is in *"the fellowship of His* [Christ's] *sufferings"* (Phil. 3:10) that the crucified Lord
can live and work out His life in us and through us.

Let us learn the lesson that the abiding in Christ Jesus, for
which we have so often prayed and worked, is nothing less than the
abiding of the crucified Lord in us, and we in Him.

THE CROSS AND THE SPIRIT

How much more shall the blood of Christ, who through
the eternal Spirit offered himself without blemish
unto God, cleanse your conscience?
—Hebrews 9:14 RV

The cross is Christ's highest glory. The glory that He received from the Father was entirely owing to His having humbled Himself to the death of the cross. *"Therefore God also has highly exalted Him"* (Phil. 2:9). The greatest work that the Holy Spirit could ever do in the Son of God was when He enabled Him to yield Himself as a sacrifice and an offering for a sweet smelling savor. And the Holy Spirit can now do nothing greater or more glorious for us than to lead us into the fellowship and likeness of that crucified life of our Lord.

Do we not have here the reason that our prayers for the mighty working of the Holy Spirit are not more abundantly answered? We have prayed too little that the Holy Spirit might glorify Christ in us in the fellowship of and the conformity to His sufferings. (See Philippians 3:10.) The Spirit who led Christ to the cross desires and is able to maintain in us the life of abiding in the crucified Jesus.

The Spirit and the cross are inseparable. The Spirit led Christ to the cross; the cross brought Christ to the throne to receive the fullness of the Spirit to impart to His people. The Spirit taught Peter to preach Christ crucified; it was through this preaching that the three thousand received the Spirit. (See Acts 2:14–41.) In the preaching of the Gospel, in the Christian life, the Spirit and the cross are inseparable; as it was in Christ, so it must be in us. The sad lack of the mind and disposition of the crucified Christ—sacrificing self and the world to win life for the dying—is one great cause of the feebleness of the church. Let us ask God fervently to teach us to say, "We have been crucified with Christ; in Him we have died to sin." Let us always carry *"about in the body the dying of the Lord Jesus"* (2 Cor. 4:10). In this way we will be prepared for the fullness of the Spirit that the Father desires to bestow.

THE VEIL OF THE FLESH

🦢

Therefore, brethren, having boldness to enter the Holiest by the blood of Jesus, by a new and living way which He consecrated for us, through the veil, that is, His flesh.
—Hebrews 10:19–20

In the temple there was a veil between the holy place and the Holiest of All. At the altar in the court, the blood of the sacrifice was sprinkled for forgiveness of sins. This gave the priest entrance into the holy place to offer incense to God as part of a holy worship. But into the Holiest of All, behind the veil, the high priest alone might enter once a year. This veil was the symbol of sinful human nature; even though it had received the forgiveness of sin, full access and fellowship with God was impossible.

When Christ died, the veil was torn in two. Christ dedicated *"a new and living way"* to God through the torn veil of His flesh. This new way, by which we now can enter into the Holiest of All, always passes through the torn veil of the flesh. Every believer has *"crucified the flesh with its passions and desires"* (Gal. 5:24). Every step on the *"new and living way"* for entering into God's holy presence maintains the fellowship with the cross of Christ. The torn veil of the flesh refers not only to Christ and His sufferings, but also to our experience in the likeness of His sufferings.

Is this not the reason why many Christians can never attain close fellowship with God? They have never yielded the flesh as an accursed thing to the condemnation of the cross. They desire to enter into the Holiest of All, yet they allow *"the flesh with its passions and desires"* (Gal. 5:24) to rule over them. God grant that we may rightly understand, in the power of the Holy Spirit, that Christ has called us to hate our lives, to lose our lives, and to be dead with Him to sin so that we may live to God with Him.

There is no way to a full, abiding fellowship with God except through the torn veil of the flesh, through a life with the flesh crucified in Christ Jesus. God be praised that the Holy Spirit always dwells in us to keep the flesh in its place of crucifixion and condemnation, and to give us the abiding victory over all temptations.

LOOKING TO JESUS

❧

Let us run with patience the race that is set before us, looking unto Jesus the author and perfecter of our faith, who for the joy that was set before him endured the cross, despising shame.
—Hebrews 12:1–2 RV

In running a race, a person's eyes and heart are always set upon the goal and the prize. In Hebrews 12, the Christian is called to keep his eyes focused on Jesus, who endured the cross, as the one object of imitation and desire. In our whole lives, we are always to be animated by His Spirit as He bore the cross. This was the way that led to the throne and the glory of God. This is the *"new and living way"* (Heb. 10:20) that He opened for us through the veil of the flesh. As we study and realize that God so highly exalted Him because He bore the cross (Phil. 2:9), we will walk in His footsteps, bearing our own crosses as He did, with our flesh condemned and crucified.

The powerlessness of the church is greatly owing to the fact that this cross-bearing mind of Jesus is so little preached and practiced. Most Christians think that as long as they do not commit obvious sins, they are at liberty to possess and enjoy as much of the world as they please. There is so little insight into the deep truth that the world, and the flesh that loves the world, is *"enmity against God"* (Rom. 8:7). Hence, for years many Christians seek and pray for conformity to the image of Jesus, and yet they fail so entirely. They do not know, they do not seek with the whole heart to know, what it is to die to self and the world.

It was for *"the joy that was set before him,"* the joy of pleasing and glorifying the Father, the joy of loving and winning souls for Himself, that Christ endured the cross. We have a great need for a new crusade with the proclamation, "This is the will of God: just as Christ, through His endurance of the cross, found His highest happiness and received from the Father the fullness of the Spirit to pour down on His people, so it is only in our fellowship of the cross that we can really become *'conformed to the image of His* [God's] *Son'* (Rom. 8:29)." As believers awake to this blessed truth, and as they always look to the crucified Jesus while running the race, they will receive power to win for Christ the souls He purchased on the cross.

OUTSIDE THE GATE

✣

For the bodies of those animals, whose blood is brought into the
sanctuary by the high priest for sin, are burned outside the camp.
Therefore Jesus also, that He might sanctify the people with His
own blood, suffered outside the gate. Therefore let us go forth to
Him, outside the camp, bearing His reproach.
—Hebrews 13:11–13

The body of the sacrifice was *"burned outside the camp,"* and
the blood of the sin offering was brought into the holy place. Similarly, Christ's body was cast out as an accursed thing, *"outside the*
camp," but His blood was presented to the Father.

And so we read in Hebrews 13, *"Let us go forth to Him, outside*
the camp, bearing His reproach." Let us enter into the holy place by
the blood of Jesus. The deeper my insight is into the boldness that
His blood gives me in God's presence, so much greater will be the
joy with which I enter the holy place. And the deeper my insight is
into the shame of the cross that He bore *"outside the camp"* on my
behalf, the more willing I will be, in the fellowship of His cross, to
follow Him *"outside the camp, bearing His reproach."*

Many Christians love to hear of the boldness with which we
can enter into the holy place through His blood, but they have little
desire for the fellowship of *"His reproach"* and are unwilling to
separate themselves from the world with the same boldness with
which they enter the sanctuary. The Christian suffers inconceivable loss when he thinks of entering into the holy place and then
feels free to enjoy the friendship of the world, as long as he does
nothing too obviously sinful. But the Word of God has said, *"Do you*
not know that friendship with the world is enmity with God?"
(James 4:4); *"Do not love the world or the things in the world. If*
anyone loves the world, the love of the Father is not in him" (1 John
2:15); *"Do not be conformed to this world"* (Rom. 12:2).

To be a follower of Christ implies a heart given up to testify for
Him in the midst of the world, if by any means some may be won.
To be a follower of Christ means to be like Him in His love of the
cross and in His willingness to sacrifice self so that the Father may
be glorified and men may be saved.

Blessed Savior, teach me what it means that I am called to
follow You *"outside the camp, bearing* [Your] *reproach."* Teach me
to bear witness of Your holy redeeming love as it embraces worldly
men to win them back to the Father. Blessed Lord, let the spirit
and the love that was in You be in me, too, so that I may at any cost
seek to win the souls for whom You have died.

ALIVE UNTO RIGHTEOUSNESS

🜊

Who his own self bare our sins in his body upon the tree, that
we, having died unto sins, might live unto righteousness.
—1 Peter 2:24 RV

Here in the epistle of Peter we have the same lessons that Paul
taught us. First is the atonement of the cross: *"Who his own self*
bare our sins in his body upon the tree." And then comes the fellowship of the cross: *"That we, having died unto sins, might live unto*
righteousness."

In this last expression, we have the great thought that a Christian cannot live to righteousness unless he knows that he has died
to sin. We need the Holy Spirit to make our death to sin such a reality that we know we are forever free from its power and will
therefore yield our *"members as instruments of righteousness to*
God" (Rom. 6:13).

Dear Christian, it cost Christ much to bear the cross and then
to yield Himself so that it could bear Him. It cost Him much when
He cried, *"Now My soul is troubled, and what shall I say? 'Father,*
save Me from this hour'? But for this purpose I came to this hour"
(John 12:27).

Let us not imagine that the fellowship of the cross—concerning which Peter wrote the words, *"That we, having died unto sins,*
might live unto righteousness"—is easily understood or experienced. It means that the Holy Spirit will teach us what it is to be
identified with Christ in His cross. It means that we realize by faith
how we truly shared with Christ in His death, and now, as He lives
in us, we abide in unceasing fellowship with Him, the Crucified
One. This costs self-sacrifice; it costs earnest prayer; it costs a
wholehearted surrender to God, to His will, and to the cross of Jesus; it costs abiding in Christ and having unceasing fellowship with
Him.

Blessed Lord, reveal to us each day through the Holy Spirit the
secret of our lives in You—we in You, and You in us. Let Your
Spirit reveal to us that as truly as we died in You, You now live in
us the life that was crucified and now is glorified in heaven. Let
Your Spirit burn the words deep into our hearts. Having died to
sin, and being forever set free from its dominion, let us know that
sin can no more reign over us or have dominion (Rom. 6:14). In the
power of Your redemption, let us yield ourselves to God as those
who are alive from the dead, ready and prepared for all His will.

FOLLOWERS OF THE CROSS

*Hereby know we love, because he laid down his life for us:
and we ought to lay down our lives for the brethren.*
—1 John 3:16 RV

"Greater love has no one than this, than to lay down one's life for his friends" (John 15:13). Here our Lord revealed to us the inconceivable love that moved Him to die for us. And now, under the influence and in the power of that love dwelling in us, comes the message: *"We ought to lay down our lives for the brethren."* Nothing less is expected of us than a Christlike life and a Christlike love, proving itself in all our fellowship with our fellow believers.

The cross of Christ is the measure by which we know how much Christ loves us. That cross is also the measure of the love that we owe to the believers around us. Only as the love of Christ on the cross possesses our hearts and daily animates our whole beings will we be able to love others. Our fellowship in the cross of Christ is to manifest itself in our sacrifice of love, not only to Christ Himself, but also to all who belong to Him.

The life to which John here called us is something entirely supernatural and divine. Only the faith of Christ Himself living in us can enable us to accept this great command in the assurance that Christ Himself will work it out in us. It is He Himself who calls us: *"If anyone desires to come after Me, let him deny himself, and take up his cross, and follow Me"* (Matt. 16:24). Nothing less than this— a dying to our own natures; a faith that our *"old man"* (Rom. 6:6), our flesh, has been crucified with Christ, so that we no longer need to sin—nothing less than this can enable us to say, "We love His commandments; this commandment, too, is not grievous." (See 1 John 5:3.)

But for such fellowship and conformity to the death of Christ, nothing will be effective except the daily, unbroken abiding in Christ Jesus that He has promised us. By the Holy Spirit revealing and glorifying Christ in us, we may trust Christ Himself to live out His life in us. He who proved His love on the cross of Calvary, He alone can enable us to say in truth, *"He laid down his life for us: and we ought to lay down our lives for the brethren."* Only as the great truth of the indwelling Christ obtains a place in the faith of the church that it does not have now, will the Christlike love for other believers become the mark of true Christianity, by which all men will know that we are Christ's disciples (John 13:35). This is what will bring the world to believe that God has loved us even as He loved Christ (John 17:23).

FOLLOWING THE LAMB

These are the ones who follow the Lamb wherever He goes.
—Revelation 14:4

It may not be easy to say exactly what is implied in this following of the Lamb in the heavenly vision. But of this we may be sure: it will be the counterpart in heaven of what it is to follow in the footsteps of the Lamb here upon earth. As the Lamb on earth revealed what the Lamb in heaven would be, so His followers on earth can show forth something of the glory of what it will be to follow Him in heaven.

And how may the footsteps of the Lamb be known? *"He humbled Himself"* (Phil. 2:8). *"As a lamb to the slaughter...He opened not His mouth"* (Isa. 53:7). The meekness, gentleness, and humility that marked Him are the very things that call His followers to walk in His footsteps.

Our Lord Himself said, *"Learn from Me, for I am gentle and lowly in heart, and you will find rest for your souls"* (Matt. 11:29). Paul wrote, *"Let this mind be in you which was also in Christ Jesus"* (Phil. 2:5). And then he taught us what that mind consisted of: *"Being in the form of God...[He] made Himself of no reputation, taking the form of a bondservant, and coming in the likeness of men....He humbled Himself and became obedient to the point of death, even the death of the cross"* (vv. 6–8). The Lamb is our Lord and Lawgiver. He opened the only path that leads to the throne of God. As we learn from Him what it means to be meek and lowly, what it means to empty ourselves, to choose the place of the servant, to humble ourselves and become obedient, even to the death of the cross, we will find the *"new and living way"* (Heb. 10:20) that leads us through the torn veil into the Holiest of All.

"Therefore God also has highly exalted Him and given Him the name which is above every name" (Phil. 2:9). Because Christians so little bear the mark of this self-emptying and humiliation even unto death, the world refuses to believe in the possibility of a Christ-filled life.

O child of God, come and study the Lamb who is to be your model and your Savior. Let Paul's words be the keynote of your life: *"I have been crucified with Christ; it is no longer I who live, but Christ lives in me"* (Gal. 2:20). This is the way to follow the Lamb even to the glory of the throne of God in heaven.

TO HIM BE THE GLORY

*To Him who loved us and washed us from our sins in His own
blood, and has made us kings and priests to His God and Father, to
Him be glory and dominion forever and ever. Amen.
—Revelation 1:5–6*

Some of my readers may feel that it is not easy to understand
the lesson of the cross or to carry it out in their lives. Do not think
of it as a heavy burden or yoke that you have to bear. Christ has
said, *"My yoke is easy and My burden is light"* (Matt. 11:30). Love
makes everything easy. Do not think of your love for Him, but of
His great love for you, given through the Holy Spirit. Meditate on
this day and night, until you have the assurance that He loves you
unspeakably. It is through the love of Christ on the cross that souls
are drawn to Him.

We have here the answer as to what will enable us to love the
fellowship of the crucified Jesus. It is nothing less than His love
poured out through the continual inspiration of the Holy Spirit into
the heart of every child of God.

"To Him who loved us." Be still, dear soul, and think what this
everlasting love is that seeks to take possession of you and fill you
with unspeakable joy.

"And washed us from our sins in His own blood." Is this not
proof enough that He will never reject you, that you are precious in
His sight, and that through the power of His blood you are well
pleasing to God?

"And has made us kings and priests to His God and Father."
He now preserves us by His power. He will strengthen us through
His Spirit to reign as kings over sin and the world and to appear as
priests before God in intercession for others. O Christian, learn this
wonderful song, and repeat it until your heart is filled with love
and joy and courage, and it turns to Him in glad surrender every
day. *"To Him be glory and dominion forever and ever. Amen."*

Yes, to Him, who has loved me, has washed me from my sins in
His blood, and has made me a king and a priest—to Him be the
glory in all ages. Amen.

THE BLESSING OF THE CROSS

But God forbid that I should boast except in the cross of
our Lord Jesus Christ, by whom the world has been
crucified to me, and I to the world.
—Galatians 6:14

One of the blessings of the cross consists in this: it teaches us to know the worthlessness of our efforts and the utter corruption of our own natures. The cross does not offer to improve human nature or to supply what man is unable to do. Indeed, many people use it in this way, like patching a new cloth on an old garment. But this tears the garment, and such people walk around in torn clothes, going from one minister to another, without finding what they seek. No, the old garment, our *"old man"* (Rom. 6:6), must be laid aside and given over to the death of the cross. And the cross causes all that is of the lost nature of man to die the accursed death, and the "I" takes the place of an evildoer; all that is of the old nature is broken by the cross.

Whoever has been brought to the cross through the Spirit has learned to pronounce the death sentence on his old nature; he has broken the staff over himself, for whatever does not bear the mark of the cross lies under the curse. He who wishes to save his life remains under the curse. If we have learned through the Spirit to understand the cross, then we have lost our lives. We will no longer expect any good from our old natures, and will not judge others, but only ourselves.

But as long as we have not been taught this lesson through the Spirit, we will try to find good in ourselves, something of worth in God's sight, upon which the sentence of death need not be passed. And if we find nothing at all, we fall into a false grief, which the Evil One eagerly uses to make us despair by saying, "You may as well give up; God will not bother with you; there is nothing for you but failure."

This is not what God desires, however. What we possess by nature must be nailed to the cross, and we must put on the new man. The cross brings us to utter bankruptcy of ourselves, and then God can come to our aid. The cross brought the disciples of Jesus to an end of themselves; even the words of the Master had failed to do this. It took from them the halo of holiness they thought they had won in the three years they followed Jesus, and it taught them to know themselves. And so they were prepared to receive the Holy Spirit, who would impart a new nature and a new life to them. For we cannot separate the cross from the Spirit. We can have no Easter and no Pentecost until we have first had a Good Friday.

Through the cross alone are we prepared for life in the fullness of God; only he who is crucified with Christ can become a *"vessel for honor"* (2 Tim. 2:21).

Our *"old man"* (Rom. 6:6) must be crucified with Christ. In the resurrection of Christ we find the roots of our new life. (See 1 Peter 1:3). Whoever loses his life will find it (Matt. 10:39). We must learn the lesson of the cross, as condemned and rejected ones who have been crucified with Christ. Then the door will be open for a life of power and blessing. All that belongs to death must be given over to death, even as the body is buried in the earth because it belongs to the earth.

The Holy Spirit, the eternal Spirit, is unchangeable. He brought Christ our Head to the cross, and us His children with Him. This work in us is twofold. On the one hand, it leads us to death and all that belongs to death; and on the other hand, it leads us to the life that God has placed within us and that leads from glory to glory.

Section Seven

❧

The Secret of the Abiding Presence

A PRAYER

How will I praise You, O my God, for the gift of the Holy Spirit, who will reveal to me the secret of the cross of Christ? The Spirit strengthened Christ to offer Himself to God on the cross. The cross gave Christ the right to receive the fullness of the Spirit from the Father to pour out on all flesh. The cross gives us the right to receive the Spirit. And the Spirit teaches us to love the cross and to partake of the life crucified with Christ.

O my Father, I thank You that You give the direct continual working of the Spirit in my heart, that the crucified Christ may be formed within me, and His life maintained within me.

Father, I ask You humbly, teach me and Your people so to know this work of the Spirit and to yield ourselves to Him to take full possession of us, that the crucified Lord Jesus may be glorified in us. Amen.

THE SECRET OF THE ABIDING PRESENCE

In the *International Review of Missions,* the editor printed an article on "The Missionary and His Task." He told of a pamphlet that had been issued to a large number of missionaries, inviting them to state the problems that, within the past year or two, had chiefly claimed their attention. In answer, 233 replies had been received from missionaries belonging to 50 different missionary societies. The editor thought that these responses were a sample of missionary thought that could seriously represent what missionaries as a whole were thinking.

After a short survey of the chief problems to which the missionaries referred, the article tells us that the most difficult problems were those dealing with the personal life of the missionary, according to many of the correspondents. A few quotations from their letters, showing their needs and desires, follow.

"One of the most pressing problems of late years has been the possibility of getting one person to do three people's work. And the question to be faced is how to live so that the things of heaven will not be crowded out by the things of earth. One's duties are so multitudinous that it is often impossible to make those opportunities for personal contact which are so important," wrote one of the respondents.

A missionary of more than ordinary ability, who had seen twenty years of service in India, wrote, "The problem is the personal one. I am the greatest problem I have to deal with in my work. Spiritually, I am always ready to be offered, but missionary work means more than this. It means adequate and real effectiveness as a source of spiritual inspiration to my work, to my people, to my brethren. What we need to face is the problem of how to make and keep the average missionary a more spiritual man, a bigger and more constant spiritual force in what the man himself is."

Another writer referred to the temptation to secularity that is always present in missionary work: "How to do the day's work and get sufficient sleep, and also get the time for Bible study and prayer that is essential—these are often the hardest battles that the missionary has to fight."

A leading missionary wrote, "The most pressing problem here, as at home, would seem to be the difficulty of avoiding such overactivity as saps the springs of spiritual life in missionaries themselves—of perseverance in following the hidden, childlike life of our Lord, and so manifesting His life to the people around."

Another experienced missionary wrote, "Within the mission field, the greatest problem would seem to be that of securing real

Christian love and unity among the workers themselves, foreigners and Indians together, *'That the world may know that You have sent Me'* (John 17:23). Supernatural power alone can bring this about."

Another correspondent said, "There is only one problem, and that is faith. We do not believe that God is in control, and so there are infinite problems, as we try to run the church or the work ourselves. Yet they are really not problems of ours at all, but His problems."

It is difficult to express what I felt as I read this article more than once and wondered what was to be done to meet this need of God's dear children, men and women who have not considered their lives dear to themselves, but have sacrificed all to bring His blessed Gospel to the unsaved.

One missionary felt that the first thing to be done was to pray. And yet, what to pray? Where to begin, and what to expect? Would our prayers reach these men and women? We might just put the 233 correspondents on our prayer list and ask God to guide us and show us what we ought to think, what to desire, and what to hope for.

Then the thought came to me that these 233 are only the evidence of how many of the multitudes of missionaries scattered throughout the world may also share the difficulties and the burdens I have mentioned, and may deeply need to know the secret of being kept and guided in the light and the joy of abiding communion with their blessed Lord. Prayer came more fervently than ever, and then I had the further thought: it is not in the missionaries, but in the home church that has sent them, that the root of the trouble is to be found. The church does not live in that full experience of the knowledge of Jesus as its life and strength that would sustain its messengers to the unsaved and would keep them, in the midst of all their trials, in perfect peace.

The closing words in the article give us in one sentence what the real lack is and what is the only way of deliverance: "I believe that when we see with real intensity of vision what the life of faith is, and as a consequence feel with real intensity how full of unbelief our lives are, both as a church and as individuals, and frankly confess it as a practical matter, then life will be aglow with the presence of God."

But it is exactly the vision of the life of faith that is so little known. When that is really given, when we begin to be ashamed of our unbelief, and when we frankly confess that we have been living lives of unbelief in not fully accepting what Christ is willing to be to us, deliverance is drawing near. On His last night, our Lord spoke distinctly about the life of the Father in Him here on earth being the very life that He would live in His disciples: *"I in them, and You in Me"* (John 17:23). This is the life of faith: to believe not only that Christ has died for us, pardoned us, and made us God's children, but also that He lives in us and keeps us in abiding and unbroken fellowship with Himself. When a child of God sees that this is what Christ has promised, and sees what He is able by His almighty power to perform and make real in us, he will be prepared to understand how his life every hour of the day can be in the power of Christ's keeping and guidance. And however difficult it may appear to act this faith and to commit oneself in the surrender of an absolute helplessness to this almighty Christ, *"they shall not be ashamed who wait for* [the Lord]*"* (Isa. 49:23).

Later on, another article appeared in the *International Review of Missions* entitled "The Devotional Life of the Missionary," in which many of the same ideas were expressed as in the extracts given above. The writer, Miss A. H. Small, was a missionary in India for sixteen years, and principal of a women's missionary college in Edinburgh for ten years. She wrote of having a large and intimate correspondence with missionaries of the younger generation in almost every mission field—a correspondence that she felt gave her a very fair indication of the minds and desires of younger missionaries at any given time.

She wrote, "There is one subject that recurs constantly and with great urgency of feeling. It is a matter for serious consideration and deeply concerns the whole of life, relationship, and service. It is the subject of the devotional life. How to secure time for the quiet hour with God in an overcrowded day, and how best to use it when secured, are the anxious considerations of a large number of men and women in every field. Indeed, many frankly state that their own feebleness as missionaries and the comparative inadequacy of missionary results in proportion to missionary endeavors, are almost entirely caused by their failure, both individually and collectively, to make the time for daily communion with God and to rightly use that time." The following quotations from letters will better illustrate what is meant.

"I would need to have time to pray until love burns away the sloth and the weariness and the sin."

"Our greatest need is to resist the temptations to do more than we can do in the right spirit and to crush out with actual work the time that should be spent in waiting on God in quietness."

"The lack of quiet time with God is at the root of all my failure, and the struggle to get it is sometimes desperate."

"Since I have been able to think about the future of the work here, I am acutely alive to the fact that it is not costing me enough spiritually. It must, even if some of the work has to go."

"I am afraid of losing sight of the vision while teaching English, arithmetic, and geography week after week. Is it not hard to shake oneself up and to look for the glory and the gleam in each lesson? I have no doubt it is there, if only I had eyes to see!"

"No man or woman, whether at home or abroad, who knows anything at all of the present missionary situation, will question that if this problem exists, the solution of it must lie heavily upon the conscience of the whole church....If prayer in these conditions, or in any conditions, is to be anything, it must be everything. If the purpose of God is to be in the missionary movement, He must move in the heart of it. If the missionary is to represent and to introduce Jesus Christ our Lord as the Savior into all holy living, he must be so filled with Him that there can be no mistake regarding the truth of his Gospel. He must himself be the living illustration, the very instrument of the spiritual power that he is there to reveal.

"The Christian belief is that the only preparation and method for such high service is to dwell with the Lord in all quietness of spirit; for only in this way is the whole being set free from the law, to live in love. The difficulties that beset us in striving after such a life of inward devotion are admittedly very great, but there is no question that they must be faithfully met, dealt with, and overcome if the kingdoms of this world are to become the kingdom of our God and of His Christ.

"If time and place can be made in the daily routine for quiet, unhurried, uninterrupted communion with God—even though it may seem at grave expense to work or needful rest—the immediate reward will be twofold. Problems of overwork will solve themselves in His presence, and the quiet hour will itself become a constant source of renewal of strength, courage, and love. One very busy missionary was often heard saying, 'Our Master never asks of us so much work that we are left with no leisure for sitting at His feet.'"

After I read the article, the question came to me: Does not the root of the difficulty lie in the failure of the church as a whole to enter into the abundance of the life that is in Christ, and to teach the fullness of His power to redeem and to save? Must not the church stand behind its missionaries with a more triumphant Gospel if the dead weight of dullness, unspirituality, unbelief, and heathen tradition is to be lifted from the church in the mission field? The tides would surely run more strongly if the church as a whole had a firmer and clearer faith in God, who, as revealed in the New Testament, is overflowing and alive. Here in this personal challenge, we seem to probe the real depths of the problem of the church in the mission field.

THE ABIDING PRESENCE

🥀

Lo, I am with you always, even to the end of the age.
—Matthew 28:20

When the Lord chose His twelve disciples, it was so *"that they might be with Him and that He might send them out to preach"* (Mark 3:14). A life in fellowship with Him was to be their preparation for the work of preaching.

The disciples were so deeply conscious of having this great privilege that when Christ spoke of His leaving them to go to the Father, their hearts were filled with great sorrow. The presence of Christ had become indispensable to them; they could not think of living without Him. To comfort them, Christ gave them the promise of the Holy Spirit, with the assurance that they then would have Himself in His heavenly presence in a far deeper and more intimate sense than they ever had known on earth. Their first calling remained unchanged; to be with Him, to live in unbroken fellowship with Him, would be the secret of power to preach and to testify of Him.

When Christ gave them the Great Commission to *"go therefore and make disciples of all the nations, baptizing them in the name of the Father and of the Son and of the Holy Spirit, teaching them to observe all things that I have commanded you"* (Matt. 28:19–20), He added the words, *"Lo, I am with you always, even to the end of the age."*

This principle holds good for all Christ's servants for all time, as it did for the twelve disciples: without the experience of His presence always abiding with them, their preaching would have no power. The secret of their strength would be the living testimony that Jesus Christ was with them every moment, inspiring, directing, and strengthening them. It was this reality that made them so bold in preaching Him as the Crucified One in the midst of His enemies. They never for a moment regretted His bodily absence; they had Him with them and in them, in the divine power of the Holy Spirit.

In all the work of the minister and the missionary, everything depends on an awareness, through a living faith, of the abiding presence of the Lord with His servant. The living experience of the presence of Jesus is an essential element in preaching the Gospel. If this is clouded, our work becomes a human effort, without the freshness and the power of the heavenly life. And nothing can bring back the power and the blessing besides a return to the Master's feet, so that He may breathe into the heart, in divine power, His blessed words: *"Lo, I am with you always."*

THE OMNIPOTENCE OF CHRIST

❧

All authority has been given to Me in heaven and on earth.
—Matthew 28:18

Before Christ gave His disciples their Great Commission to begin the great world conquest that aimed to bring His Gospel to every creature, He first revealed Himself in His divine power as a partner with God Himself, the Almighty One. It was their faith in this that enabled the disciples to undertake the work in all simplicity and boldness. They had begun to know Him in the mighty resurrection power that had conquered sin and death; there was nothing too great for Him to command or for them to undertake.

Every disciple of Jesus Christ who desires to take part in *"the victory that has overcome the world"* (1 John 5:4) needs time, faith, and the Holy Spirit. These things are needed so that he may come under the full conviction that he is to take his part in the work as a servant of the omnipotent Lord Jesus. He is to depend on the daily experience of being *"strong in the Lord and in the power of His might"* (Eph. 6:10). God's promises give us the courage to unquestioningly obey His commands.

Just think of what the disciples had learned to know of the power of Christ Jesus here on earth. And yet that was such a little thing as compared with the greater works that He was now to do in and through them (John 14:12). He has the power to work even in the feeblest of His servants with the strength of the almighty God. He has power even to use their apparent powerlessness to carry out His purposes. He has the power over every enemy and every human heart, over every difficulty and danger.

But let us remember that this power is never meant to be experienced as if it were our own. Only as Jesus Christ as a living person dwells and works with His divine energy in our own hearts and lives can there be any power in our preaching as a personal testimony. It was when Christ had said to Paul, *"My strength is made perfect in weakness"* (2 Cor. 12:9), that Paul could say what he never learned to say before: *"When I am weak, then am I strong"* (v. 10).

The disciple of Christ who fully understands that all power has been entrusted to Christ, to be received from Him hour by hour, is the disciple who will feel the need and experience the power of these precious words: *"Lo, I [the Almighty One] am with you always"* (Matt. 28:20).

THE OMNIPRESENCE OF CHRIST

🦋

I will certainly be with you.
—Exodus 3:12

The first thought of man when he imagines a god is that of power, however limited. The first thought of the true God, in contrast, is His omnipotence: *"I am God Almighty"* (Gen. 35:11). The second thought is God's omnipresence. God always gave His servants the promise of His unseen presence with them. To His *"I am with you"* (Gen. 26:24), their faith responded, *"You are with me"* (Ps. 23:4).

When Christ said to His disciples, *"All authority has been given to Me in heaven and on earth"* (Matt. 28:18), the promise immediately followed: *"I am with you always"* (v. 20). The Omnipotent One is surely the Omnipresent One.

The psalmist spoke of God's omnipresence as something beyond his comprehension: *"Such knowledge is too wonderful for me; it is high, I cannot attain it"* (Ps. 139:6).

The revelation of God's omnipresence in the Man Christ Jesus makes the mystery still deeper. It also makes the grace that enables us to claim this presence as our strength and our joy something inexpressibly blessed. Yet how many servants of Christ, when the promise is given to them, find it difficult to understand all that is implied in it and how it can become the experience of their daily lives!

Here, as elsewhere in the spiritual life, everything depends on faith, on accepting Christ's words as a divine reality, and on trusting the Holy Spirit to make it true to us from moment to moment.

When Christ said *"always"* (Matt. 28:20), He meant to assure us that there is not a day of our lives in which that blessed presence is not with us. It is ours every day and all day long. There does not need to be a moment in which that presence cannot be our experience. This does not depend on what we can do, but on what He undertakes to do. The omnipotent Christ is the omnipresent Christ; the ever present is the everlasting. As surely as He is the Unchangeable One, His presence, as the power of an endless life, will be with each of His servants who trusts Him for it.

"Rest in the LORD, and wait patiently for Him" (Ps. 37:7). *"Lo, I am with you always"* (Matt. 28:20). Let your faith in Christ, the Omnipresent One, be in the quiet confidence that He will every day and every moment keep you as the apple of His eye (Ps. 17:8), in perfect peace and in the sure experience of all the light and strength you need in His service.

CHRIST, THE SAVIOR OF THE WORLD

✺

This is indeed the Christ, the Savior of the world.
—John 4:42

Omnipotence and omnipresence are considered natural attributes of God. They have their true worth only when linked to and inspired by His moral attributes of holiness and love. When our Lord spoke of the omnipotence and omnipresence that had been given to Him—*"All authority...in heaven and on earth"* (Matt. 28:18); *"Lo, I am with you always"* (v. 20)—His words pointed to what lies at the root of all: His divine glory as the Savior of the world and the Redeemer of men. Because *"He humbled Himself and became obedient to the point of death, even the death of the cross...God...highly exalted Him"* (Phil. 2:8–9). While He was on earth, His share in the attributes of God was owing to the work He had done in His perfect obedience to the will of God and the finished redemption He had worked out for the salvation of men.

It is this that gives meaning and worth to what He said of Himself as the Omnipotent and Omnipresent One. Between His mention of these two attributes, He gave His command that they should go out into all the world and preach the Gospel: *"Go therefore and make disciples of all the nations, baptizing them in the name of the Father and of the Son and of the Holy Spirit, teaching them to observe all things that I have commanded you"* (Matt. 28:19–20). As the Redeemer who saves and keeps us from sin, as the Lord who requires obedience to all that He has commanded, He promises His divine presence to be with His servants.

Of course, only when His servants show that they obey Him in all His commands can they expect the fullness of His power and presence to be with them. Only when they themselves are living witnesses to the reality of His power to save and to keep from sin can they expect the full experience of His abiding presence and will they have power to demonstrate to others the life of obedience that He asks.

Yes, it is Jesus Christ who saves His people from their sin, who rules over a people who volunteer themselves in the day of His power (Ps. 110:3), who proves in them that He enables them to say, *"I delight to do Your will, O my God"* (Ps. 40:8), and who says, *"Lo, I am with you always"* (Matt. 28:20). The abiding presence of the Savior is promised to all who have accepted Him in the fullness of His redeeming power from sin and who preach by their lives as well as by their words what a wonderful Savior He is.

CHRIST CRUCIFIED

✿

*God forbid that I should boast except in the cross of our
Lord Jesus Christ, by whom the world has been
crucified to me, and I to the world.*
—*Galatians 6:14*

Christ's highest glory is His cross. It was in this that He glorified the Father, and the Father glorified Him. In the fifth chapter of Revelation, it is as the Lamb slain in the midst of the throne that He receives the worship of the ransomed, the angels, and all creation. And it is because He is the Crucified One that His servants have learned to say, *"God forbid that I should boast except in the cross of our Lord Jesus Christ, by whom the world has been crucified to me, and I to the world."* Is it not reasonable that Christ's highest glory should be our only glory, too?

When the Lord Jesus said to His disciples, *"Lo, I am with you always"* (Matt. 28:20), He gave the promise as the Crucified One, who had shown them His pierced hands and feet. And each one who seeks to claim the promise must realize that it is the crucified Jesus who promises, who offers, to be with him every day.

We do not glory in the cross by which we are crucified to the world. Is this not one of the reasons why we find it so difficult to expect and enjoy the abiding presence of Christ? We *"have been crucified with Christ"* (Gal. 2:20); our *"old man was crucified with Him"* (Rom. 6:6); *"those who are Christ's have crucified the flesh with its passions and desires"* (Gal. 5:24); and yet how little we have learned that the world has been crucified to us, and that we are free from its power. How little we have learned, as those who are crucified with Christ, to deny ourselves, and to have the mind that was in Christ when He took *"the form of a bondservant, and…humbled Himself and became obedient to…the death of the cross"* (Phil. 2:7–8).

Oh, let us learn the lesson: it is the crucified Christ who comes to walk with us every day and in whose power we, too, are to live the life that can say, *"I have been crucified with Christ…Christ [crucified] lives in me"* (Gal. 2:20).

CHRIST GLORIFIED

The Lamb who is in the midst of the throne will shepherd.
—Revelation 7:17

These are the ones who follow the Lamb wherever He goes.
—Revelation 14:4

"*Lo, I am with you always*" (Matt. 28:20). Who spoke these words? We must take time to know Him well if we are to understand what we may expect from Him as He offers to be with us all day long. Who is He? None other than the Lamb standing "*in the midst of the throne...as though it had been slain*" (Rev. 5:6). He is the Lamb in His deepest humiliation, enthroned in the glory of God. This is He who speaks and invites us to the closest fellowship and likeness to Himself.

It takes time, deep reverence, and adoring worship to fully understand what it means that He who dwells in the glory of the Father, before whom all heaven bows in prostrate adoration, is none other than He who offers to be your companion, to lead you like a shepherd who cares for each individual sheep, and so to make you one of those "*who follow the Lamb wherever He goes.*"

Read and reread the fifth chapter of Revelation, until your heart is filled with the thought of how all heaven falls prostrate, how the elders "*cast their crowns before the throne*" (Rev. 4:10), and how the Lamb reigns amid the praises and the love of His ransomed ones and all creation. If this is He who comes to you in your daily life and offers to walk with you, to be your strength, your joy, and your almighty Keeper, surely you cannot expect Him to abide with you unless your heart bows in a still deeper reverence and in a surrender to a life of praise and service that may be worthy of the love that has redeemed you.

O Christian, the Lamb in the midst of the throne is indeed the embodiment of the omnipotent glory of the everlasting God and of His love. To have this Lamb of God as your almighty Shepherd and your faithful Keeper does indeed make it possible that the thoughts and cares of earth will not separate you from His love for a single moment. (See Romans 8:38–39.)

THE GREAT QUESTION

🥀

"Do you believe that I am able to do this?"
They said to Him, "Yes, Lord."
—Matthew 9:28

"If you can believe, all things are possible to him who believes."
Immediately the father of the child cried out and said with
tears, "Lord, I believe; help my unbelief!"
—Mark 9:23–24

Jesus said to her... "He who believes in Me, though he
may die, he shall live....Do you believe this?" She
said to Him, "Yes, Lord, I believe."
—John 11:25–27

To what we have seen and heard of Christ Jesus, our hearts are ready to say with Martha, *"Yes, Lord, I believe that You are the Christ, the Son of God"* (John 11:27). But when it comes to believing in Christ's promises of the power of the resurrection life and of His abiding presence with us, we do not find it so easy to say, "I believe that this omnipotent, omnipresent, unchangeable Christ, our Redeemer God, will actually walk with me all day long and will give me the unceasing awareness of His holy presence." It almost looks too good to be true. And yet it is just this faith that Christ asks for and is waiting to work within us.

It is well that we understand clearly the conditions on which Christ offers to reveal to us in our daily lives the secret of His abiding presence. God cannot force His blessings on us against our will. He seeks in every possible way to stir our desire and to help us to realize that He is able and most willing to make His promises true. The resurrection of Christ from the dead is His great plea, His all-prevailing argument. If He could raise that dead Christ, who had died under the burden of all our sin and curse, surely now that Christ has conquered death and is to us the Resurrection and the Life, He can fulfill in our hearts His promise that Christ can be so with us and in us that He will be our life all day long.

And now, in view of what we have said and seen about Christ as our Lord, as our Redeeming God, the great question is whether we are willing to take His word in its divine fullness of meaning and to rest in the promise: *"Lo, I am with you always"* (Matt. 28:20). Christ's question comes to us: *"Do you believe this?"* Let us not rest until we have bowed before Him and said, *"Yes, Lord, I believe."*

CHRIST MANIFESTING HIMSELF

*He who has My commandments and keeps them, it is he who
loves Me. And he who loves Me will be loved by My Father,
and I will love him and manifest Myself to him.*
—*John 14:21*

Christ had promised the disciples that the Holy Spirit would
come to reveal His presence and would always be with them. When
the Spirit came, Christ through the Spirit would manifest Himself
to them. They would know Him in a new, divine, spiritual way; in
the power of the Spirit they would know Him, and He would be far
more intimately and unceasingly with them than ever He had been
on earth.

The condition of this revelation of Himself is comprised in the
word *love:* "*He who has My commandments and keeps them, it is he
who loves Me. And he who loves Me will be loved by My Father, and
I will love him.*" This is to be the meeting of divine and human
love. The love with which Christ had loved them had taken possession of their hearts and would show itself in the love for a full and
absolute obedience. The Father would see this, and His love would
rest upon the soul; Christ would love him with the special love
drawn out by the loving heart and would manifest Himself. The
love of heaven poured out in the heart (see Romans 5:5) would be
met by the new and blessed revelation of Christ Himself.

But this is not all. When the question was asked, "What is it?"
the answer came in the words, "*If anyone loves Me, he will keep My
word; and My Father will love him, and We will come to him and
make Our home with him*" (John 14:23). In the heart thus prepared
by the Holy Spirit, showing itself in loving obedience in a fully surrendered heart, the Father and the Son will make their residence.

And now, Christ promised them nothing less: "*Lo, I am with
you always*" (Matt. 28:20). That word "*with*" implies "in"—Christ
with the Father, dwelling in the heart by faith. Oh, that everyone
who wishes to enter into the secret of the abiding presence would
study, believe, and claim in childlike simplicity the blessed promise:
"*I will...manifest Myself to him*"!

MARY: THE MORNING WATCH

🦡

Jesus saith unto her, Mary. She turned herself, and saith
unto him, Rabboni; which is to say, Master.
—John 20:16 KJV

Here we have the first manifestation of the risen Savior, to
Mary Magdalene, the woman who *"loved much"* (Luke 7:47).

Think of what the morning watch meant to Mary. Is it not evidence of the intense longing of a love that would not rest until it
had found the Lord it sought? It meant a separation from all else,
even from the chief of the apostles, in her longing to find Christ. It
meant the struggle of fear against a faith that refused to let go its
hold of a wonderful promise. It meant Christ's coming and fulfilling
the promise: *"If anyone loves Me, he will keep My word...and I will*
love him and manifest Myself to him" (John 14:23, 21). It meant
that her love was met by the love of Jesus, and she found Him, the
living Lord, in all the power of His resurrection life. It meant that
she now understood what He had said about ascending to the Father, to the life of divine and omnipotent glory. It meant, too, that
she received her commission from her Lord to go and tell His disciples of what she had heard from Him.

That first morning watch, waiting for the risen Lord to reveal
Himself, became a prophecy and a pledge of what the morning
watch has been to thousands of souls since! In fear and doubt, and
yet with a burning love and strong hope, they waited until He
breathed on them the power of His resurrection life and manifested
Himself as the Lord of Glory. They had scarcely known Him because of their feeble human understanding; but when He breathed
on them, they learned—not in words or thought, but in the reality
of a divine experience—that He to whom had been given *"all*
authority...in heaven and on earth" (Matt. 28:18) had now taken
them into the keeping of His abiding presence.

And what are we now to learn? That there is nothing that can
prove a greater attraction to our Lord than the love that sacrifices
everything to Him and rests satisfied with nothing less than Himself. It is to such a love that Christ manifests Himself. He *"loved us*
and [has] *given Himself for us"* (Eph. 5:2). Christ's love needs our
love in which to reveal itself. It is to our love that He speaks the
words, *"Lo, I am with you always"* (Matt. 28:20). It is love that accepts, rejoices in, and lives in that word.

EMMAUS: THE EVENING PRAYER

They constrained Him, saying, "Abide with us...." And He
went in to stay with them....As He sat at the table with
them...their eyes were opened and they knew Him.
—Luke 24:29–31

Mary taught us what the morning watch can be for the revelation of Jesus to the soul. Emmaus reminds us of the place that the evening prayer may have in preparing for the full manifestation of Christ in the soul.

To the two disciples on the way to Emmaus, the day had begun in thick darkness. When they finally heard about the angel who had said that Jesus was alive, they did not know what to think. When *"Jesus Himself drew near"* (v. 15), their eyes were blinded, and they did not recognize Him (v. 16). How often Jesus comes near to us with the purpose of manifesting Himself but is hindered because we are so slow to believe what the Word has spoken! But as the Lord talked with the two disciples, their hearts began to burn within them, and yet they never once thought that it might be Him. It is often the same with us today. The Word becomes precious to us in the fellowship of the saints; our hearts are stirred with the new vision of what Christ's presence may be; and yet our eyes are blinded, and we do not see Him.

When the Lord acted as though He would have gone farther, their request, *"Abide with us,"* constrained Him. On His last night, Christ had given a new meaning to the word *abide*. They did not yet understand this, but by using the word they received far more than they expected—a foretaste of the life of abiding, which the Resurrection had now made possible. Let us learn the lesson of how necessary it is that, toward the close of each day, there should be a pause, perhaps in fellowship with others, when the whole heart takes up anew the promise of the abiding presence of Christ and prays with the urgency that constrains Him: *"Abide with us."*

And what is the chief lesson of the story? What was it that led our Lord to reveal Himself to these two men? Nothing less than their intense devotion to Him. There may be much ignorance and unbelief, but if there is a burning desire for Him above everything else—a desire that is always fostered as the Word is heard or spoken—we may be assured that He will make Himself known to us. To such intense devotion and constraining prayer, the Lord's message will be given in power: *"Lo, I am with you always"* (Matt. 28:20). Our eyes will be opened, and we will know Him and the blessed secret of the ever abiding presence.

THE DISCIPLES: THEIR DIVINE MISSION

🦚

Then, the same day at evening...when the doors were shut
where the disciples were assembled, for fear of the Jews, Jesus came
and stood in the midst, and said to them, "Peace be with you."
—John 20:19

The disciples had received the message of Mary. Peter had told them that he had seen the Lord. Late in the evening, the men from Emmaus told how He had been made known to them. The disciples' hearts were prepared for what now came, when Jesus stood in the midst of them and said, *"Peace be with you,"* and showed them His hands and His feet. This was to be not only a sign of recognition, but also the deep eternal mystery of what would be seen in heaven when He was standing *"in the midst of the throne...[as] a Lamb as though it had been slain"* (Rev. 5:6).

"Then the disciples were glad when they saw the Lord" (John 20:20). And He spoke again: *"Peace to you! As the Father has sent Me, I also send you"* (v. 21). With Mary He revealed Himself to the fervent love that could not rest without Him. With the men at Emmaus, it was their constraining request that received the revelation. Here He met the willing servants whom He had trained for His service, and He handed over to them the work He had done on earth. He changed their fear into the boldness of peace and gladness. He ascended to the Father; the work the Father had given Him to do He now entrusted to them. The divine mission was now theirs to make known and carry out to victory.

For this divine work they needed nothing less than divine power. He breathed upon them the resurrection life He had won by His death. He fulfilled the promise He gave: *"Because I live, you will live also"* (John 14:19). The *"exceeding greatness of...power"* (Eph. 1:19) by which God raised Christ from the dead was the same spirit of holiness by which Christ, as the Son of God, was raised from the dead and would work in them. And all that was bound or loosed in that power would be bound or loosed in heaven (Matt. 16:19).

The story comes to every messenger of the Gospel with wonderful power. Christ says the same words to us: *"As the Father has sent Me, I also send you....Receive the Holy Spirit"* (John 20:21–22). We can have the same personal manifestation of Jesus as the Living One, with His pierced hands and feet. If our hearts are set on nothing less than the presence of the living Lord, we may be assured that it will be given to us. Jesus never sends His servants out without the promise of His abiding presence and His almighty power.

THOMAS: THE BLESSEDNESS OF BELIEVING

❧

Jesus said to him, "Thomas, because you have seen Me,
you have believed. Blessed are those who have not
seen and yet have believed."
—*John 20:29*

We all consider the blessedness of Thomas as something very wonderful—Christ manifesting Himself and allowing Thomas to touch His hands and His side. It is no wonder that this blessedness could find no words except those of holy adoration: *"My Lord and my God!"* (v. 28). Has there ever been a higher expression of the overwhelming nearness and glory of God?

And yet Christ said, *"Because you have seen Me, you have believed. Blessed are those who have not seen and yet have believed."* True and living faith gives a sense of Christ's divine nearness far deeper and more intimate than even the joy that filled the heart of Thomas. Here, even now, after the lapse of all these centuries, we may experience the presence and power of Christ in a far deeper reality than Thomas did. *"Those who have not seen and yet have believed"*—those who believe simply, truly, and fully in what Christ is and can be to them every moment—to these He has promised that He will manifest Himself and that the Father and He will come and dwell in them. (See John 14:21, 23.)

Have we not often been inclined to think of this full life of faith as something beyond our reach? Such a thought robs us of the power to believe. Let us turn to take hold of Christ's word: *"Blessed are those who have not seen and yet have believed."* This is indeed the heavenly blessing, filling the whole heart and life—the faith that receives the love and the presence of the living Lord.

You ask how you may obtain this childlike faith. The answer is very simple. Where Jesus Christ is the one object of our desire and our confidence, He will manifest Himself in divine power. Thomas had proved his intense devotion to Christ when he said, *"Let us also go, that we may die with Him"* (John 11:16). To such a love, even when it is struggling with unbelief, Jesus Christ will manifest Himself. He will make His holy promise an actual reality in our conscious experience: *"I am with you always"* (Matt. 28:20). Let us see to it that our faith in His blessed Word, in His divine power, and in His holy abiding presence, is the one thing that masters our whole beings. Then Christ will indeed manifest Himself, abide with us, and dwell in our hearts as His home.

PETER: THE GREATNESS OF LOVE

🕊

Peter was grieved because He said to him the third time, "Do you love Me?" And he said to Him, "Lord, You know all things; You know that I love You." Jesus said to him, "Feed My sheep."
—John 21:17

It was to Mary who *"loved much"* (Luke 7:47) that Christ first revealed Himself. He also revealed Himself in Peter's first vision (John 21:1–14), to the two disciples on the road to Emmaus (Luke 24:13–31), in His appearance to the ten (John 20:19–23), and in the revelation of Himself to Thomas (vv. 24–28). It was always to the intense devotion of a prepared heart that Christ manifested Himself. And here in His manifestation of Himself to Peter, love is again the keynote.

We can easily understand why Christ asked the question three times, *"Do you love Me?"* It was to remind Peter of the terrible self-confidence in which he had said, *"Even if I have to die with You, I will not deny You!"* (Matt. 26:35); of the need for quiet, deep heart-searching before he could be sure that his love was real and true; of the need for deep penitence in the consciousness of how little he could trust himself; and then of love being the one thing needed for the full restoration to his place in the heart of Jesus, the first condition for feeding His sheep and caring for His lambs.

"God is love" (1 John 4:8). Christ is the Son of His love. *"Having loved His own who were in the world, He loved them to the end"* (John 13:1) and said, *"As the Father loved Me, I also have loved you"* (John 15:9). He asked them to prove their love to Him by keeping His commandments and by loving each other with the love with which He loved them (vv. 10, 12). In heaven and on earth, in the Father and in the Son, in us, in all our work for Him, and in our care for souls, the greatest thing is love.

To everyone who desires to have Jesus manifest Himself, the prerequisite is love. Peter taught us that such love is not in our power to offer. But such love came to him through the power of Christ's death to sin—the power of His resurrection life, of which Peter became partaker. Peter said in his first epistle, *"Whom having not seen you love. Though now you do not see Him, yet believing, you rejoice with joy inexpressible and full of glory"* (1 Pet. 1:8). Thank God, if Peter could be so changed, Christ will certainly work the wondrous change in us, too, and will manifest Himself to a loving heart in all the fullness of His precious word: *"Lo, I am with you always"* (Matt. 28:20). Such love, to which Christ will reveal Himself, is the only preparation for feeding His sheep and tending His lambs.

JOHN: LIFE FROM THE DEAD

❦₧

*And when I saw Him, I fell at His feet as dead. But He laid
His right hand on me, saying to me, "Do not be afraid; I
am the First and the Last. I am He who lives, and was
dead, and behold, I am alive forevermore."*
—Revelation 1:17–18

Here we have Christ manifesting Himself, sixty or more years
after the Resurrection, to the beloved disciple. John *"fell at His feet
as dead."* In answer to Moses' prayer to *"show me Your glory"*
(Exod. 33:18), God had said to him, *"You cannot see My face; for no
man shall see Me, and live"* (v. 20). Man's sinful nature cannot receive the vision of the divine glory, and live; it needs the death of
the natural life for the life of God in glory to enter in. When John
fell at Christ's feet *"as dead,"* it proved how little he could endure
the wonderful heavenly vision.

When Christ laid His right hand upon John and said, *"Do not
be afraid....I am He who lives, and was dead, and behold, I am
alive forevermore,"* He reminded him that He Himself had passed
through death before He could rise to the life and glory of God. For
the Master Himself and for every disciple, for Moses and for John,
there is only one way to the glory of God. That way consists of
death to all the nature that has been in contact with sin and cannot
enter heaven.

This lesson is a deep and necessary one for all who desire Jesus
to manifest Himself to them. The knowledge of Jesus, fellowship
with Him, and the experience of His power are not possible without
the sacrifice of all that is worldly in us. The disciples experienced
this. When Christ spoke about forsaking one's father and mother,
about taking up the cross, about losing one's life for His sake—in
everything He said, down to the days before His death, when He
said, *"Unless a grain of wheat falls into the ground and dies, it remains alone; but if it dies, it produces much grain. He who loves his
life will lose it"* (John 12:24–25)—He made this the one great
charge: deny self; bear the cross, and follow Me.

What is the secret of getting into touch with the Lord Jesus, so
that His abiding presence will be our daily portion? Let us accept
the lesson—through death to life. In the power of Christ Jesus,
with whom we have been crucified and whose death now works in
us, if we will yield ourselves to it, death to sin and to the world is to
be the deepest law of our spiritual lives. The disciples had followed
Christ to the cross. That was what prepared them to receive the
Master's words: *"Lo, I am with you always"* (Matt. 28:20).

PAUL: CHRIST REVEALED IN HIM

🥀

It pleased God...to reveal His Son in me.
—Galatians 1:15–16

In all our study and worship of Christ, we find our thoughts gathering round these five points: the incarnate Christ, the crucified Christ, the enthroned Christ, the indwelling Christ, and Christ coming in glory. If the first is the seed, the second is the seed cast into the ground, and the third is the seed growing up to heaven. Then follows the fruit through the Holy Spirit, which is Christ dwelling in the heart, and then the gathering of the fruit when Christ appears.

Paul told us that it pleased God to reveal His Son in him. And he gave his testimony of the result of that revelation: *"Christ lives in me"* (Gal. 2:20). Of that life, he said that its chief mark was that he was *"crucified with Christ"* (v. 20). It was this that enabled him to say, *"It is no longer I who live"* (v. 20); in Christ he had found the death of self. Just as the cross is the chief characteristic of Christ Himself—*"in the midst of the throne...stood a Lamb as though it had been slain"* (Rev. 5:6)—so the life of Christ in Paul made him inseparably one with his crucified Lord. So completely was this the case that he could say, *"God forbid that I should boast except in the cross of our Lord Jesus Christ, by whom the world has been crucified to me, and I to the world"* (Gal. 6:14).

If you had asked Paul, "If Christ so actually lives in you that you no longer live, what responsibility do you have in living your life?" the answer was ready and clear: *"I live by faith in the Son of God, who loved me and gave Himself for me"* (Gal. 2:20). His life was every moment a life of faith in Him who had loved him and given Himself completely. Christ had undertaken at all times to be the life of His willing disciple.

This was the sum and substance of all Paul's teaching. He asked for intercession so that he might speak *"the mystery of Christ"* (Col. 4:3), *"the riches of the glory of this mystery among the Gentiles: which is Christ in you, the hope of glory"* (Col. 1:27). The indwelling Christ was the secret of his life of faith, the one power, the one aim of all his life and work, *"the hope of glory."* Let us believe in the abiding presence of Christ as the sure gift to each one who trusts Him fully.

WHY COULD WE NOT?

🐾

*Then the disciples came to Jesus privately and said, "Why
could we not cast it out?" So Jesus said to them,
"Because of your unbelief....However, this kind does
not go out except by prayer and fasting."*
—Matthew 17:19–21

The disciples had often cast out devils, but here they had been powerless. They asked the Lord what the reason might be. His answer was very simple: *"Because of your unbelief."*

We have here the reply to the question that is so often asked, "Why can we not live the life of unbroken fellowship with Christ that the Scriptures promise?" Simply because of our unbelief. We do not realize that faith must accept and expect that God will, by His almighty power, fulfill every promise He has made. We do not live in the utter helplessness and dependence on God alone that is the very essence of faith. We are not *"strong in faith...fully persuaded that, what he* [God] *had promised, he was able also to perform"* (Rom. 4:20–21 KJV). We do not give ourselves with our whole hearts to believe that God, by His almighty power, will work wonders in our hearts.

But what can be the reason that this faith is so often lacking? *"However, this kind does not go out except by prayer and fasting."* A strong faith in God needs a life in close touch with Him by persistent prayer. We cannot call up faith at our bidding; it requires close fellowship with God. It requires not only prayer, but also fasting, in the larger and deeper meaning of that word. It requires the denial of self, the sacrifice of pleasing of *"the lust of the flesh, the lust of the eyes, and the pride of life"* (1 John 2:16), which are the essence of a worldly spirit. To gain the prizes of the heavenly life here on earth, one needs to sacrifice all that earth can offer. Just as one needs God to satisfy the human heart and work His mighty miracles in it, the whole man must be utterly given up to God in order to have the power of the faith that can cast out every evil spirit. *"Prayer and fasting"* are essential.

THE POWER OF OBEDIENCE

He who sent Me is with Me. The Father has not left Me alone,
for I always do those things that please Him.
—John 8:29

In these words, Christ not only tells what His life with the Father was, but He also reveals at the same time the law of all communion with God—simple obedience.

We see in the Farewell Discourse how strongly Christ insisted upon it. In John 14 He said, *"If you love Me, keep My commandments. And I will pray the Father, and He will give you another Helper* [the Holy Spirit]*"* (vv. 15–16). He stressed this point twice more: *"And he who loves Me will be loved by My Father, and I will love him and manifest Myself to him"* (v. 21); *"And We will come to him and make Our home with him"* (v. 23). Christ also mentioned obedience three times in chapter 15: *"If...My words abide in you, you will ask what you desire, and it shall be done for you"* (v. 7); *"If you keep My commandments, you will abide in My love, just as I have kept My Father's commandments and abide in His love"* (v. 10); *"You are My friends if you do whatever I command you"* (v. 14).

Obedience is the proof and the exercise of the love of God that has been *"poured out in our hearts by the Holy Spirit"* (Rom. 5:5). It comes from love and leads to love, a deeper and a fuller experience of God's love and indwelling. It assures us that what we ask will be given to us. It assures us that we are abiding in the love of Christ. It seals our claim to be called the friends of Christ. And so it is not only a proof of love, but also of faith, as assuring us that *"whatever we ask we receive from Him, because we keep His commandments and do those things that are pleasing in His sight"* (1 John 3:22).

For the abiding enjoyment of the holy presence, simple, full obedience is necessary. The new covenant has made full provision for this: *"I will put My law in their minds, and write it on their hearts"* (Jer. 31:33); *"I will put My fear in their hearts so that they will not depart from Me"* (Jer. 32:40); *"I will...cause you to walk in My statutes, and you will keep...them"* (Ezek. 36:27).

Obedience enables us to abide in His love and gives us the full experience of His unbroken presence. Christ did not speak of an impossibility; He saw what we might confidently expect in the power of the Spirit. Remember, it is to the obedient disciple that Christ says, *"Lo, I am with you always"* (Matt. 28:20), and to whom all the fullness of its meaning will be revealed.

THE POWER OF INTERCESSION

We will give ourselves continually to prayer.
—Acts 6:4

Constant prayer was offered to God for him by the church.
—Acts 12:5

Dr. John Mott, an American Methodist leader, urged us to believe in the unlimited power of united intercession. While travelling in Asia, he was charged to press upon the missionary societies the imperative need of more intercession—above all, of united intercession. He wrote, "We can in no way better serve the deepest interest of the churches than by multiplying the number of real intercessors and by focusing the prayers of Christendom upon those great situations that demand the almighty working of the Spirit of God. Far more important and vital than any service we can render to missions is that of helping to release the superhuman energy of prayer, and, through uniting in this holy ministry true intercessors of all lands, to help the ushering in of a new era abounding in signs and wonders characteristic of the working of the living Christ. Immeasurably more important than any other work is the linking of all we do to the fountain of divine life and energy. The Christian world has a right to expect mission leaders to set forth not only the facts and methods of the work, but also a larger discovery of superhuman resources and a greater irradiation of spiritual power."

And where is there a greater need of focusing the united intercession of Christendom than on the great army of missionaries, of whom I wrote in the introduction to this section? They confess the need for the presence and the power of God's Spirit in their lives and work. They long for the experience of the abiding presence and power of Christ every day. They need it; they have a right to it. Will you, my dear reader, be a part of the great army that pleads with God for that infilling of power that is so absolutely necessary for effective work? Will you, like the early apostles, *"continue earnestly in prayer"* (Col. 4:2), until God sends an abundant answer? As we *"give ourselves continually to prayer,"* the power of the promise, *"Lo, I am with you always"* (Matt. 28:20), will be proved in our lives.

THE POWER OF TIME

My times are in Your hand.
—Psalm 31:15

The plural in this Scripture verse implies the singular: "All my time is in Your hands, O God. It belongs to You; You alone have the right to command it. I yield it wholly and gladly to Your disposal." What mighty power time can exert if wholly given up to God!

Time is lord of all things. What is all the history of the world if not proof of how, slowly but surely, time has made man what he is today? All around us we see the evidence. In the success of every pursuit, in all our efforts and accomplishments, it is under the law of time and its inconceivable power that we spend our lives.

This is especially true in religion and in our fellowship with God. Time is master here, too. Our communion with God, our likeness to His image, and our power in His service all depend on one condition: that we have sufficient time with God for His holiness to shine on us with its light and to make us partakers of His Spirit and His life. The very essence of religion lies in how much time we spend with God. Yet so many of God's servants, while giving their lives to His service, frankly confess that the feebleness of their spiritual lives and the inadequate results of their mission work as a whole are due to the failure to make the time—and to use it wisely—for daily communion with God.

What can be the cause of this sad confession? Nothing but a lack of faith in the God-given assurance that time spent alone with Him will indeed bring into the lives of His servants the power to enable them to use all their time in His fellowship. Then His abiding presence will be with them all day long.

O my fellow Christian, you complain that you are overworked, or that your zeal hinders your spiritual effectiveness. Do you not see that if you would only submit your time to the inspection of Christ and His Holy Spirit, you would find that a new life would be yours if you fully believed and put into practice this Scripture: *"My times are in Your hand"*?

THE POWER OF FAITH

All things are possible to him who believes.
—Mark 9:23

Scripture teaches us that there is not one truth on which Christ insisted more frequently, both with His disciples and with those who came seeking His help, than the absolute necessity of faith and its unlimited possibilities. And experience has taught us that there is nothing in which we come so short as the simple and absolute trust in God to literally fulfill in us all that He has promised. A life in the abiding presence must be a life of unceasing faith.

Think for a moment of the marks of a true faith. First of all, faith depends on God to do all that He has promised. A person with true faith does not rest content with taking some of the promises; he seeks nothing less than to claim every promise that God has made in its largest and fullest meaning. Under a sense of the nothingness and utter powerlessness of his faith, he trusts the power of an almighty God to work wonders in the heart in which He dwells.

The person of faith does this with his whole heart and all his strength. His faith yields to the promise that God will take full possession, and throughout the day and night will inspire his hope and expectation. By faith, he recognizes the inseparable link that unites God's promises and His commands, and he yields to do the one as fully as he trusts the other.

In the pursuit of the power that such a life of faith can give, there is often a faith that seeks and strives but cannot grasp. This is followed by a faith that begins to see that waiting on God is needed, and quietly rests in the hope of what God will do. This should lead to an act of decision, in which the soul takes God at His word and claims the fulfillment of the promise and then looks to Him, even in utter darkness, to perform what He has spoken.

The life of faith to which the abiding presence will be granted must have complete mastery of the whole being. It is such a wonderful privilege—Christ's presence actually keeping us all day long in its blessedness—that it needs a parting with much that was formerly thought lawful, if He is indeed to be the Lord of all, the blessed Friend who is our companion, the joy and light of our lives. By such faith, we will be able to claim and experience the words of the Master: *"Lo, I am with you always"* (Matt. 28:20).

JOHN'S MISSIONARY MESSAGE

🕮

*That which we have seen and heard we declare to you, that you
also may have fellowship with us; and truly our fellowship
is with the Father and with His Son Jesus Christ.*
—1 John 1:3

What a revelation of the calling placed on every preacher of the Gospel! His message is nothing less than to proclaim that Christ has opened the way for us to have daily, living, loving fellowship with the holy God. He is to preach this as a witness to the life he himself lives in all its blessed experience. In the power of that testimony, he is to prove its reality and show how a sinful man upon earth can indeed live in fellowship with the Father and the Son.

The message suggests to us that the very first duty of the missionary every day of his life is to maintain such close communion with God that he can preach the truth in the fullness of joy, with the knowledge that his life and conversation are the proof that his preaching is true, so that his words appeal with power to the heart: *"And these things we write to you that your joy may be full"* (v. 4).

The October 1914 issue of the *International Review of Missions* contained an article on the influence of the Keswick Convention on mission work. Keswick is well-known as the English town in which a great revival began. The article provides the substance of Keswick teaching in these words: "A life of communion with God through Christ is a reality to be entered upon, and constantly maintained, by the unconditional and habitual surrender of the whole personality to Christ's control and government, in the assurance that the living Christ will take possession of the life thus yielded to Him." It is such teaching, revealing the infinite claim and power of Christ's love as maintained by the power of the Holy Spirit, that will encourage and compel men to make the measure of Christ's surrender for them the only measure of their surrender to Him and His service.

It is this intimate fellowship with Christ as the secret of daily service and testimony that has power to make Christ known as the Deliverer from sin and the Inspiration of a life of wholehearted devotion to His service. It is this intimate and abiding fellowship with Christ that the promise, *"I am with you always"* (Matt. 28:20), secures for us. This is what every missionary needs, what every missionary has a right to claim. By this alone, he maintains the spiritual effectiveness that will influence the workers and the converts with whom he comes into contact.

PAUL'S MISSIONARY MESSAGE

*Continue earnestly in prayer...meanwhile praying also for us, that
God would open to us a door for the word, to speak the mystery of
Christ...that I may make it manifest, as I ought to speak.*
—Colossians 4:2–4

The mystery which...now has been revealed to His saints.
To them God willed to make known what are the riches of the glory
of this mystery among the Gentiles: which is Christ
in you, the hope of glory.
—Colossians 1:26–27

To Paul, the very center and substance of his Gospel was the indwelling Christ. He spoke of the *"riches of the glory of this mystery...Christ in you, the hope of glory."* Though he had been a preacher of this Gospel for so many years, he still asked for prayer, so that he might correctly make known the mystery of it.

I often hear complaints that, after a time, there appears to be no further growth in many churches, and very little of the joy and power for bearing witness to Christ Jesus. The question arises whether the home church is living in the experience of the indwelling Christ, so that the missionaries whom she sends out know the secret and make it the substance of their message.

Some years ago, I knew a minister who went to the mission field. Before he left, there was a little gathering for prayer, at which he asked what his message should be. The thought was expressed that, in speaking to Christians, it was desirable to present a message of a full salvation, so that people would be roused to believe in, and to accept, an indwelling Christ. On his return, he told with what deep interest the presentation of this truth had been received, many saying that they had never before understood this.

Dr. Alexander Maclaren, a Baptist preacher, once said that it seemed as if the church had lost the truth of the indwelling Christ. We speak of Paul's missionary methods, but is there not a greater need for Paul's missionary message, which culminates in the words, *"Christ in you, the hope of glory"*? Are not all missionary intercessors, and missionaries themselves, called to make it a matter of first importance to lead Christians into the enjoyment of their rightful heritage? *"If anyone loves Me, he will keep My word; and My Father will love him, and We will come to him and make Our home with him"* (John 14:23). And it may be the home church that will also share in the blessing, the restoration of this truth to its right place: *"Christ in you, the hope of glory."*

THE MISSIONARY'S LIFE

🦋

Ye are witnesses, and God also, how holily and righteously and unblameably we behaved ourselves toward you that believe.
—*1 Thessalonians 2:10 RV*

Paul more than once appealed to what his converts had seen of his own life. He said, *"Our boasting is this: the testimony of our conscience that we conducted ourselves in the world in simplicity and godly sincerity, not with fleshly wisdom but by the grace of God, and more abundantly toward you"* (2 Cor. 1:12). Christ had taught His disciples as much by His life as by His teaching. Paul had sought to be a living witness to the truth of all that he had preached about Christ—that He is able to save and to keep from sin, that He renews the whole nature by the power of His Holy Spirit, and that He Himself becomes the life of those who believe in Him.

One writer, expressing his ideas about world missions, has said, "It has come to pass that our representatives on the field, just because they are what we have made them, have far too often hidden the Christ whom they are giving their lives to reveal. Only to the degree that the missionary manifests the character of Christ in and through his own life can he gain an audience for the Gospel. Only as far as he can live Christ before their eyes can he help them to understand his message."

Paul referred to his life as holy, righteous, and blameless; this gave him courage to put a high standard before his converts. In the same epistle, he called them to trust God, to *"establish [their] hearts blameless in holiness before our God"* (1 Thess. 3:13). And later in the epistle he wrote, *"The God of peace Himself sanctify you completely...who also will do it"* (1 Thess. 5:23–24). In Philippians 4:9 he wrote, *"The things which you learned and received and heard and saw in me, these do, and the God of peace will be with you."* And in 1 Timothy 1:14–16 we find, *"The grace of our Lord was exceedingly abundant, with faith and love which are in Christ Jesus. This is...a pattern to those who are going to believe on Him for everlasting life."* Let us believe that when Paul said, *"It is no longer I who live, but Christ lives in me"* (Gal. 2:20), he spoke of an actual, divine, unceasing abiding of Christ in him, working in him from hour to hour all that was well pleasing to the Father. And let us not rest until we can say, "The Christ of Paul is my Christ! All that filled his soul from heaven is mine, too."

THE HOLY SPIRIT

❧

He [the Holy Spirit] *will glorify Me, for He will take
of what is Mine and declare it to you.*
—*John 16:14*

When our Lord said to the disciples, *"Lo, I am with you always"* (Matt. 28:20), they did not at first understand or experience
the full meaning of His words. It was at Pentecost, when they were
filled with the Holy Spirit from heaven who brought down into
their hearts the glorified Lord Jesus, that they began the new life
in the joy of the abiding presence.

All our attempts to live this life of continuous, unbroken communion will be in vain unless we, too, yield ourselves wholly to the
power and the indwelling of the ever blessed Spirit. Throughout the
church of Christ, there is an apparent lack of faith in what the
Spirit is as God, in what He can enable us to be, and in how completely He demands full and undisturbed possession of our whole
beings. All our faith in the fulfillment of Christ's glorious promises,
especially that of the Father and Son making their abode in us
(John 14:23), is subject to one essential and indispensable condition: a life utterly and unceasingly yielded to the rule and leading of
the Spirit of Christ.

I hope no one will say, "The experience of Christ's being with
us every day and all day long is impossible." Christ meant His
words to be a simple and eternal reality. He meant the promises to
be accepted as absolute divine truth: *"He who loves Me will be loved
by My Father, and I will love him and manifest Myself to him"* (v.
21); *"We will come to him and make Our home with him"* (v. 23).
But such truth can only be experienced where the Spirit, in His
power as God, is known, believed in, and obeyed. What Christ spoke
of in John 14 is what Paul testified of when he said, *"Christ lives in
me"* (Gal. 2:20), or, as John expressed it, *"And by this we know that
He abides in us, by the Spirit whom He has given us"* (1 John 3:24).

Christ came as God to make known the Father, and the Spirit
came as God to make known the Son in us. We need to understand
that the Spirit, as God, claims absolute surrender and is willing to
take possession of our whole beings and enable us to fulfill all that
Christ asks of us. It is the Spirit who can deliver us from all the
power of the flesh, who can conquer the power of the world in us. It
is the Spirit through whom Christ Jesus will manifest Himself to us
in nothing less than His abiding presence: *"Lo, I am with you always"* (Matt. 28:20).

FILLED WITH THE SPIRIT

✖

Be filled with the Spirit; speaking one to another in psalms and hymns and spiritual songs, singing and making melody in your heart to the Lord, giving thanks always for all things.
—Ephesians 5:18–20

If the expression, *"filled with the Spirit,"* could be applied only to the story of Pentecost, we might think that it was something special, and not meant for ordinary life. But the above Scripture teaches us that it is meant for every Christian and for everyday life.

To realize this more fully, think of what the Holy Spirit was in Christ Jesus and what the conditions were under which He, as man, was filled with the Spirit. He received the Spirit when He was praying and had yielded Himself as a sacrifice to God—when He was baptized in the sinner's baptism. Full of the Holy Spirit, Jesus was led to the forty days' fasting, sacrificing the needs of the body to be free for fellowship with the Father and the victory over Satan. He even refused, when He was extremely hungry, to listen to the temptation of the Evil One to use His power to make bread to supply His hunger. And so He was led by the Spirit all through life until He, by the eternal Spirit, offered Himself without blemish to God. In Christ, the Spirit meant prayer, obedience, and sacrifice.

Likewise, if we are to follow Christ, to have His mind in us, and to live out His life, we must seek to regard the fullness of the Spirit as a daily supply, a daily provision. In no other way can we live the life of obedience, of joy, of self-sacrifice, and of power for service. There may be occasions when that fullness of the Spirit will become especially manifested, but only as we are led by the Spirit every day and all day long can we abide in Christ Jesus, conquer the flesh and the world, and live the life with God in prayer and with our fellowmen in humble, holy, fruitful service.

Above all, it is only as we are filled with the Spirit that the words of Jesus can be fully understood and experienced: *"Lo, I am with you always"* (Matt. 28:20). Let no one think this is too high or that this is impossible. *"The things which are impossible with men are possible with God!"* (Luke 18:27). And if we cannot attain it immediately, let us at least, in an act of holy decision, make it our definite aim, our unceasing prayer, our childlike expectation. *"Lo, I am with you always"* (Matt. 28:20) was meant for daily life, with the sure and all-sufficient aid of the blessed Spirit. Our faith in Christ will be the measure of our fullness of the Spirit. The measure of the power of the Spirit in us will be the measure of our experience of the presence of Christ.

THE CHRIST LIFE

❧

Christ...is our life.
—Colossians 3:4

Christ's life was more than His teaching, more than His work, more than even His death. It was His life in the sight of God and man that gave value to what He said, did, and suffered. And it is this life, glorified in the Resurrection, that He imparts to His people and enables them to live out before men.

"By this all will know that you are My disciples, if you have love for one another" (John 13:35). It was the life in the new brotherhood of the Holy Spirit that made both Jews and Greeks feel that there was some superhuman power about Christ's disciples; they gave living proof of the truth of what they said, that God's love had come down and taken possession of them.

It has often been said that, unless the missionary lives out the Christ life on an entirely different level from that on which other men live, he misses the deepest secret of power and success in his work. When Christ sent His disciples forth, it was with the command, *"Tarry...until you are endued with power from on high"* (Luke 24:49); *"But you shall receive power when the Holy Spirit has come upon you; and you shall be witnesses to Me...to the end of the earth"* (Acts 1:8). Many missionaries have felt that it is not learning, zeal, or the willingness for self-sacrifice in Christ's service, but the secret experience of the life *"hidden with Christ in God"* (Col. 3:3), that enables them to meet and overcome every difficulty.

Everything depends on the life with God in Christ being right. It was so with Christ, with the disciples, and with Paul. The simplicity and intensity of our lives in Christ Jesus, and of the life of Christ Jesus in us, sustains us in the daily drudgery of work, makes us conquer self and everything that could hinder the Christ life, and gives victory over the powers of evil and over the hearts from which the evil spirits have to be cast out.

The life is everything. It was so in Christ Jesus. It must be so in His servants, too. It can be so, because Christ Himself will live in us. When He said, *"Lo, I am with you always"* (Matt. 28:20), He meant nothing less than this: "Every day and all day long, I am with you, the secret of your life, your joy, and your strength."

Oh, to learn what hidden treasures are contained in the blessed words we love to repeat: "Lo, I am with you all the days!"

THE CHRISTLIKE LIFE

🕊

Let this mind be in you which was also in Christ Jesus.
—Philippians 2:5

What was the mind that was in Christ Jesus? *"Taking the form of a bondservant, and coming in the likeness of men...He humbled Himself and became obedient to the point of death, even the death of the cross"* (vv. 7–8). Self-emptying and self-sacrifice, obedience to God's will, and love for men, even to the death of the cross—such was the character of Christ for which God so *"highly exalted Him"* (v. 9). Such is the character of Christ that we are to imitate. He was made in the likeness of men, so that we might be conformed into the likeness of God.

Self-effacement, self-sacrifice, so that God's will might be done and man might be saved—such was the life of Christ. Love *"does not seek its own"* (1 Cor. 13:5). This was His life; He lived only to please God and to bless men.

Let no one say that this is an impossibility. *"The things which are impossible with men are possible with God"* (Luke 18:27). We are called to *"work out"* (Phil. 2:12) this salvation of a Christlike character *"with fear and trembling; for it is God who works in you both to will and to do for His good pleasure"* (vv. 12–13). He of whom Christ said, *"The Father who dwells in Me does the works"* (John 14:10), is He who works in us *"to will and to do."*

It has been said that the "missionary who is to commend the Gospel must first embody it in a character fully conformed to the likeness of Jesus Christ. Only as far as he can live Christ before the eyes of the converts can he help them to understand his message. At times our representatives on the field, just because they are what we have made them, have far too often hidden the Christ whom they are giving their lives to reveal."

As the church aims to make some noticeable degree of likeness to Christ's character the standard for Christian teachers, our missionaries will be able to pass this on to their converts and say to them, *"Imitate me, just as I also imitate Christ"* (1 Cor. 11:1).

Let us not rest until our faith lays hold of the promise, *"It is God who works in you"* (Phil. 2:13). The confidence will be aroused that, as the character of Christ is the revelation with which every missionary has been entrusted, so the power will be given to fulfill this high and holy calling. Let ministers and missionaries and all intercessors make this their one great plea and aim to have this mind *"which was also in Christ Jesus."*

CHRIST, THE NEARNESS OF GOD

ເເ

Draw near to God and He will draw near to you.
—James 4:8

It has been said that the holiness of God is the union of God's infinite distance from sinful man with His infinite nearness to man in His redeeming grace. Faith must always seek to realize both the distance and the nearness.

In Christ, God has come near, so very near to man, and now the command comes: if you want to have God come still nearer, you must draw near to Him. The promised nearness of Christ Jesus expressed in the promise, *"Lo, I am with you always"* (Matt. 28:20), can only be experienced as we draw near to Him.

This means, first of all, that we must yield ourselves afresh at the beginning of each day for His holy presence to rest upon us. It means a voluntary, intentional, and wholehearted turning away from the world, to wait on God to make Himself known to our souls. It means giving time, and all our hearts and strength, to allow Him to reveal Himself. It is impossible to expect the abiding presence of Christ with us throughout the day unless there is a definite daily exercise of strong desire and childlike trust in His word: *"Draw near to God and He will draw near to you."*

Furthermore, this means the simple, childlike offering of ourselves and our lives in everything, in order to do His will alone and to seek above everything to please Him. His promise is sure: *"If anyone loves Me, he will keep My word; and My Father will love him, and We will come to him and make Our home with him"* (John 14:23).

Then comes the quiet assurance of faith, even if there is not much feeling or sense of His presence, that God is with us and that He will watch over us and keep us as we go out to do His will. Moreover, He will strengthen us *"in the inner man"* (Eph. 3:16) with divine strength for the work we have to do for Him.

Child of God, let these words come to you with a new meaning each morning: *"Draw near to God and He will draw near to you."* Wait patiently, and He will speak in divine power: *"Lo, I am with you always"* (Matt. 28:20).

LOVE

🎕

Having loved His own who were in the world,
[Jesus] *loved them to the end.*
—John 13:1

These are the opening words of the holy, confidential talk of Christ with His disciples, as He discoursed with them out of the depths of eternity in the last hours before He went to Gethsemane. (See John 13–17.) They are the revelation and full display of the divine love that was manifested in His death on the cross.

He began with the new commandment: *"That you love one another; as I have loved you"* (John 13:34). Later, He told His disciples, *"If you love Me, keep My commandments....He who loves Me will be loved by My Father, and I will love him and manifest Myself to him....And We will come to him and make Our home with him"* (John 14:15, 21, 23). The new life, the heavenly life in Christ Jesus, is to be the unfolding of God's love in Christ. Then, farther on, we read, *"As the Father loved Me, I also have loved you; abide in My love. If you keep My commandments, you will abide in My love....This is My commandment, that you love one another as I have loved you. Greater love has no one than this, than to lay down one's life for his friends"* (John 15:9–10, 12–13). *"That the world may know that You have sent Me, and have loved them as You have loved Me....I have declared to them Your name, and will declare it, that the love with which You loved Me may be in them, and I in them"* (John 17:23, 26).

Can words make it plainer that God's love for Christ is meant to pass into us and to become our life, so that the love with which the Father loved the Son can be in us? If the Lord Jesus is to manifest Himself to us, it can only be to the loving heart. If we are to claim His daily presence with us, it can only be as a relationship of infinite, tender love is formed between Him and us—love rooted in the faith of God's love for Christ coming into our hearts and showing itself in obedience to His commandments and in love for one another.

In the early church, the *"first love"* (Rev. 2:4) was forsaken after a time, and confidence was put in all the activities of service instead of in God. It is only in the atmosphere of a holy, living love that the abiding presence of the loving Christ can be known, and the depth of divine love expressed in Christ's promise, *"Lo, I am with you always"* (Matt. 28:20), will be realized.

THE TRIAL AND TRIUMPH OF FAITH

🦋

Jesus said to him, "If you can believe, all things are possible to him who believes." Immediately the father of the child cried out and said with tears, "Lord, I believe; help my unbelief!"
—Mark 9:23–24

What a glorious promise: *"All things are possible to him who believes"*! And yet it is just the greatness of this promise that constitutes the trial of faith. At first we do not really believe its truth. But when we have grasped it, then comes the real trial in the thought, "Such a wonder-working faith is utterly beyond my reach."

But what constitutes the trial of faith soon becomes its triumph. How can this be? When the father of the child heard Christ say to him, *"If you can believe, all things are possible to him who believes,"* he felt that this was only casting him into deeper despair. How could his faith be able to work the miracle? But as he looked into the face of Christ, and as the love of His tender eyes touched his heart, he felt sure that this blessed Man had not only the power to heal his child, but also the power to inspire him with the needed faith. The impression Christ produced upon him made possible not only the one miracle of the healing, but also the second miracle that he should have so great a faith. And with tears he cried, *"Lord, I believe; help my unbelief!"* The very greatness of faith's trial was the greatness of faith's triumph.

What a lesson! Of all things that are possible to faith, we think the most impossible is that we should be able to exercise such faith. But the abiding presence of Christ is possible to faith, and this faith is possible to the soul that clings to Christ and trusts Him. As surely as He will lead us into His abiding presence all day long, so surely will He strengthen us with divine power for the faith that claims and receives the promise. Blessed is the hour when the believer sees how entirely he is dependent on Christ for the faith as well as the blessing. In the consciousness of the unbelief that is still struggling within, he casts himself on the power and the love of Jesus, saying, "Lord, I believe! Lord, I believe!"

Through such trial and through such triumph—sometimes the triumph of despair—we enter into our inheritance, which is the abiding presence of Him who speaks to us now: *"Lo, I am with you always"* (Matt. 28:20). Let us wait at His feet until we know that He has blessed us. *"I can do all things in him that strengtheneth me"* (Phil. 4:13 RV).

EXCEEDINGLY ABUNDANTLY

🥁

Now to Him who is able to do exceedingly abundantly above
all that we ask or think, according to the power that works in us,
to Him be glory in the church by Christ Jesus to all
generations, forever and ever. Amen.
—Ephesians 3:20–21

In the above prayer, Paul had apparently reached the highest expression possible of the life to which God's mighty power could bring the believer. But Paul was not content. In this doxology, he rose still higher and lifted us up to give glory to God as *"able to do exceedingly abundantly above all that we ask or think."* Pause a moment to think what that *"exceeding abundantly"* means.

Think of the words *"exceedingly great and precious promises"* (2 Pet. 1:4). Think of *"the exceeding greatness of His power toward us who believe, according to the working of His mighty power which He worked in Christ when He raised Him from the dead"* (Eph. 1:19–20). Think of the grace of our Lord as *"exceedingly abundant, with faith and love which are in Christ Jesus"* (1 Tim. 1:14), so that *"where sin abounded, grace abounded much more"* (Rom. 5:20). He lifts our hearts to give glory to God as able to do *"exceedingly abundantly above all that we ask or think, according to the* [greatness of the] *power that works in us"*—nothing less than the power that raised Christ from the dead. And as our hearts begin to feel that this is an indication of something that God will work in us beyond all our imagination, He lifts our hearts to join in the universal chorus: *"To Him be glory in the church by Christ Jesus to all generations, forever and ever. Amen."*

As we worship and adore, the call comes to believe in this almighty God who is working in our hearts according to His mighty power, able and willing to fulfill every one of His *"exceedingly great and precious promises"* (2 Pet. 1:4), and, where sin abounds, to prove that grace abounds more exceedingly (Rom. 5:20).

Paul began his great prayer, *"I bow my knees to the Father"* (Eph. 3:14). He ended it by bringing us to our knees, to give glory to Him as able to fulfill every promise, to reveal Christ dwelling in our hearts, and to keep us in the life of love that leads to being *"filled with all the fullness of God"* (v. 19).

Child of God, bow in deep adoration, giving glory to God, until the prayer is fulfilled and Jesus dwells in your heart by faith. Faith in this almighty God, and the exceeding abundance of His grace and power, will teach you that the indwelling of Christ is the secret of the abiding presence.

Section Eight

The Secret of Inspiration

What a mistake it is to confine inspiration to particular times and occasions, to prophets and apostles and extraordinary messengers of God, and to call it fanaticism when the common Christian looks and trusts to be continually led and inspired by the Spirit of God! For though all are not called to be prophets or apostles, yet all are called to be holy as God is holy, to be perfect as their heavenly Father is perfect. Now the holiness of the common Christian is not an occasional thing that begins and ends with a certain time, place, or action, but is the holiness of the thoughts and emotions that are stirring in us. If, therefore, these are always governing our lives; if we have no holiness apart from this life of will and emotion working in us; if we are all called to this inward holiness, then a perpetual, always-existing operation of the Spirit of God within us is absolutely necessary. Perpetual inspiration, therefore, is as necessary to a life of holiness as the perpetual respiration of the air is necessary to physical life.

—WILLIAM LAW

THE SECRET OF INSPIRATION

In this section I present excerpts from the writings of William Law—excerpts that deal with the three great divisions of our faith: the Spirit of God, the spirit of love, and the spirit of prayer.

The Spirit of God was the subject of his last work, *An Humble, Earnest, and Affectionate Address to the Clergy,*[2] in which he explained that the one thing needed to raise the church out of its fallen state is for the Holy Spirit to have the same place in the church that He had in Adam before the Fall. With wonderful power, Law unfolded the great truth that the Holy Spirit does not occasionally dwell or work in the Christian, but that, by direct and continual inspiration, He is always working toward bringing him to the full knowledge and experience of the life of God. William Law called the leaders of the church to cease preaching in the power of human wisdom and to bear witness of the spiritual experience of Christ in the heart. Nothing less than this, Law insisted, can restore the church to the place Christ gave it at Pentecost. Such thoughts are needed by the church of our day, as well.

The second of William Law's books from which I have taken excerpts is *The Spirit of Love.* In it the wonderful glory and power of God's love are set forth, to prove that God delights in making us partakers of the love and happiness with which He is filled. Law pointed out how our human nature has fallen into entire and utter selfishness and worldliness, and how nothing but the denial and death of the self-life can enable us to receive and act out the love with which God, by His Holy Spirit, seeks to fill us. *The Spirit of Love* also points us to our Lord Jesus as the Lamb of God, who calls us to learn from Him what the lowliness and meekness are that will prepare us for receiving the fullness of divine love.

Then follows *The Spirit of Prayer,* which Law defined as the spirit of man rising out of the vanity of time into the riches of eternity. In the course of that book, the terrible power of self, with the kingdom it has established in the attractions and lusts of the world, is more fully exposed. And the way is paved for showing us how our hearts can be prepared to make prayer, as an unceasing hunger for God, the means of the full union and communion between the God of love and His creatures here upon earth.

I have only one more thought, a word of advice to every reader. William Law repeatedly warned us against having any delight in

---

[2] Editor's note: *An Humble, Earnest, and Affectionate Address to the Clergy* is published by Whitaker House under the title *You Will Receive Power,* which also contains excerpts from letters written by William Law. Excerpts from *The Spirit of Love* and *The Spirit of Prayer* are published in the Whitaker House book *God's Power in You.*

hearing or understanding religious truth, unless we also have an entire denial of the world and a real death to self. It is only then that the Holy Spirit can do His blessed work. Only then can the Spirit reveal Christ, not to the mind, but as an inborn life dwelling in the heart and proving its truth by nothing less than a life that shares in the mind of Christ. Take heed of this loving counsel. When you read a page of this book each day, do not be content with having read it and with being satisfied that you know what it contains and what it means. You must do more than this. Take some of the words or expressions; take them into the heart, and meditate on them. Bring them in prayer to God, and yield yourself, in simple dependence and full obedience to the Holy Spirit, in the assurance that He will make the truth a living reality and a true blessing.

My humble, loving prayer is that God may teach His church and every reader the threefold blessing of the power of the Spirit of God, of the spirit of love, and of the spirit of prayer.

A PRAYER

“O heavenly Father, infinite, fathomless depth of never ceasing Love, save me from myself, from the disorderly workings of my fallen, long corrupted nature, and let my eyes see, let my heart and spirit feel and find, my salvation in Christ Jesus.

“O God, who made me for Yourself to show forth Your goodness in me, I humbly pray that You will manifest the life-giving power of Your holy nature within me. Help me to such a true and living faith in You, such strength of hunger and thirst after the life, birth, and spirit of Your Son Jesus in my soul, that all that is within me may be turned from every thought or action that is not of You and Your heavenly working in my soul. Amen.”

—WILLIAM LAW

THE ONE ESSENTIAL THING

An Humble, Earnest, and Affectionate Address to the Clergy was the dying legacy of William Law to the church. He had corrected the proofs of the greater part when he was taken away. In this book, Law invited all church leaders to consider the one thing that is essential, and the only thing that is available, for us to rise out of our fallen state and become as we were at our creation—the holy offspring of God and real partakers of the divine nature.

"What is this one thing? It is the renewal of the original life and power of the Spirit of God in us. Everything else, no matter what it is—however glorious and divine in outward appearance, even if it is part of the church—is dead and helpless unless it has the Spirit of God breathing and living in it.

"Everything written in the Bible was written only to call us back from the spirit of Satan, the flesh, and the world, to be again fully dependent upon and obedient to the Spirit of God. Out of love and thirst for our souls, the Holy Spirit seeks to have His original power of life in us. Delight in whatever passage of Scripture you can find, and your delight will be nothing unless it has strengthened your union with and dependence upon Him. For when delight in matters of Scripture is a delight that is merely human, it is only the self-love of fallen man. It can have no better nature than this until it proceeds from the inspiration of God, awakening His own life and nature within us, which alone can bring forth a godly love in us.

"Because it is an immutable truth that *'no one can say that Jesus is Lord except by the Holy Spirit'* (1 Cor. 12:3), it must be an equally immutable truth that no one can have a Christlike mind or the power of goodness unless he is led and governed by the Holy Spirit."

Let us remember that it is of little profit to know the meaning of what we read; the great question is whether we have taken the instruction to heart. Do we indeed believe that the one essential thing for the church and ourselves is that the Holy Spirit should have the place in us that He had in Adam before the Fall? God's one desire is that the direct work of the Spirit of God will be the only thing that gives value to our religion.

OUR TOTAL DEPENDENCE ON GOD ALONE

❧

"All that is called divine goodness and virtue in us is nothing but the goodness of God manifesting itself according to how our created nature is able to receive it. This is the unalterable relationship between the Creator and the creature. Forever and ever, goodness can only belong to God. It is as essential to Him and inseparable from Him as His own unity.

"All that is divine, great, and glorious in us is only a reflection of the greatness, glory, majesty, and blessedness of God dwelling in us and giving forth His own triune life, light, and love. As much as we are able to receive these things, we may infallibly see the true ground and nature of all true faith, including when and how we may fulfill all our duties to God. Man's true religion is in rendering to God all that is God's, and in continually acknowledging that everything he is, has, and enjoys is from God.

"The one relationship that is the ground of all true religion and is the same between God and all intelligent creatures is a total and unalterable dependence upon God; it is continually receiving directly from God every kind and degree of goodness, blessing, and happiness that ever could be found.

"The angels are ever abiding flames of pure love, always ascending up to and uniting with God, because the wisdom, power, glory, majesty, love, and goodness of God alone are all that they see and know. Their adoration never ceases because they never cease to acknowledge the *all* of God—the entirety of God in the whole creation. This is the one religion of heaven, and nothing else is the truth of religion on earth.

"The benefit that we receive from faith is the power and presence of God living and working in our beings. Because this is the unchangeable blessedness that may be gained from faith in God, we must receive all our religious goodness wholly and solely from God's direct operation in our hearts, just as Adam received all his goodness directly from God at his creation."

Ever Blessed Father, we thank You for the wonderful relationship with You for which You created us. And we thank You still more for the wonderful redemption that has restored us by the gift of the Holy Spirit into the blessed union and communion with Yourself, in which You will enable us always to live. We humbly pray that You will keep this thought in the hearts of Your people.

CONTINUAL INSPIRATION

✿

"All true religion is, or brings forth, an essential union and communion of the spirit of the creature with the Spirit of the Creator. God in us, and we in God—one life, one light, one love. Divine inspiration is inseparable from true religion.

"All that the natural or uninspired man does in the church has no more of the truth or power of divine worship in it than that which he does in the field or the shop through a desire for more money. Self-love, self-esteem, self-seeking, and living wholly to oneself are all that is or possibly can be in the natural man. No creature can be in a better or higher state than this until something supernatural is found in it, and this supernatural something is called the Word or Spirit or Inspiration of God. This alone can give man the first good thought about God. The Holy Spirit of God is the only force that can cause man to have more heavenly desires than fleshly ones.

"No one, therefore, can reach God with his love or have union with Him by it besides the person who is inspired by the one Spirit of love—the Spirit with which God loved Himself from all eternity, before there were any created beings. Infinite hosts of newly created heavenly beings could not begin any new kind of love for God, nor could they begin to love Him at all if His own Holy Spirit of love had not been brought to life in them.

"This love, with which God loved Himself from all eternity and which was then in God alone, is the only love in us that can draw us to God. We can have no power to cleave to Him, to will what He wills, or to adore the divine nature, except by partaking of that eternal Spirit of love.

"Therefore, the continual, direct inspiration or operation of the Holy Spirit is the only possible ground for our continual love for God."

Let us meditate and pray, until this blessed truth begins to take possession of our hearts. The direct, continual inspiration of God—our only power of goodness—is our birthright and must be our experience if we are to live out God's will. To an extent that we have very little realized, the Holy Spirit waits to fill our lives all day long with the love of God.

THE SPIRIT OF GOD IN ADAM

"Divine inspiration was indeed essential to man's first created state. The Spirit of the triune God, which breathed life into him, was the only force that made man a holy creature in the image and likeness of God. If he had not been like this at the very beginning—God in him and he in God, brought into the world as a true offspring of the Holy Spirit—no dispensation or revelation would have directed fallen man to the Holy Spirit. I sometimes wonder if there would have been any mention of the Spirit's inspiration in man.

"Consequently, it is clear that the gospel state is God's last dispensation and the finishing of man's redemption, because its whole work is a work of the Spirit of God in the spirit of man. All God's dispensations have been for the sake of that first godly and holy life that was born in the soul of the first man, Adam, and to which he died. Therefore, the direct inspiration of the Holy Spirit is as necessary to make fallen man alive again unto God as it was to create man as a living soul after the image and likeness of God.

"The necessity of continual inspiration from the Spirit of God, both to begin and to continue every step of the divine life in man, is a truth to which every life in nature, as well as all Scripture, bears full witness. No life can continue in the goodness of its first created or redeemed state except by continuing under the influence of the spirit that first created or redeemed it. Because we can do nothing without Christ, we should expect, believe in, wait for, and depend upon His continual, direct operation in everything that we do."

Let us pause to consider how little this direct, continual inspiration of the Holy Spirit in the heart of God's child is believed or accepted. And let us, from the very beginning of our readings, make this the one object of our desires and prayers: the full experience of what the Holy Spirit is meant to be to us.

THE MINISTRATION OF THE SPIRIT

"All natural life can subsist only when it is directly and continually under the working power of the root or source from which it sprang. Hence, nothing but obedience to the Spirit, trusting in the Spirit, walking in the Spirit, praying with and for His continual inspiration, can possibly keep either men or churches from being sinners or idolaters in all that they do. The truth and perfection of the Gospel could not be shown until it became solely a ministration of the Spirit, or a kingdom in which the Holy Spirit of God could be credited for all that was done in it.

"When Christ said to His disciples, *'I tell you the truth. It is to your advantage that I go away'* (John 16:7), He taught them to believe in and joyfully expect the coming of a higher and more blessed state than that of His bodily presence with them. They could not have the Holy Spirit as their Guide until Christ's outward teaching was changed into the inspiration and operation of His Spirit in their souls.

"Here, two fundamental truths are fully demonstrated. First, the perfection of the Gospel could not take place until Christ had been glorified and His kingdom among men had been made a continual, direct ministration of the Spirit. This last dispensation carried man into the real possession and enjoyment of a divine life.

"The second truth is that no man can have any true and real knowledge of the spiritual blessings of redemption except by the divine Spirit opening all the mysteries of a redeeming Christ. It was the same with the apostles, evangelists, and first ministers of the Gospel; and it is so from the beginning of their lifetimes to the end of the world. No man can have a divine call or a capacity to preach and bear witness of such spiritual blessings to the world unless the Holy Spirit first ministers to his heart."

Let us confess how much we have thought of the working of the Spirit as an occasional thing, meant only for certain times or duties. It will be no easy thing for us to be delivered from this thought and to yield ourselves wholly to the great truth that the direct and continual inspiration of the Holy Spirit is what is absolutely needed, is promised by God, and is made possible to us. Let us make this the one aim of our desires and prayers.

OUR DEATH AND LIFE IN CHRIST

🙷

"The apostles were eyewitnesses to the whole life and ministry of Christ. Why, then, with their human understanding, could they not declare and testify the truth of such things until they were baptized *'with the Holy Spirit and fire'* (Luke 3:16)? Because the truth and the mysteries of Christ's life and His redeeming act, as they may be known by man, are the very things that are accomplished by this heavenly fire and Spirit of God in our souls.

"Therefore, every natural man, no matter who he is or how educated he is, is an entire stranger to all the mysteries of gospel redemption. He can only talk about them as he would of any other tale he has been told, until the mystery of a redeeming Christ is brought forth, verified, fulfilled, and witnessed in him by the Holy Spirit being reborn in his soul.

"Redemption is entirely an inward, spiritual work. It works by altering, changing, and regenerating the life of the soul, bringing forth a spiritual death of the old and a spiritual birth of the new. Thus, no one can know or believe the mysteries of Christ's redeeming power without inwardly finding and experiencing the operation of those mysteries by the new death and the new life, both of which must be brought about in the soul of man. Otherwise, Christ cannot be found and known by the soul as its salvation.

"Our salvation is in the life of Jesus Christ in us. This truth of truths, fully possessed and firmly adhered to, turns the whole faith of man to a Christ who can be a Savior to him only in the inmost part of his being. It is not possible for Christ to be born within man by any other means than the direct inspiration and working power of the Holy Spirit.

"Only to this spiritually reborn man do the words of Christ and His apostles fall like a fire into him. What do these words kindle there? A holy flame of love to be always with Christ and His Holy Spirit. This alone can cause a man to be and to do all that the words of Christ and His apostles have taught. For there is no possibility of being like-minded with Christ in anything that He taught, or having the truth of even a single Christian virtue, unless the nature and Spirit of Christ become alive in your soul."

We need to remember that the great work of the Holy Spirit is to reveal Christ in us, not as a matter of knowledge in the mind, but in the heart, communicating to us the death and life of our Lord. In this way, Christ is formed in us, lives in us, and works in us all that is pleasing to the Father. Take time to yield yourself to this blessed truth; in it lies the true secret of the Christian life.

HUMILITY

After writing the preceding material, from which I have taken excerpts, William Law went on to prove how in the church of Christ, the gifts of human learning and wisdom soon took the place of entire dependence upon the Holy Spirit, of which Christ had spoken. As a natural consequence, self was exalted, and the whole difference became the question between pride, in the power of human learning and wisdom, and humility, in the absolute dependence on the teaching of the Holy Spirit.

"In order to know this as the truth, you need to know these two things: first, that our salvation consists wholly in being saved from ourselves, or from what we are by nature; and, secondly, that this salvation is only manifested in us by the sort of godly humility that is beyond all expression. Hence, the first unalterable condition of salvation to fallen man is this, as spoken by the one and only Savior: *'If anyone comes to Me and does not hate his father and mother, wife and children, brothers and sisters, yes, and his own life also, he cannot be My disciple'* (Luke 14:26). To show that this is only the beginning of and the foundation for man's salvation, the Savior added, *'Learn of me; for I am meek and lowly in heart'* (Matt. 11:29 KJV).

"What light is here for those who can bear it; what light for those who love the light! Self is the whole evil of our fallen nature, but self-denial is our capacity for being saved; humility is our savior.

"All the vices of fallen angels and men originate with the pride of self. In other words, all our vices get their power from the atheism and idolatry of self, for self is indeed both an atheist and an idolater. It is an atheist because it has rejected God, and it is an idolater because it is its own idol. On the other hand, all the virtues of the heavenly life are the virtues of humility. There is not a joy or glory or praise in heaven that does not come out of humility. It is humility alone that can traverse the otherwise unpassable gulf between heaven and hell. The plainest and most vital truth of the Gospel is that there is only one true humility in the whole world, and that is the humility of Christ."

In the life of faith, humility has a far deeper place than we think. Not only is it a great virtue, but it is also the first and chief need of the soul. It leads us to know our absolute and entire powerlessness to do any good of ourselves. It leads us to look to the humility of our Lord Jesus—the same humility that He has prepared for us and will most surely work in us in response to our faith.

THE KINGDOM OF HEAVEN

🦋

"The light and Spirit that were from all eternity, before angels or any heavenly beings were created, must to all eternity be the light and Spirit by which angels and men can ever have any union or communion with God. What, therefore, can have the least share of power in man's redemption, besides the light and Spirit of God being born again in him as they were in his first glorious creation?

"Our Lord affirmed the gospel state to be the kingdom of heaven at hand, or the kingdom of heaven that has come among men. This kingdom has the nature of no worldly thing or creaturely power, receives nothing from man except the full denial of himself, and has no existence except in the working power of God that created and upholds heaven and earth. It is a kingdom of a God who became man, and a kingdom of men united to God through direct and continual divine illumination. Is there any Scripture of the New Testament that does not prove this to be the gospel state—a kingdom of God into which no one can enter unless he is born of the Spirit? The Scriptures affirm that no one can continue to be alive unless he is led by the Spirit. And no thought, desire, or action can have any part in the gospel state unless it is a fruit of the Spirit.

"*Your kingdom come. Your will be done on earth as it is in heaven*' (Matt. 6:10). God's kingdom in heaven is the manifestation of what God is and what He does in His heavenly creatures. His will is done there because His Holy Spirit is the life, the power, and the mover of everything that lives in heaven. We may recite the Lord's Prayer every day, and yet, for the sake of 'orthodoxy,' we may preach and write against all that is prayed for in it. For nothing but a continual, direct, divine illumination can do what we pray will be done. God's kingdom comes where every other power besides His is at an end and has been driven out. His will can only be done where the Spirit that wills in God also wills in the creature.

"This is the truth of the kingdom of God that has come unto men. The birthright privilege of all who are living members of it is deliverance from the nature that they received from Adam, from the spirit and wisdom of this world. Through the whole course of their lives, they may now say and do and be all that the Spirit of their Father works in them."

Much has been written about what the kingdom of heaven means, but here we have what it really is. As God rules in His kingdom in heaven, so He lives and rules in us when the kingdom comes into our hearts. The kingdom of God consists of the men in whom God rules as He does in heaven.

THE NATURE OF LOVE

🐌

"The spirit of love originates in God's eternal will, which only desires all goodness. God considers this eternal will in His holy being before anything is brought forth by Him or out of Him. He is the one eternal, immutable God, who does not change from eternity to eternity, who can desire neither more nor less nor anything else than all the goodness that is in Himself and can come from Him. The creation of worlds or systems of creatures adds nothing to and takes nothing from this immutable God. He always was and always will be the same immutable Will for all goodness. As certainly as He is the Creator, He is the One who blesses every created thing and can give forth nothing but blessing, goodness, and happiness because He has nothing else to give.

"Now this is the basis for and origin of the spirit of love in created beings. It is and must be a desire for all goodness, and you do not have the spirit of love until you have this desire for all goodness at all times and on all occasions. You may indeed do many works of love, and delight in them, especially when they are not inconvenient to you or contradictory to your condition, mood, or circumstances in life. But the spirit of love is not in you until it is the spirit of your life, until you live freely, willingly, and universally according to it. This spirit knows no difference of time, place, or persons; but, whether it gives or forgives, suffers or escapes suffering, it is equally doing its own delightful work, equally blessed in and of itself. For the spirit of love, wherever it is, is its own blessing and happiness because it is the truth and reality of God in the soul. Love has no ulterior motives and desires nothing but its own enrichment, so everything is like oil to its flame. The spirit of love does not want to be rewarded, honored, or esteemed. Its only desire is to propagate itself and to become the blessing and happiness of everyone who lacks it. Therefore, it meets wrath and evil and hatred and opposition with the same one will as the light meets the darkness—only to overcome any opposition with all of its blessings. The infinitely perfect and happy God is entirely love, an unchangeable Will toward all goodness. Therefore, every creature must be corrupt and unhappy as far as it is led by any other will than the one Will to all goodness."

May God teach us that as glorious and holy as His love is to us, so is the love with which He promises by His Holy Spirit to fill our hearts.

THE NECESSITY OF LOVE

"The necessity of this spirit is absolute and unchangeable. No one can be a child of God unless the goodness of God is in him, and he cannot have any union or communion with the goodness of God until his life is a spirit of love. This is the only bond of union between God and man. Since God unchangeably desires all goodness, the divine will cannot unite or work with any human will unless it desires with Him only what is good. Since the desire for all goodness is the whole nature of God, it must be the whole nature of every service or religion that can be acceptable to Him. For nothing serves God or worships and adores Him except what wills and works with Him. God can delight in nothing except His own will and His own Spirit, because all goodness is included in it and can be nowhere else. Therefore, everyone who follows his own will or his own spirit forsakes the one Will to all goodness, and while he does so, he has no capacity for the light and Spirit of God.

"The spirit of love, therefore, is such a necessity that God cannot exempt any of His created beings from it any more than He can deny Himself or act contrary to His own holy being. But since it was His desire for all goodness that brought forth the angels and the spirits of men, He can will nothing for their lives but that they should live and work and manifest the same spirit of love and goodness that brought them into being.

"There is no peace, and there never can be peace, for the soul of man except in the purity and perfection of his first created nature. He cannot have his purity and perfection in any other way than in and by the spirit of love. For since God who created all things is love (1 John 4:16), love is the purity, the perfection, and the blessing of all created things. No one can live in God unless he lives in love. Love alone, then, is the cure of every evil. Whoever lives in the purity of love has risen out of the power of evil into the freedom of the one Spirit in heaven."

Let us take time to ponder this blessed truth and promise, that the God and Father of all love is longing to fill the hearts of His children with nothing less than His own divine, eternal love!

LOVE: A NEW BIRTH FROM ABOVE

❧

"This spirit of love, which I have been talking about, is the most delightful subject in the world. I am writing all this to help us rejoice in that Deity who is so worthy of adoration. His infinite being is an infinity of love and love alone, a never-beginning, never-ceasing, forever-overflowing ocean of meekness, sweetness, delight, blessing, goodness, patience, and mercy. All this is like many blessed streams breaking out of the abyss of universal love: Father, Son, and Holy Spirit, a triune infinity of love and goodness, forever giving forth nothing but the same gifts of light and love, blessing and joy to both angels and men, whether before or after the Fall.

"You can know as a certain truth that no good can come into your soul except by its being born from above, from the entrance of the Deity into the properties of your own soul. Nature must be set right; it must enter into the process of a new birth, and it must work for the production of light before the spirit of love can be born in it. For love is delight, and delight cannot arise in any soul until it is in a delightful state or one in which it must rejoice.

"This is the reason why God had to become man. It is because a new birth of Deity must be found in the soul, giving to nature all that it needs. Otherwise, the soul can never find itself in a delightful state and in a state in which it can work with the spirit of love.

"And now you see the absolute necessity of the gospel doctrine of the cross, that is, of dying to self as the only way to life in God. This is the needed response to the spirit of love. This cross, or dying to self, is the one moral principle that does man any good. Therefore, the one work of true morality is the one doctrine of the cross, that is, to resist and deny nature so that a supernatural power leading to divine goodness may take possession of it and bring a new light into it.

"Goodness is only a sound, and virtue is a mere struggle of natural passions, until the spirit of love is the breath of everything that lives and moves in the heart. For love is the one and only blessing, goodness, and God of nature. You have no true religion and you are no worshipper of the one true God unless the spirit of love that is God Himself is living and working in you."

Let us bow in deep humility to adore God for this wonderful love, and let us ask for grace to yield ourselves completely to the denial and the death of self.

THE TWOFOLD LIFE

❧

"No intelligent creature, whether angel or man, can be good and happy except by partaking of a twofold life. It is an absolute necessity that everyone who wants to be good and happy has this twofold life. The twofold life is the following: man must have in himself the life of nature and the life of God who created him. Man needs to see himself as a creature of various capabilities who has the powers of understanding, willing, and desiring. This is his creaturely life, which, by the creating power of God, he has because he is human. God Himself cannot make man through man's nature to be anything else but a state of emptiness, want, and appetite. Therefore, the highest life that is still natural and creaturely can have no more than only a bare capacity for goodness and happiness. This life cannot possibly be good and happy unless the life of God dwells in it and has union with it.

"There can be no goodness and happiness for any intelligent creature, except in this twofold life; therefore, the union of the divine and human life, or the Son of God incarnate in man to make man once again a partaker of the divine nature, is the one possible salvation for all the sons of fallen Adam, that is, of Adam dead to or fallen from his first union with the divine life.

"This is all clear proof that there can be no happiness, blessing, or goodness for any creature in heaven or on earth except by having, as the Gospel says, Jesus Christ made unto him wisdom, righteousness, sanctification, and peace with God (1 Cor. 1:30). The reason is that goodness and happiness are absolutely inseparable from God, and they can be nowhere except in God.

"This clearly gives the solid distinction between inward holiness and all outward, creaturely practices. All that God has done for man by any particular dispensations, whether by the law or the prophets, by the Scriptures or the ordinances of the church, are only aids to a holiness that they cannot supply in and of themselves. Such things are only suited to the death and darkness of the earthly, creaturely life, to turn man from himself, from his own workings, and to awaken in man a faith and hope, a hunger and thirst, after that first union with the Deity's life that was lost in the fall of the first father of mankind."

May God bring us to know fully that, because goodness and happiness are absolutely inseparable from God, our only hope is to be found in unceasing fellowship with Him and His love. Let this be our one desire and continual prayer—the life and the love of God dwelling in our hearts.

PERPETUAL INSPIRATION

"It is quite unreasonable to call those who are perpetually inspired through the twofold life 'fanatics,' because the only true goodness or happiness that can be in any intelligent being is merely and truly the breath, the life, and the operation of God. If goodness can only be in God; if it cannot exist separately from Him; if He can only bless and sanctify not by a creaturely gift, but by Himself becoming man's blessing and sanctification, then it is the highest degree of blindness to look for any goodness and happiness from anything except the direct indwelling, union, and operation of God in man's life. Perpetual inspiration, therefore, is as necessary in man's nature for a life of goodness, holiness, and happiness, as the perpetual respiration of air is necessary to physical life.

"It is a mistake, therefore, to confine spiritual inspiration to particular times and occasions, as only being for prophets or apostles, when the common Christian depends on being continually led and inspired by the Spirit of God. Even though all are not called to be prophets or apostles, all are called to be holy as He who has called them is holy (Lev. 11:44), to be perfect as their heavenly Father is perfect (Matt. 5:48), and to be like-minded with Christ (Phil. 2:5). All Christians are to desire only as God desires, to do everything to His honor and glory, to renounce the spirit of this world, and to love God with all their hearts, souls, and spirits, and their neighbors as themselves (Matt. 22:37, 39).

"When we look at a work as great, divine, and supernatural as that of a prophet and an apostle, we must remember that the holiness of a common Christian is not an occasional thing that begins and ends or is only for a particular time, place, or action. Rather, it is the holiness of what is always alive and stirring in us, namely, of our thoughts, wills, desires, and holy inclinations. If we are all called to this inward holiness and goodness, then a perpetual, ever existing operation of the Spirit of God within us is absolutely necessary. If our thoughts and inclinations are to be holy and good always, then the holy and good Spirit of God should always be operating as a principle of life within us."

Ever blessed God and Father, we pray that You will reveal to us in power this blessed truth, that the direct and continual leading and working of Your Holy Spirit is indeed what You long to give and what we may confidently claim.

TWO KINDS OF KNOWLEDGE

🕉

"Every kind of virtue and goodness may be brought into us by two different ways. They may be taught to us outwardly by men, by rules and precepts; they may also be inwardly born in us, as the genuine birth of our own renewed spirits. In the former way, as we learn them from men by rules and documents of instruction, they at best only change our outward behavior and leave our hearts in their natural states. This way of learning and attaining goodness, though thus imperfect, is absolutely necessary and must have its time, place, and work in us.

"Yet this is only for a time, just as the law was our schoolmaster to bring us to the Gospel (Gal. 3:24). But it must be said of all this outward instruction, whether from good men or the letter of Scripture, what the apostle said of the law: that it *"made nothing perfect"* (Heb. 7:19) and yet is highly necessary in order for perfection to come about. All Scriptures have had no other good in them except to lead and direct us to a salvation that is not to be had in the Scriptures themselves but from faith in Christ Jesus. Their teaching is meant only to teach us where to seek and find the Fountain and Source of all light and knowledge. Such things can only direct us to something that is better than themselves, that can be the true light, life, spirit, and power of holiness in us.

"From this twofold teaching, there necessarily arises a twofold state of virtue and goodness. If you learn virtue and goodness only from outward means, from men or books, you may be virtuous and good according to outward forms. You may do works of humility, works of love and benevolence, use times and forms of prayer; all this virtue and goodness is suitable to this kind of teaching and may very well be gained from it. But the spirit of prayer, the spirit of love, and the spirit of humility, or of any other virtue, are only to be attained by the operation of the light and Spirit of God, not outwardly teaching but inwardly bringing forth a newborn spirit within us."

Alas, how much there is in the church of the outward teaching with its intermittent states of goodness! Let us with our whole hearts believe in the direct teaching and working of the Holy Spirit that brings the life of heaven as a newly born spirit within us.

THE MONSTER OF SELF

"Until this birth of the spirit of divine love is found in you, you cannot know what divine love is. Divine love is perfect peace and joy, a freedom from all disquiet, making everything to rejoice in it. It is the Christ of God, and wherever it comes, it comes as the blessing and happiness of every natural life; as the restorer of every lost perfection; a redeemer from all evil; a fulfiller of all righteousness; and a *'peace of God, which surpasses all understanding'* (Phil. 4:7).

"When the intelligent creature turns from God to self or nature, he finds nature only as it is in itself and without God. Nothing is to be gained from it or found in it except the work of every kind of evil. Covetousness, envy, pride, and wrath are the four elements of self, nature, or hell; all of them are inseparable from self. If we were truly affected by things and recognized their inherent good or evil, we would be much more afraid of having the serpents of covetousness, envy, pride, and wrath well nourished and kept alive in us than of being cast into a dungeon full of venomous beasts. This monster of self can hide under all forms of goodness, can watch and fast, can pray much and preach long, and he often gets more life and strength and a more permanent place of residence through these forms of virtue than he has through more obvious forms of sin.

"To die to self or to come from under its power cannot be done by any active resistance that we can make to it by the powers of nature. The one true way of dying to self is most simple and plain; it is equally practicable by everybody, and it is always at hand. It meets you in everything and is never without success. If you ask what this one true, simple, plain, immediate, and unerring way is, it is the way of patience, meekness, humility, and yieldedness to God. This is the truth and perfection of dying to self."

There is not a more difficult lesson in the Christian life than to attain a true knowledge of self. Its terrible power, its secret and universal rule, and the blinding influence it exerts in keeping us from the knowledge of what it is, are the causes of all our sin and evil. This is why so few really believe in their absolute powerlessness to obey God or to believe in His love. And there is nothing that can deliver us from it except an entire willingness to die to self, which comes when by faith we understand that we died in Christ Jesus. It is this alone that can make us partakers, through faith and the Holy Spirit, of the meekness and humility that gave Christ's death its worth and its beauty in the sight of the Father.

DYING TO SELF

🐜

"Many wonder how these virtues—patience, meekness, humility, and yieldedness to God—will prove that the way of overcoming self is so simple, plain, and immediate. This is because the doctrine of almost all men is that a great length of time and effort and a variety of methods are necessary and scarcely sufficient in order to attain any one of these four virtues. When I refer you to patience, meekness, humility, and yieldedness to God as the one simple, plain, immediate, and unerring way of dying to self or being saved from it, it is because you can have all the benefits of these virtues as easily and immediately, without plan or method, as the tax collectors and sinners could turn to Christ and be saved. You have only to turn your faith to Christ, and you will die to self and be saved from it. The reason why you or anyone else is vainly endeavoring for a long time and hardly ever attaining these first-rate virtues is that you seek them in the way they are not to be found. You seek them in the multiplicity of human rules, methods, and contrivances, and not in the simplicity of faith in which those who applied to Christ immediately obtained what they asked of Him.

"*'Come to Me, all you who labor and are heavy laden, and I will give you rest'* (Matt. 11:28). How short, simple, and certain a way to peace and comfort from the misery and burden of sin! What will now become of your rules and methods and roundabout ways to be delivered from self and the power of sin and to find the redeeming power and virtue of Christ? It would be foolish to suppose that Christ, after having finished His great work, overcome death, and ascended into heaven with all power in heaven and on earth, has become less of a Savior and gives less certain and immediate help to those who by faith turn to Him now than when He was clothed with the infirmity of our flesh and blood upon earth.

"You may then ask, 'Will turning in faith and desire toward patience, meekness, humility, and yieldedness to God do as fully for me now all that faith in Christ did for those who became His disciples?'

"When I exhort you to give yourself up, in faith and hope, to patience, meekness, humility, and yieldedness to God, what else do I do but turn you directly to so much faith and hope in the true Lamb of God? If I ask you what the Lamb of God is and means, you must tell me that He is and means the perfection of patience, meekness, humility, and yieldedness to God. Consequently, you must also say that every sincere wish and desire, every inward inclination of your heart that presses after these virtues and longs to be governed by them, is an immediate, direct application to Christ, is worshipping and falling down before Him, is giving up yourself unto Him and the very perfection of faith in Him."

We too often think of faith in Christ only in connection with the work He did for us on the cross. But its meaning is far larger and richer. It is by faith that we can claim all the grace that was in Him, along with the mind that was in Him, and receive these through the Spirit as ours. Faith then becomes the daily exercise by which the virtues and the graces that are in Christ can become ours. And so we receive the mind of Christ.

OF FAITH IN CHRIST

"In the words of Christ—*'Learn from Me, for I am gentle and lowly in heart, and you will find rest for your souls'* (Matt. 11:29)—the plain truth is fully asserted of what it means to give yourselves up in faith. First of all, to be given up to, or to strongly desire patience, meekness, humility, and yieldedness to God, is strictly the same thing as to learn from Christ or to have faith in Him. The inclination of your heart to these virtues is truly giving up all that you are and all that you have from fallen Adam. It is perfectly leaving all that you have to follow and be with Christ; it is your highest act of faith in Him. Therefore, all the good and blessing, pardon and deliverance from sin that ever happened to anyone from any degree of faith and hope in Christ are sure to come from this state of heart that continually turns to Him in a hunger and desire for being led and governed by His spirit of patience, meekness, humility, and yieldedness to God.

"While you shut yourself up in patience, meekness, humility, and yieldedness to God, you are in the very arms of Christ. Your whole heart is His dwelling place, and He lives and works in you. When these heavenly inclinations live and abide in you as the spirit and aim of your life, then Christ is truly in you, and the life that you then lead is not yours but Christ's, who lives in you (Gal. 2:20). The spirit of divine love can have no possibility of existing in any fallen man until he desires and chooses to be dead to all self in a patient, meek, humble resignation to the good power and mercy of God. When your own impatience, wrath, pride, and unyieldedness attack you, stand turned toward this patient, humble resignation, and give yourself up to be helped by the mercy of God. And be assured of this as a most certain truth: we have the divine operation within us to the degree to which our faith, hope, trust, and dependence upon God are in us.

"These are short but full points of true faith that carry salvation along with them, that make a true and full offering of our whole natures to the divine operation, and that make a true and full confession of the Holy Trinity in unity."

Let your one thought be, "It is now the whole aim of my soul to seek my salvation only through the mediation of the meek, humble, patient, resigned Lamb of God, who alone has power to bring forth the blessed birth of these heavenly virtues in my soul."

THE LAMB OF GOD

"The Lamb of God is the eternal love and meekness who left the bosom of His Father to be the resurrection of meekness and love in all the darkened, wrathful souls of fallen men. What a comfort it is to think that this Lamb of God, the Son of the Father, the Light of the world, who is the glory of heaven and the joy of angels, is as near to us and as truly in the midst of us as He is in the midst of heaven.

"Oh, sweet resignation of myself to God—happy death of every selfish desire, blessed unction of a holy life, the only driver of all evil out of my soul—be my guide and governor wherever I go! Nothing but this can take me from myself; nothing but this can lead me to God. Hell has no power where such resignation is, and heaven cannot hide from it. Oh, may I never indulge a thought, bring forth a word, or do anything for myself or others but under the influence of this blessed inspiration! The sight of this Sabbath of the soul, freed from the miserable labor of self, to rest in meekness, humility, patience, and yieldedness under the Spirit of God is like the joyful voice of the Bridegroom to my soul, and it leaves no wish in me but to be at the Marriage Supper of the Lamb.

"The marriage feast signifies the entrance into the highest state of union that can be between God and the soul in this life. Or, in other words, it is the birthday of the spirit of love in our souls. When this happens, the spirit of love will fill our souls with such peace and joy in God as will blot out the remembrance of everything that we once called peace or joy.

"If you ever go aside from the path of meekness, humiliation, and patience, even if the occasion may seem ever so glorious, or the effects ever so wonderful to you, it is only preparing for yourself a harder death. For you must die to everything that you have done under any other spirit except that of the meekness of the Lamb. As the Lamb of God, He has all power to bring forth in us an awareness and a weariness of our own wrathful state and a willingness to fall from it into His meekness and humility."

Let us listen to the blessed Lamb of God as He calls us: *"Learn from Me, for I am gentle and lowly in heart"* (Matt. 11:29). It was for His humility that God so highly exalted Him (Phil. 2:5–11). Only as our lives become the unceasing expression of a longing for His humility and meekness will we find rest for our souls.

PRAYER: THE KEY TO THE TREASURES OF HEAVEN

🕊

"Man has been sent into the world on no other errand except to rise out of the vanity of time into the riches of eternity. As poor and miserable as this life is, we have free access to all that is great and good, and we carry within ourselves a key to all the treasures that heaven has to bestow upon us.

"God, the only good of all intelligent natures, is not an absent or distant God, but is more present in and to our souls than our own bodies are. We are strangers to heaven, and we are without God in the world, because we are void of the spirit of prayer that alone can and never fails to unite us with the only good and that can open heaven and the kingdom of God within us. A root set in the finest soil, grown in the best climate, and blessed with all that sun and air and rain can do for it, is not as sure to grow to perfection as every man may be whose spirit aspires after all that God is ready to give to him. For the sun does not meet the springing bud that stretches toward him with half the certainty that God, the source of all good, communicates Himself to the soul that longs to partake of Him.

"All of us are the offspring of God by birth, more nearly related to Him than we are to one another, *'for in Him we live and move and have our being'* (Acts 17:28). The first man who was brought forth from God had the breath and spirit of the Father, Son, and Holy Spirit breathed into him, and so he became a living soul (Gen. 2:7). He was the image and likeness of God, not with regard to his outward shape or form—for no shape has any likeness to God—but he was in the image and likeness of God because the Holy Trinity had breathed their own nature and spirit into him. And as the Deity—Father, Son, and Holy Spirit—is always in heaven and makes heaven to be everywhere, so this spirit, breathed into man, brought heaven into man along with it. Thus, man was in heaven, as well as on earth, that is, in Paradise, which signifies a heavenly state of life."

The lesson of the sun is one of the deepest truths of God's Word. As the sun is unceasingly willing to shine forth its light and warmth on the waiting earth, so is the living God waiting unceasingly to work in the hearts of His children. Or, rather, He is always working within us unless we hold Him back and hinder Him by our unbelief and our surrender to the spirit of the world. Oh, that we could learn to say every day, "As sure as the sun shines on this earth, my God is sending forth His light and His love into my heart for me to receive and to rejoice in!"

THE GOODNESS OF GOD

🐚

"The goodness of God breaking forth into a desire to communicate good was the cause and the beginning of creation. Therefore, for all eternity, God can have no thought or intent toward His creation except to communicate good, because He made the creature for the sole purpose of receiving good. God must always desire for His creation what He desired at the creation of it. As the sun has only one nature and can give forth nothing but the blessings of light, so the holy triune God has only one nature and intent toward all creation, which is to pour forth the riches and sweetness of His divine perfections upon everything that is capable of receiving them, according to its capacity to receive them.

"This is the amiable nature of God: He is the good, the unchangeable, overflowing fountain of good, who sends forth nothing but good for all eternity. He is the love itself, the unmixed, immeasurable love, doing nothing except what comes from love, giving nothing except gifts of love to everything that He has made. And He requires nothing of all His creatures except the spirit and fruits of the love that brought them into being.

"Oh, how sweet is this contemplation of the height and depth of the riches of divine love! With what attraction it must draw every thoughtful man to return love for love to this overflowing fountain of boundless goodness! What charms there must be in the religion that makes us aware of our existence in, relation to, and dependence upon this ocean of divine love! Look closely at every part of our redemption, from Adam's first sin to the resurrection of the dead, and you will find nothing but successive mysteries of that first love that created angels and men. All the mysteries of the Gospel are only many marks and proofs of God's desiring to make His love triumph in the removal of sin and disorder from all nature and creation."

What journeys are undertaken to the heights in Switzerland where the sun gives its warmth best! Unfortunately, how rarely God's children understand that this is the one thing they need: to wait before God in quiet until His light shines upon them, into them, and through them. How little it is understood that unless we take time, time enough, with God for His light to shine into the depths of our hearts, it is futile for us to expect that His immeasurable love can enter our hearts and fill our lives. O Father, teach us, we pray, to believe in Your love, and not to rest until our hearts are filled with it!

THE KINGDOM OF SELF

🦚

"Man, by his fall, had fallen from a life in God into a life of self, into an animal life of self-love, self-glorification, and self-seeking in the poor, perishing enjoyments of this world. All sin, death, damnation, and hell are nothing else but this kingdom of self, or the various operations of self-love, self-glorification, and self-seeking, which separate the soul from God and end in eternal death and hell.

"On the Day of Pentecost, a new dispensation of God came forth, which on God's part was the operation of the Holy Spirit in gifts and graces upon the whole church. On man's part, it was the adoration of God in spirit and in truth. All this was done to make way for the direct and continual operation of God upon the soul. Then man, baptized with the Holy Spirit and born again from above, would absolutely renounce self and wholly give up his soul to the operation of God's Spirit. He would do so in order to use all the faculties of his mind and all the outward things of this world in a way that is enlightened, inspired, moved, and guided by the Holy Spirit.

"The kingdom of self is the fall of man or the great apostasy from the life of God in the soul. The kingdom of Christ is the Spirit and power of God dwelling and manifesting itself in the birth of a new inward man. When the call of God to repentance first arises in your soul, you are to be silent, passive, and humbly attentive to this newly risen light within you. You should do so by wholly stopping or disregarding the workings of your own will, reason, and judgment.

"Why is it so necessary, then, that we universally mortify and deny ourselves with regard to all our senses, appetites, tempers, passions, and judgments? Our own lives are to be hated. The reason for this is plain: there is nothing lovely in them. By thus knowing and acknowledging our own nothingness and incapacity for good except that of receiving it from God alone, self is wholly denied; its kingdom is destroyed.

"You now know to what you are daily to die and daily to live. Therefore, consider every day as lost unless it helps to forward both this death and this life in you. Casting yourself with a broken heart at the feet of divine mercy, desire nothing but that every moment of your life may be given to God, and pray from the bottom of your heart that the seed of eternity, the spark of life that had so long been smothered under earthly rubbish, might breathe and come to life in you."

Let us take hold of the central thought here: in order to make way for the direct and continual operation of God in our souls, we need, in the power of the Holy Spirit, to renounce self absolutely and yield our whole beings for God to dwell and work in. This universal mortification and self-denial is indispensable if God's redeeming love is to display its power and shed forth all its blessing. Let us cast ourselves with broken hearts at the feet of divine mercy, and let us desire nothing except that every moment of our lives may be given to God.

CONTINUAL SELF-DENIAL

🐝

"We are called to as real and total a death to the life of corrupt nature as that which Adam died in Paradise to the life of heaven. To the end of our earthly lives, every step we take, every inch of our road, is to be made up of denial and of dying to ourselves. Therefore, to think of anything but the continual, total denial of our earthly nature is to overlook the one thing on which all depends.

"You might rejoice in thinking, 'Now that I know these truths, I have found the pearl of great price' (Matt. 13:45–46). But remember, it is not yours until you sell all that you have in order to buy it. Self is all that you have; you have no good of your own. All this self is to be parted with before the pearl can be yours. Therefore, die to all your possession of self; all of it is to be given up. Self is a continual departure from God; it corrupts everything that it touches. All evil inclinations are born and nourished in self. Die to this self, to this inward nature, and all outward enemies will be overcome.

"This, my friend, is the true ground of all true religion: it means nothing, it intends nothing, but to overcome the earthly life that overcame Adam in the Fall. Therefore, you may see and know for certain that the one thing necessary for every fallen soul is to die to all the life that we have from this world. The Son of God calls us to die to this life and take up His cross. When the human soul turns from itself and turns to God, dies to itself and lives to God in the Spirit of Jesus, only then is it delivered from covetousness and the flesh, from a worldly spirit, from all self-interest and self-exaltation, and from all hatred and envy.

"To have any pretenses of being holy or religious, without totally dying to this old man, is building castles in the air. To think of being alive in God before we are dead to our own nature is as impossible as for a grain of wheat to be alive before it dies. The total dying to self is the only foundation for solid piety. Only in this way can the spiritual life begin at the true root, grow out of death, and be born in a heart that is broken off from all its own natural life."

Jesus could not be raised from the dead into the glory of the Father's right hand until He had died on the cross. This is the *"new and living way"* (Heb. 10:20) that He opened up through the torn veil of the flesh into the Holiest of All. And it is in this *"new and living way,"* with our flesh crucified and given over to death, that we can enter into the life and joy of God's presence here on earth. The continual denial of self is one of the secrets of the continual enjoyment of God's presence and power working in our hearts.

PRAYER: A STATE OF THE HEART

"Our Savior, though He had all wisdom, gave only a small number of moral teachings to mankind. This is because He knew that our malady lies in the fact that the will of our minds, the lust of our lives, is turned to this world, and nothing can set us right besides the turning of our minds and our hearts to God and the heaven that we lost. Hence, He calls us to nothing but a total denial of ourselves and the life of this world, and to a faith in Him as the Worker of a new birth and life in us. He teaches us every reason for renouncing ourselves and loving the whole nature of our redemption as the greatest joy and desire of our hearts.

"We see that all our religion is only the religion of the heart. We see with open eyes that a spirit of longing for the life of this world made us to be the poor pilgrims on earth that we are. Similarly, the spirit of prayer, or the desire of the heart for Christ and God and heaven, breaks all our bonds and raises us out of the miseries of time into the riches of eternity. Thus seeing and knowing our first state and our present one, everything calls us to prayer, and the desire of our hearts becomes the spirit of prayer. When the spirit of prayer is born in us, then prayer is no longer considered as only the business of this or that hour, but it is the continual breathing of the heart after God. The spirit of prayer, as a state of the heart, becomes the governing principle of the soul's life.

"An honest man may prove his honesty by actions. At other times, there is no special call to show his honesty. But in both situations, he possesses the same inward living principle. In the same way, the spirit of prayer may possess the heart without interruption, and yet at other times may have its specific hours of prayer. But its own life and spirit are vastly superior to, are independent of, and stay for no particular hours or forms of work."

It would be worthwhile to study the place that, according to William Law, the word *continual* ought to have in our lives. First, there is the continual streaming forth of the infinite love of God toward men. Then there is the continual, unalterable dependence upon God every hour of our lives. Then comes the continual receiving of goodness and happiness from God alone, followed by the continual mortification of our evil natures. Next is the continual and direct inspiration of the Holy Spirit, maintaining the life of Christ in us. Then is the continual breathing of the heart after God in prayer. Finally, we see the continual loving of Him with our whole hearts.

A WORLDLY SPIRIT

"From what has been said about the first state and fall of man, it plainly follows that the sin of all sin, or the heresy of all heresies, is a worldly spirit. We are apt to consider this only as an infirmity, but it is indeed the great apostasy from God and the divine life.

"Choose any life but the life of God and heaven, and you choose death; for death is nothing else but the loss of the life of God. The spirit of the soul is in itself nothing else but a spirit breathed forth from the life of God, for the sole purpose that the life of God, the nature of God, the working of God, and the inclinations of God might be manifested in it.

"Therefore, all the religion of fallen man, all the methods of our redemption, have only this one end: to take from us the strange and earthly life we have gotten by the Fall, and to kindle again the life of God and heaven in our souls. *'All that is in the world; the lust of the flesh, the lust of the eyes, and the pride of life; is not of the Father'* (1 John 2:16), is not the life that we had from God by creation, but is of this world, is brought into us by our fall from God into the life of this world. Therefore, a worldly spirit is not to be considered as a single sin, but as a state of real death to the kingdom of life and God in our souls.

"This is a certain truth: the heresy of all heresies is a worldly spirit. It is the whole nature and misery of our fall, and it keeps up the death of our souls. Of all things, therefore, detest the spirit of this world, or there is no help for you; you will live and die an utter stranger to all that is divine and heavenly, for a worldly, earthly spirit can know nothing of God. All real knowledge is life. We understand and know only as far as our lives reach, and no further. Everything beyond this is only our imagination amusing itself with the dead pictures of its own ideas."

When our Lord spoke of the world, its prince, and its spirit, He emphasized its hatred of Him and His church. His apostles, too, warned most earnestly against being conformed to the world: *"If anyone loves the world, the love of the Father is not in him"* (v. 15). We need to yield ourselves to the Holy Spirit from heaven in order to discover the evil and the danger of the spirit of the world, to give us the victory over it, and to fill us with the life of heaven.

OF THE DESPAIR OF SELF

"When the truth touches a man's heart, he feels that he cannot overcome the hardness of his heart and his pride by the force of his reason. Nature becomes its own torment and burden before it can willingly surrender to the death through which alone it can pass into life. There is no true conversion from the life of sin and death until a man knows and feels that nothing less than his whole nature is to be parted with, and yet finds in himself no possibility of doing it. This is the despair by which we lose all our own life to find a new one in God. Here, faith, hope, and true seeking of God and Christ are born. But until all is despair in ourselves, faith and hope and turning to God in prayer are only things practiced by rule and method; they are not born in us, are not living qualities of a new birth, until we no longer have any trust or confidence in ourselves.

"A man must feel that he is still within the reach of divine love, that God created him for Himself to be a habitation of His own life and Holy Spirit. In dealing with such souls, love must be our bait; it will put its hook into the heart and will force men to know that nothing is so strong, so irresistible, as divine love.

"What is God? His name is Love; He is the good, the perfection, the peace, the joy, the glory, and the blessing of every life. What is Christ? He is the universal remedy of all evil that has broken forth in nature and creatures. He is the unwearied compassion, the long-suffering pity, the never ceasing mercifulness of God to every need and weakness of human nature.

"Let us surround and encompass men with these flames of love until they become willing victims to their power. All religion is the spirit of love; all its gifts and graces are love; it has no breath, no life, besides the life of love. Love is heaven revealed in the soul; it is light and truth; it is infallible. Love is the Christ of God; it is the resurrection and life of every divine virtue, a fruitful mother of true humility, boundless benevolence, unwearied patience, and the center of compassion."

Let us seek above everything to believe that God is love and that He longs intensely to fill every heart with its blessedness. As the sun shines with the purpose of shedding its light and life on the earth, may we believe that the great God of love is shining upon us every moment of the day. If we will give Him time and patient waiting, this love will enter our hearts with all its gifts and graces and its unspeakable blessedness. We will be made willing to part utterly with self and to yield ourselves as a continual sacrifice to the God who loves us.

TRUE RELIGION

🦚

"Here we see once and for all what the true nature of religion is. Its work and effect is within; its glory, its life, and its perfection are all within. It is solely the raising of a new life, new love, and new birth in the inward spirit of our hearts. This was the spiritual nature of religion in its beginning, and this alone is its whole nature to the end of time. It is nothing else but the power, life, and Spirit of God, as Father, Son, and Holy Spirit, working, creating and reviving life in the fallen soul, and driving all its evil out of it. Religion is no true divine service, no proper worship of God, has no good in it, can do no good to man, can remove no evil out of him, can raise no divine life in him, but insofar as it serves, worships, conforms to, and gives itself up to this operation of the holy, triune God as living and dwelling in the soul.

"Keep close to this idea of religion as an inward spiritual life in the soul. Observe all its works within you, the death and life that are found there. Seek no good, no comfort, but in the inward awakening of all that is holy and heavenly in your heart. And then, inasmuch as you have this inward religion, so much you have of a real salvation. For salvation is nothing but a victory over nature. Insofar as you resist and renounce your own vain, selfish, and earthly nature; insofar as you overcome all your own natural inclinations of the old man; insofar as God enters into, lives in, and operates in you, He will be the light, the life, and the spirit of your soul, and you will be in Him the new creature that worships Him in spirit and in truth.

"All Scripture brings us to the conclusion that all religion is but a dead work unless it is the work of the Spirit of God. All our sacraments, prayers, singing, preaching, and hearing are only so many ways of being fervent in the spirit and of giving up ourselves more and more to the inward working, enlightening, quickening, sanctifying Spirit of God within us—all so that a true, real, Christlike nature may be formed in us by the Spirit."

So much of religion consists of man's thoughts of what it should be. Let us seek to study what God considers as true religion. It is nothing less than that He Himself, by His Spirit, should live and work in us as the light and life of our souls. As we take these thoughts of God into our hearts, we will see that a continual depending upon Him, a continual receiving of His Holy Spirit, and a continual breathing of our hearts after Him, is the life of Christ in us. This is what will enable us to continually worship, pray, and work in His holy presence.

THE PRACTICE OF PRAYER

"The best instruction I can give you in preparation for the spirit of prayer is already fully given where the original perfection, the miserable fall, and the glorious redemption of man are set forth. It is the true knowledge of these great things that can do everything for you that human instruction can do. These things must fill you with a dislike of your present state, drive all earthly desires out of your soul, and create an earnest longing after man's first perfection. For you can only learn prayer by truly sensing and knowing what you are and what you should be, and by being filled with a continual desire for God, His life, and Holy Spirit. When you begin to pray, ask your heart what it desires, and have nothing in your prayer except what the state of your heart causes you to ask, say, or offer to God.

"The one and only infallible way to go safely through all the difficulties, trials, dryness, or opposition of our evil inclinations is this: to expect nothing from ourselves, but in everything to depend on God for relief. Take hold of this thought, and then no matter how much temptation or rebellion of nature you encounter, you will be led through all into a union with God. For the only thing that ever hurts us is an expectation of something when we should only expect that something from God. And it will continue to be this way until our minds are so changed that we fully see and know our inability to have any goodness of our own, just as we cannot have any life of our own. When we are happily brought to this conviction, the whole spirit of our minds becomes a true faith, hope, and trust in the sole operation of God's Spirit."

What a universal confession there is that we pray too little! How strange that our highest privilege—holding fellowship with God in prayer—is to so many a burden and a failure, and to so many more a matter of form without the power! Let us learn the lesson that the first step is to expect nothing from ourselves. And then we are to expect everything from God. These two thoughts lie at the root of all true prayer. Instead of our thoughts being centered on man, ourselves, and our needs, let them become centered on God in His glory and His love, and prayer will become a joy and a power. Then our trials will become our greatest blessings, because they compel us to wait on God.

A TOUCHSTONE OF TRUTH

"I will here give you an infallible touchstone that will bring you to the truth if you try it. It is this: retire from the world and all associations with it for one month; stop all the former workings of your heart and mind; and, with all the strength of your heart, spend as much of the month as you can in prayer to God. Offer it frequently on your knees; but, whether sitting, standing, or walking, be always inwardly longing and earnestly praying this one prayer to God: 'I pray that God, in His great goodness, would make known to me and take from my heart every bit of pride, whether it is from evil spirits or my own corrupt nature. I pray that He will awaken in me the deepest depth and truth of all the humility that can make me capable of His light and Holy Spirit.'

"Reject every thought that is contrary to wishing and praying in this manner from the bottom of your heart. Pray with the kind of truth and earnestness with which people in torment wish and pray to be delivered.

"The painful sense of what you are, kindled into an awareness of the light of God within you, is the fire and light from which your spirit of prayer proceeds. In its first kindling, nothing is found or felt except pain, wrath, and darkness, as is to be seen in the first kindling of every heat or fire. Therefore, your first prayer is nothing but a sense of penitence, self-condemnation, confession, and humility. It feels nothing but its own misery, and so is all humility.

"This prayer of humility is met by divine love. The mercifulness of God embraces it, and then its prayer is changed into songs and thanksgiving. When this state of fervor has done its work, has melted away all earthly passions and affections, and has left no inclination in the soul but to delight in God alone, then its prayer changes again.

"It now comes so near to God and has found such union with Him, that it does not so much pray as live in God. Its prayer is not any particular action; it is not confined to times, words, or place; but it is the work of the whole being who continually stands in fullness of faith, in purity of love, in absolute resignation to do and be what the Beloved pleases. This is the last state of the spirit of prayer and is its highest union with God in this life."

Prayer is not merely bringing certain requests to God. It is the highest revelation of our capacity for fellowship with God. It begins with the deep humility that knows that it is nothing and has no desire except to meet God in the fellowship of His love. Then it desires to live in absolute surrender to the Lord.

THE SPIRIT OF PRAYER

"The spirit of the soul is in itself nothing else but a spirit breathed forth from the life of God, for the sole purpose that the life, nature, working, and inclinations of God might be manifested in it.

"The spirit of prayer is a pressing forth of the soul out of this earthly life; it is a stretching with all its desires after the life of God; it is a leaving, as far as it can, all its own spirit, in order to receive a Spirit from above—to be one life, one love, one spirit with Christ in God. This prayer, which is an emptying of all its own natural desires and an opening of itself for the light and love of God to enter into it, is the prayer in the name of Christ to which nothing is denied. The love that God has for the soul—His eternal, never ceasing desire to enter into it, to dwell in it, and to open the birth of His Holy Word and Spirit in it—stays until the door of the heart opens for it. For nothing can keep God out of the soul, or hinder His holy union with it, except the heart that is turned away from Him.

"A will that is surrendered to worldliness is much like Nebuchadnezzar, who *'was driven from men and ate grass like oxen'* (Dan. 4:33). Such a will has the same life as the beasts of the field, for earthly desires maintain the same life in a man and an ox. It is suitable for earthly food to be only desired and used for the support of the earthly body; but when the desire, the delight, and the longing of the soul is set upon earthly things, then humanity is degraded, is fallen from God, and the life of the soul is made as earthly and animal as the life of the body."

Child of God, I pray that you will rise to a right conception of what it means that the eternal Father, by the Holy Spirit, breathes into us and is seeking to have His life, His nature, and His work revealed within us. In earthly things, we are not unwilling to make sacrifices for the objects of our desire. Will we not therefore begin, as never before, to make the knowledge, love, will, and pleasure of God the great purpose of our study and our efforts? God is waiting to bless us, to reveal Himself to us, to fill us with His life, to use us for His glory, if we will simply yield ourselves to the life of continual dependence and adoration. We will then prove how possible it is for a man to walk in the footsteps of Christ Jesus, living His life on earth every day in the love of the Father and to His glory.

THE PRAYER OF THE HEART

🙘

"Turning to God according to the inward desire of your own heart—in love, in trust, and in faith of having from Him all that you need and wish to have—this turning to God, whether it is with or without words, is the best form of prayer in the world. This is because prayers that are not formed according to the real state of your heart are like a prayer to be pulled out of a deep well when you are not in it.

"When the heart really pants and longs after God, its prayer is moved and animated by the Spirit of God; it is the breath or inspiration of God, stirring, moving, and opening itself in the heart. It is a certain truth that nothing ever did or can have the least desire or tendency to ascend to heaven except that which came down from heaven. Therefore, every time a good desire stirs in the heart, a good prayer goes out of it that reaches God as being the fruit and work of His Holy Spirit.

"When the heart stands continually in this state of wishing to have what may be expressed in just a few words, then the reality, the steadiness, and the continuity of the desire are the goodness and perfection of the prayer.

"You have already taken the first step in the spiritual life: you have devoted yourself absolutely to God, to live wholly to His will under the light and guidance of His Holy Spirit. Your next step is this: to continue this first resolution and donation of yourself to God. This second step cannot be taken except purely by prayer; nothing else has any power here but prayer—prayer of the heart, a prayer of your own, proceeding from the state of your heart and its tendency toward God. Look at this prayer of the heart; consider it an infallible guide to heaven. As a man who has some great worldly matter on his mind will ignore everything that is not related to it, so our hearts will maintain a state of prayer as soon as God is the great object or our hearts are wholly given up to Him as the one great good."

Our times of prayer are meant to lead us on to a life of prayer in which the heart will continually live and rejoice in God's presence, just as the eye rejoices all day in the sunshine that gives it light. Let us believe that God, *"who is able to do exceedingly abundantly above all that we ask or think"* (Eph. 3:20), is indeed able and willing by the power of His Holy Spirit to strengthen us for this life of unceasing prayer as we walk in the light of His countenance.

THE PROOF OF THE SPIRIT

❧

"The Holy Spirit of God is as necessary to our spiritual lives as the air of this world is necessary to our physical lives. It is as distinct from us as the air of this world is distinct from the creatures that live in it. And yet our own good spirits are the Spirit of God moving and stirring in us—not God, but the Spirit of God breathed into a creaturely form. This good Spirit, divine in His origin and His nature, is the only thing in us that can reach God, unite with Him, and be moved and blessed by Him.

"You ask, 'How can I know when, and how far, I am led and governed by the Spirit of God?' Just as a man knows when he is hungry or pleased, the knowledge of the Spirit of God can be perceived. For the Spirit of God is more distinguishable from all other spirits than any of your natural emotions are from one another. Let me illustrate this.

"God is unwearied patience, a meekness that cannot be provoked. He is an ever enduring mercifulness; He is unmixed goodness and universal love. His delight is in the communication of Himself and His own happiness to everything according to its capacity. He is the good from which nothing but good comes, and He resists all evil only with goodness. This is the nature and Spirit of God, and here you have your infallible proof as to whether you are moved and led by the Spirit of God. If it is the earnest desire of your heart to be merciful as He is merciful, to be full of His unwearied patience, to dwell in His unalterable meekness; if you long to be like Him in universal, impartial love; if you desire to communicate every good to every creature as you are able, then you may be certain that the Spirit of God lives, dwells, and governs in you.

"Now, if you lack any of these qualities, if the whole bent of your heart and mind is not set upon them, then you cannot even pretend to have the direct inspiration and continual operation of the Spirit of God in your soul. Nothing is proof of the Spirit or the work of God in your soul except these virtues and the works that they produce. When you stay within these bounds, then, and not until then, you may safely say with John, *'By this we know that He abides in us, by the Spirit whom He has given us'* (1 John 3:24)."

Let us believe that the Spirit bears witness with our spirits and gives us the assurance of His own presence. To the person who yields himself in childlike trust and obedience, the knowledge will not be withheld that he is indeed led by God and is transformed from glory to glory as by the Spirit of the Lord.

A PRAYER

"O my God, with all the strength of my soul, assisted by Your grace, I desire and resolve to resist and deny all my own will, earthly tempers, selfish views and inclinations—everything that the spirit of this world and the vanity of fallen nature draws me to. I give myself up wholly and solely to You; to be all Yours; to have, do, and be, inwardly and outwardly, according to Your good pleasure. I desire to live for no other purpose than to accomplish the work that You require of me—a humble, obedient, faithful, thankful instrument in Your hands, to be used as You please."

—WILLIAM LAW

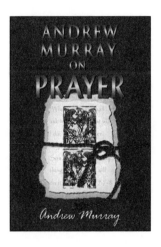

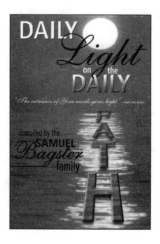